LEADING THE CUSTOMER-LED REVOLUTION

SUEANNE CARR
AND PETER TURNER

First published in 2023 by Sueanne Carr and Peter Turner

A catalogue entry for this book is available from the National Library of Australia.

ISBN: 978-1-922764-89-8

Printed in Australia by McPherson's Printing
Book production and text design by Publish Central
Cover design by Julia Kuris

Image credits:
Image on page xvi from Shutterstock.
People icons on pages 45, 207 and 258 from the Noun Project.
Photo on page 187 from Pixabay.

The paper this book is printed on is certified as environmentally friendly.

MIX
Paper | Supporting
responsible forestry
FSC® C001695
www.fsc.org

CONTENTS

'To join the industrial revolution you needed to open a factory;
to join the internet revolution you need to open a laptop;
to join the Customer-led Revolution you need to open your mind.'

– Sueanne + Peter

A GLOBAL PERSPECTIVE
by Don Peppers

The Customer-led Revolution has arrived, and your customers are now storming the gates! Their patience has never been thinner, their expectations never higher. If you don't let customers lead your business – indeed, if you don't *help* them to lead your business – then your very existence as a business will soon be in jeopardy.

This is the urgent message in Sueanne Carr and Peter Turner's book, which should serve not just as an energetic, forceful call to action, but also as a guidebook for better understanding this revolutionary terrain, and as an explanation of how to navigate it successfully.

In truth, of course, the Customer-led Revolution has been brewing and bubbling for a couple of decades now, steadily nurtured by the technologies that have connected us ever more closely together, electronically. Real-time, 24/7 interactivity has only recently come onto the historical stage, but it has already empowered customers in ways barely imagined just a few years ago.

It is now technologically cost-efficient for a business to communicate interactively with and treat all its different customers *differently*, one customer at a time, even if the business is serving millions – or billions – of customers. Leading companies, early to embrace the technology, have been pioneering new, personalised business practices, but now customers have come to expect *all* the businesses they buy from to provide the same kind of improved and individualised customer experience.

But the only way you can do this, for real, is to forsake your old-fashioned business model – you know, the one that proceeds from product to process. Give it up. Yes, it's hopeless! Because what you *need* is a business model based on following the customer's lead. Your goal should be to encourage and empower your customers to set the direction *they* want, and then to *innovate* constantly, to keep up with them – new products, new services, new interactions, all designed to satisfy whatever new needs your customers reveal to you. In other words:

> Rather than finding more customers for each of your products, find (or create) more products for each of your customers.

Consider, for instance, the relatively straightforward task of personalisation, and what it actually involves. Yes, on the one hand personalising anything at scale requires technology, but how exactly should a business *use* that technology to produce whatever personalised product or service is desired by some particular, individual customer?

Answer: By starting with the *customer!*

By its very nature, the whole process of personalisation is customer-led. There must first be some interaction of some sort, in which the customer specifies exactly what would meet *their* need. It could be a selection of options, or colors, or sizes, or a specified delivery time, or a maintenance schedule. And the specification process itself might involve one or more of a number of interactive activities, from an online enquiry to an in-app choice or a QR-code scan.

Regardless of the mechanism, however, the direction of the process is straightforward: First the customer *specifies*, and then the company *produces*. First the customer. Then the company. The customer expresses a need, and the company then scrambles to meet *that* need for *that* customer.

In the 'Customer-led Revolution' it is the customer that leads, and the business that follows. It really is that simple. And that difficult. It's time for business leaders to rise to the challenge and put the right capabilities in place. For a more complete explanation, read on...

Don Peppers is a best-selling author, blogger, widely-acclaimed keynote speaker and global CX authority. The co-founder of the Peppers and Rogers Group, one of the world's leading customer-centric management consulting firms, Don remains one of the founders of the customer experience movement and regularly takes the global stage to share his insights and expertise.

AN AUSTRALIAN PERSPECTIVE
by Andrew Griffiths

As an Entrepreneurial Futurist, I spend a great deal of my time helping Australian organisations, of all sizes, to develop strategies that will ensure they not only survive, but they are highly successful in an overwhelmingly competitive and rapidly changing world. Much of this strategy comes down to the very simple concept of differentiation.

As business and industry continues to evolve, it starts to homogenise, meaning it all starts to look the same. Take for example the franchise concept, it's built on businesses looking and being the same, that's what makes it work. But even outside of the franchise model, this move towards same/same ultimately impacts on all businesses and industries, to the point where every business within an industry sector starts to look the same and act the same and be the same. And this now provides both a challenge and an opportunity.

When we all become the same, how do we differentiate from our competitors? How do we stand out? How do we find that compelling competitive advantage that gives potential customers a reason to buy from us?

That is what this entire book is about, building a business with a customer-led strategy. As Sueanne Carr and Peter Turner have so clearly shown, the revolution is here, and it's really no surprise when you consider the homogenisation factor.

This is all about our philosophy towards the people who buy from us, regardless of what they buy and what we sell. It's about having respect for these people because they have enormous choice and they've chosen us. It's about how we engage and interact, how we adapt and evolve our product offering to meet their needs and expectations. Often this sounds like such a simple concept, yet it's so often overlooked by organisations who tend to be focused inwards as opposed to being focused outwards.

In reality, this concept is a future proofing strategy. Simple as that. The business that is always out front, leading the way, seemingly one step ahead of their competitors, deeply attuned to what their customers want and need and subsequently in a state of constant adaption and evolution, is the business that will be here for a long time to come.

The Customer-led Revolution is here in Australia, whether we're ready for it or not. We all have an extraordinary opportunity to become an organisation that embraces this, regardless of whether we're running a small business, a government organisation or a listed company. It's a culture and a driving force strategy, that can be applied regardless of what we sell, who we sell it to, where we're located, online or offline.

My advice is simple. Start reading this book with the clear knowledge that the Customer-led Revolution is here. In the coming years it's only going to become more significant and have greater impact on every organisation, including yours and including mine. We get to choose whether we take advantage of the revolution or not. I know what my choice is.

I talk a great deal about future proofing.
From now on, I'll be telling people to read this book.
The answer is here.

Andrew Griffiths
Entrepreneurial Futurist
International bestselling business author of 14 books

BEYOND PRODUCTS AND SERVICES

Have you ever encountered a business that just seemed to 'get it'? Beyond their product or service, they just seemed to do everything right? They seemed to bring – what looks like magic – to your encounter. They take standard, and make it special. They take nice, and make it remarkable.

Imagine this.

Your wedding anniversary is coming up. It's a big one so the pressure is on to make it 'next level'. You get the sweats just thinking about it. What could you possibly do to celebrate such a momentous occasion while portraying the depth of gratitude and love you have for your partner in crime and in life?

All you know is this… it probably needs to be something relatively small, definitely shiny and probably, expensive.

Cue the high-end jewellery brands. You know, the ones that grace the pages of high fashion magazines, CEO publications and Princess Di's jewellery box. Think the likes of Cartier, Tiffany and Co., Paspaley, Bvlgari.

With appointments made to visit a few of your favourites, you surprise your love with a day out in the city. A lovely lunch, a few hours surrounded by bright shiny things, being pawned over and spoiled rotten – the perfect day.

Except, it's not. In fact, two of the store experiences could be likened to shopping at a low-end jewellery retailer in your local Westfield, such is the sense of occasion, the service, the interaction that is afforded you by the sales assistants.

You begin to lose faith. Maybe this wasn't going to be as great a day as you'd hoped. Maybe you weren't going to find that perfect piece to celebrate the love of your life.

And then, you walk into your third appointment.* And there, in the store, in the greeting, in the welcome, is the magic you've been searching for.

Following the warm welcome and the big smiles, a gentle enquiry – Is this for a special occasion? Indeed it is – 20 years married, a milestone, an achievement, a big deal. Expecting the same as the other stores, you wait for the textbook congratulations gush to follow.

It doesn't.

Instead, two glasses of champagne are presented to you as you peruse the pristine displays. Not any old champs, but exquisite Ruinart French champagne, your absolute favourite since you visited the champagne house several years before. It must be a sign. You might stay just a little longer, take another look at the pieces on display.

All the while, warm, friendly conversation with our attendant, Sarah (her real name), ensues. What are we doing to celebrate our anniversary? Oh, dinner at The Spirit House, a famous Thai restaurant on Queensland's Sunshine Coast, the following night. How lovely!

Slightly overwhelmed with the love of your life's now six-figure shopping list, you reluctantly depart empty-handed, promising to return in the coming weeks for another look.

Unperturbed by your lack of purchase, Sarah rushes over as you leave the store with a gift. 'Please enjoy this on behalf of myself and the Bvlgari family. Thank you for sharing your special moment with us today.' In the gift bag, your very own bottle of Ruinart champagne to enjoy on your anniversary trip.

Wow. There's no doubt that this is a company that knows its customer. Attentive service, tick. Genuine authentic interest in the customer, tick. French champagne, tick. Absence of purchase pressure, tick. A send-off gift, tick.

In a business sense, a customer edge, tick. Deep knowledge and understanding of their customer profiles, tick. A 'see you again' mentality, tick. Perfection.

The following evening, you arrive at the Spirit House for dinner, as planned. Shown to your table beside the stunning pond, drink in hand,

---

* At Bvlgari.

you notice immediately an oversized gold envelope addressed to you in stylish sweeping handwriting.

A handwritten note. From Sarah. From Bvlgari. Wishing you the loveliest of anniversary dinners and a lifetime of love and good fortune.

What? How? When? Did she chopper it up here? Wow. You both agree, this was next level. Not only had Sarah made an incredibly impressive gesture, she had listened attentively to your conversation the day before. She had paid attention. And she managed to put Bvlgari at the heart of your celebrations, even without a bright shiny piece of jewellery adorning your wife's neck, wrist or finger.

That's the magic. That's the wow.

You can imagine the table conversation that night, the plans made to visit Sarah again in the immediate future and the expressed desire to be part of the Bvlgari tribe. What you may not imagine is all the future annual visit to Sarah for special occasion gifts, be they wedding anniversaries, birthdays or just because.

It's easy to see, now in retrospect, how beautifully choreographed and executed the whole experience was. How obsessing over the customer, having the right team members in place (here's looking at you, Sarah) and going above and beyond the customers' expectations has set Bvlgari apart in the minds of their ideal customers (us!). How viewing the customer by their lifetime value, not by an individual transaction, can lead to a long, loyal and unbreakable customer relationship. For life.

Now is the time for brave business leaders to charge forward as vanguards of the Customer-led Revolution. To change things up, to make changes, to go above and beyond. Whether you're a high-end jewellery brand or a small boutique hotel, an IT consultancy or a FMCG retailer, the opportunity exists for every leader willing to step up and out of their comfort zone to navigate the journey and smash their goals.

That's why we wrote this book. To help brave business leaders find and bring their magic to their organisations and to the world.

Now, where did we put our wand...

Warmest

Sueanne + Peter

IN THIS BOOK

In this book, we're presenting our views and perspectives on the Customer-led Revolution based on our extensive experience in customer-led organisational transformation from around the world. We are sharing the framework we use with our clients to build a roadmap that brings it all together.

While some of the concepts may not be new, how we connect them is. We help you reframe the way you see the world in relation to your organisation and how you see and relate to your customers. We'll give you a refreshed view, some gentle reminders and some head-slap moments that enable you to reconnect with the ultimate reason your organisation exists – your customer.

We have a different perspective. On business. On customer. On success. In fact, you'll find two viewpoints. The yin and the yang. Peter's strategic, data-loving brain combined with Sueanne's creative, empathetic approach brings a fresh perspective.

Figure 1: The yin and yang of customer strategy

In our experience of working with countless organisations and businesses across the world, there's one thing people say to us consistently, 'I've never thought about it like that.'

It's tempting to follow the path of our competitors, copy what they do and how they do it to stay in the race. But all that does is lead us to the same place they're going – the same finish line, the same destination. It also sees us competing head-to-head for our customers' attention, engagement and hard-earned cash.

In this book, we're going to challenge you to throw out the old ways of doing business and start your own revolution. Businesses have been playing this game for so long, it's time to change things up and change the way we see the court, the players and the prize.

HOW TO USE THIS BOOK

As the title suggests, this book is a simple and powerful roadmap for you to succeed.

There are a few ways you can use it. Some people like to read a book from front to back (hello, Ms Structure, Sueanne!), while others like to dip in and out depending on their mood and need at the time (here's looking at you, Peter). We've written this book so you can do either. We've also added page references in the margins so you can find linked material easily.

This book takes you through a process of self-discovery, a diagnostic if you like. We show you what good looks like and help you understand where you stand against best practice today.

We start out by talking you through why the Customer-led Revolution is here and why it's important. Then we'll take you through our framework of the nine key areas a business needs to be strong in, to be truly customer-led. We'll give you tips and tricks along the way and pose the hard questions.

At times you'll feel uncomfortable, even a little restless – you'll become acutely aware of what's working and not working today and what you could do in the future. Some of our clients tell us they had no idea they were on the wrong track until they met us; instead happily humming their way along what they thought was the right path. That's okay too.

As you're working through the book, try not to be hard on yourself if you realise you're not using the best practice and learnings. Instead, look at how you can adopt new ways of thinking to make improvements and inspire and motivate your team to go the extra mile.

In each of the Framework chapters, we cover the core strategic question, the five ingredients for success and ask you to do a self-assessment. This will help you to identify where you are today based on your newfound knowledge, best practice points and examples you'll find in each chapter. Self-assessment includes not just yourself, but your leadership team and customer-facing teams like Sales, Customer Service, Business Development – even Reception. And your back-office team, such as Finance, HR, IT and your web developers.

In the self-assessment sections, there are four steps you should follow:

1. Read the statement.
2. Ponder your answer – what's your gut feel?
3. Read the best practice concept.
4. Rate your organisation's strength, based on the best practice statement.

The power, friends, is not only in the questions you ask, but who you ask. In fact, many of us don't know the right questions to ask to get the answers we need to drive our business forward. That's why we're here.

By asking these questions across your organisation, you not only get a wider and deeper perspective, you get your team thinking along the same lines as you.

Be curious. Be brave. Ask the questions. Don't be afraid of the answers. The answers are the answers whether you ask them or not. These things – the good and bad – are happening in your business every day. By asking the right questions, you can find the gaps, focus your efforts and fix the issues.

We're on a journey together. And we're so glad you're here.

THE CUSTOMER-LED REVOLUTION MANIFESTO

Customers have the power, and they're beginning to know it. They're the ones with the wallets and the ones with the ability to amplify and influence. They're the ones that can make or break a business. And, they've had enough of being treated like a number, at being dehumanised. They're ready to rise up and you need to be ready to rally their cause.

The high-performing organisation in the Customer-led Revolution is one that has stepped out of the legacy of thinking of the past and truly embraced the value, importance and criticality of customers. This organisation is dynamic by nature, ever-sensing and in tune with its customers, using this insight to tweak and adjust every part of the operation.

This organisation sees customers, not as a means to an end, but the end themselves. It understands that efficiency and effectiveness come from aligning offerings to meet customer needs. That, by knowing the customer intimately, tracking performance on what matters most to customers and aligning the offering and delivery of the organisation, it has a competitive advantage that is unique and hard to copy.

The customer-led organisation is an employer of choice, attracting the best talent from within and across industries to elevate the impact even more. These people are energised to come to work, putting in discretionary effort without direct expectation of transactional reward, as they are connected to the higher purpose of the organisation – enabling the customer to succeed. There's lower staff attrition, meaning less downtime and distractions in finding resources, instead everyone getting on with the tasks at hand.

Respect and empathy are central to success, with everyone from boardroom to back office understanding their role in enabling the customer. A strong sense of pride and a bullet-proof customer culture forms the backbone that is an aspirational benchmark for others.

This is the organisation of the future. One that meets the Customer-led Revolution head on. This is the customer-led organisation.

THE CUSTOMER-LED REVOLUTION IS HERE

There is nothing new except what has been forgotten.
Marie Antionette

In our desire to be intrepid, cutting edge and different; to be disruptors and change-makers – and shake sh!t up – we've forgotten some stuff. Pretty fundamental stuff. Like our customers. Community. Connection. Where it all started. The premise of business – to offer value, to interact, to relate – to enter into a relationship where both parties benefit.

We love talking with people from prior generations. You know… 'old people' (insert eye roll here). Those who have the benefit of years of experience, who are able to share their wisdom with those of us who are willing to hear it.

*They talk about the 'good old days', with almost a golden glow around the sentiment they hold for the way things used to be. Sure, they had their struggles, but there was a **human connection** they speak of either explicitly or implicitly, a common purpose, a kinship that has seemed to dwindle over the generations since.*

You'll see as we take you on the journey through this book, we haven't landed where we are today by mistake. But one thing we are yearning for today, more than ever, is that human connection that the generations before us possibly took for granted. That connection that in the pursuit of success, of profit, of market share, has been lost.

In fact, over the last few decades the pressure for change has been rising and customers are no longer willing to forego this connection, to be at the whim of organisations. They now have the power, the wallets and the ability to choose. As a savvy, informed and intelligent business leader, it's your job to prepare your organisation for the revolution that is already upon us – the Customer-led Revolution.

Chapter 1

WHAT IS THE CUSTOMER-LED REVOLUTION?

There's no doubt that a revolution is upon us.

We're not talking bloody uprisings of the past, like the French or American Revolutions, or Tiananmen Square or the LA riots. Nothing that dramatic... or is it?

Never before in our modern age have we seen such depth and breadth of change, from technological to social, educational to environmental, all at the one time.

Some may call it natural evolution – after all, change is change. We see it more as a revolution, a bit more radical than slow moving.

The truth is that everything is changing. And every*one* is changing.

Some may think that technology is behind these changes. Everywhere we look there's some new app or new automation or new technology to make our lives 'easier' but the reality is, even though we're more 'connected' than we've ever been, we've never been more disconnected as human beings.

We believe the drivers of this change can no longer be ignored – the real change-makers, the earth-shakers, the protagonists. The people. Your customers.

We call it the Customer-led Revolution.

THE CUSTOMER-LED REVOLUTION IS HERE – WHETHER WE LIKE IT OR NOT

Whether you like it or not, the customer now has more choice at their fingertips than they've ever had before, the ability to switch providers at a mouse click and the option to publicly praise or slay you to thousands, if not millions, of people. Organisations may have lost sight of the fact that the customer is important, but those that have built the capabilities to truly respect, honour and value their customers are the ones that are continuing to smash their goals and their competitors.

The truth is, the Customer-led Revolution is here, whether we like it or not. Many will say, 'Yeah, yeah, we know – we've got this' (and continue on as before). But in our experience, most don't.

The revolution cannot be ignored. Imagine if your organisation had no customers tomorrow. What would it mean? Would you have a job? Would your team? As leaders, it's funny how you often get caught up in the operational minutiae and lose sight of what's really important.

Without customers, you have nothing.

For as long as there have been customers and providers, the power balance has tended to favour the latter – the businesses who sell and provide the products – forever the boss of how and when they interact with customers. Want a product? Sure, but you have to wait. Wait until we're ready to sell it / ship it / communicate with you. But the tables have turned. The customer has wrestled back that power and it's the customer who chooses who helps them achieve their goals, and how. It's their terms we operate on.

Customers have put themselves back in the driver's seat, no longer content to be the passenger. They control the network of people and organisations who inform, inspire and influence them. They no longer bow to brands and businesses, in fact, they expect the opposite. They're now 'the boss'.

WITHOUT CUSTOMERS, YOU HAVE NOTHING.

This might seem like something to fear – no business leader wants to hear they're not really in control. But if you're willing to learn some tools and if you have the inclination to generate enthusiasm from your whole organisation to focus on your customers, the Customer-led Revolution is something to embrace, not fear.

WHY IS THIS HAPPENING?

So, you may be wondering why this revolution is happening. Or why at least, it's so profound. The answer is dehumanisation.

Basically, it's making a human into a number, an asset, a liability even.

It's taking human-ness, individuality, basic needs and wants and converting it into something that serves the business. Not the other way around.

In reality, it looks like customers listed as names on a list, numbers on a spreadsheet, like demographics in a marketing plan or one of those shadow icons of a head instead of an actual image of a person (shudders); it's staff, treated like machines that can be easily swapped out and replaced – instead of real people, real individuals, with needs and wants and a voice of their own.

And they've had enough.

OVERCOMING THE DISCONNECT

So, what does this dehumanisation equate to? It's a disconnect. Somewhere between a little crack and a gaping chasm between the organisation and the customer, between the leaders of the organisation and their staff, between staff and the customer.

Is there any wonder that there is a Customer-led Revolution going on right now? When for so long, we as business leaders and key decision-makers have ignored the very people who make up the fabric of our operations – the customers who buy our products and the employees who create and deliver them.

BRAND REFRESH – LIPSTICK ON A PIG?

Sueanne once worked for a global organisation, a market leader in their industry. She was in a board meeting with the CEO, and the Head of Marketing was gloating about how the development of the new brand was coming along and how it was going to change the world. In charge of Customer Strategy at the time, she posed a simple question – 'The brand sounds amazing, but what are we planning to do behind the scenes to ensure our staff deliver on these new and bold promises?' Blank stares looked back at her from across the table (except for her colleague who was ill-impressed with her hijack of their 'show'). Crickets. Nothing.

Until the CEO looked her straight in the eye, nodded, smiled and said, 'Yes, what are we doing?' to the brand flag-wavers who only moments before were beaming brightly at their pretty brand logos and expensive outdoor placements. Again, crickets. Nothing. A complete disconnect between the glitz and glamour of brand and marketing, and the reality of the organisation delivering the expected customer experience.

Brand over customer. Tell over listen. This is dehumani-sation in action.

In fact, some clever people at Harvard created this model to address this dynamic. They called it the Service Profit Value Chain model. At Customer Frame, we like to call it common sense.

But they got it right. And this is one of those head-slap moments, a simple yet great reminder of the dynamics at play in our organisations today. The more you can align the three parties of this model, the better the engine will run and generate value for all involved.

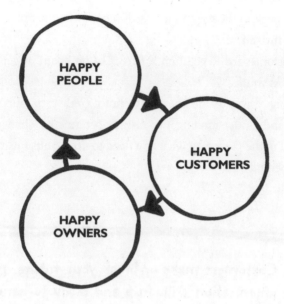

Figure 2: Service-Profit Value Chain model (aka common sense)

It's time to reconnect with people and bring back the human. We call it putting the heart back into business. The way things used to be in the 'good old days', when customers and suppliers had relationships, when they knew each others' names and supported each other regardless of who'd opened up down the road. It's all about heart.

ARM YOUR ORGANISATION FOR WHAT LIES AHEAD

Understanding where your organisation is in terms of your people – your employees and your customers – and we mean a true view of how you treat them, where they stand, how important they are – can take you in leaps and bounds towards success. In fact, we'd argue that without this, you're doomed to fail. Your customers will abandon you for a better priced competitor or a better experience, your staff will move on to an employer that values and listens to them.

We believe that people are yours to lose. And that people are yours to gain. And that's what this book is all about. People.

Let's go back to the way things used to be – when people mattered and businesses thrived.

The Customer-led Revolution is here. Get on board or get left behind. The choice is yours.

Assuming you've made the right choice, let's turn our attention to exploring and understanding the drivers behind the change. This will begin to fill in the picture of what you need to do in your business to avoid being left behind.

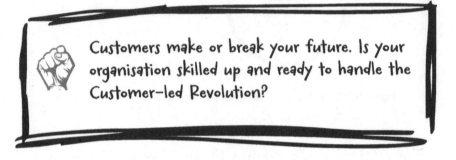

Customers make or break your future. Is your organisation skilled up and ready to handle the Customer-led Revolution?

Chapter 2

WHAT'S DRIVING THE CUSTOMER-LED REVOLUTION?

We know a revolution is coming. Let's explore what's driving the revolution so we can begin to direct your thinking on the areas to prioritise for your organisation.

EVOLUTION VERSUS REVOLUTION

A revolution is different from an evolution – the main difference is where the energy for change originates from.

Evolutions are about incremental changes. If we think about the ape to human evolution, it is a series of small changes over time. Even now, we as humans are living longer and we're taller than previous generations. The driver is internal (comes from inside) for evolution.

Revolutions on the other hand are about disruptive, step changes. When we think about revolutions, we have images in our heads of parts of history where citizens uproared to governments – like the French Revolution. The driver is external (comes from outside) for a revolution.

ARE THEY REALLY THE DISRUPTORS?

We often talk about industry disruptors (Amazon, Netflix, Jetstar, Virgin) being the drivers of revolution. Well, they are, sort of. They were the smart ones to see what customers needed and empowered the customer to revolt against the old ways.

So, why does this matter for a Customer-led Revolution? It means that the energy for change is coming from outside your organisation, shaking up the environment you work in. And, most importantly, this external energy is being driven by – your customers.

WHAT'S DRIVING THE CUSTOMER-LED REVOLUTION?

Of course, it's customers who are driving the Customer-led Revolution! Customers have been liberated by leaders in specific industries and they no longer put up with sub-standard experiences across their consumer interactions.

Take banking, for example. Historically, the retail banking experience was one fraught with visions of laser beams, attack dogs and the guillotine bullet-proof glass between you and the 'teller'. As the customer, you were powerless, they were powerful. You waited in line with intentional barriers between you and them. You almost had to beg to have your own money handed over.

Now when you walk into a bank, you're often left wondering whether you've accidentally walked into a coffee shop. There's someone to greet you at the front, coffee machines and lounges everywhere, not to mention the open-plan feel. No dogs, no glass, no barriers. Customers may wonder – if banks can transform from being closed, feared, transaction-based environments to open, engaging spaces that promote relationships, then why can't you?

These heightened expectations have become the new norm for customers. If dealing with you gets too difficult, they will choose another option and can do so within a few clicks of a mouse.

You may find yourself making excuses for not having to worry about the revolution. 'But we're different in our organisation!' we hear you say. This is one of the biggest limiting beliefs that will hold you back from discovering and embracing the opportunities that lie ahead.

In our extensive work with market leaders, government agencies and specifically local government, we often hear the disclaimer, 'Our customers don't get to choose, we're their only option!' The reality is that your customer **can** choose to go somewhere else. If you're a council, they can choose to invest in your region, or select another over you that's easier to deal with. Residents can choose to live in your region or not. If you think you're operating in a monopoly, customers can choose to search for another solution, an alternate route to achieve their outcome.

No one is immune to the Customer-led Revolution. But, you can arm yourself and your organisation to not just survive in it, but thrive in it. Even those of you who don't think you have competitors – trust us, you do! More on that later. (p143)

THE FIVE KEY CUSTOMER TRENDS DRIVING THE REVOLUTION

In any industry or sector – people buy from people. And, by understanding the trends driving personal behaviours, you can better prepare yourself as a leader and set up your organisation for success.

#1 The paradox of choice

One of the great things about the revolution is that today we have an amazing level of choice. We have the ability to find anything we need at any time of the day, but in doing so we also find everything. We have choice in most aspects of our lives. We have an increasingly seamless global marketplace at our fingertips, amplifying it even further.

Isn't it great? Well actually, it's not. Humans get overwhelmed with lots of options or choices. We freeze up, and in most cases, go for the familiar or the (perceived) less risky option.

Think about the last Chinese restaurant you went to. Chances are they had LOTS of options on the menu (our fave has 144!). And, if you're like us, you scan the menu, find a few appealing options, mull over them, hit overwhelm, then order... beef in black bean sauce. Again. Why? Because there's simply too much choice.

The problem behind this trend is that customers like the IDEA of choice, but can easily get paralysed by it (hence the paradox!). The same goes for dealing with your organisation. Do you give customers so many options that it overwhelms them? Or have you curated their needs into simple options you know will be spot-on for them?

#2 Your customer has the knowledge

No longer is your organisation holding the position of power when it comes to knowledge about your offering. In many cases, your customer will know more about your products, processes and services than you do! They also know how you stack up against alternate offerings. They have access to a vast array of knowledge within a few clicks. Not just the technical aspects either. They see reviews, comparisons, opinions – all at the click of a mouse. It's where the ultimate test comes from the customer – is your organisation going to treat me as an equal or not?

Customers are pre-armed with detailed knowledge, insights and perceptions, well before they make contact with you. The challenge is to keep your entire organisation at least up to speed with them, if not ahead of them when it comes to knowledge.

This can go horribly wrong at the coal face – where your teams are interacting with customers. We had a coal face experience when purchasing a high-end computer from one of Australia's most respected retailers. As informed customers, we knew what we *needed*, down to the product specs. But we wanted to ensure they knew the product, so we could trust their recommendation. So, it came down to one simple question. 'Is this LRF compatible?'

Instead of the sales rep delving deeper to clarify what we meant, he indignantly answered, 'Well, of course it is – we're the market leader.' Long story short – we walked out of that store and bought from another supplier, one who was less arrogant and treated us as equals.

What was LRF? It's not a technical computer term. It's simply Little Rubber Feet. You know, the ones on the bottom of the box!

Your team needs to be informed, up-to-speed and on the pulse – be it the latest expert review or opinion in the news. But they also have to be real or customers will see through them. This is where strong internal communications around your customer is key to leading the way through the revolution. And being honest when you don't know or seeking clarification, goes a long way to building customer trust and connection.

#3 Stories over stuff

In an age of increasing dehumanisation, customers are craving more meaningful connection. In previous eras, features and benefits sold products and services. In the next era, it is more about the stories attached to the stuff that are of value. No longer is it enough to say, 'We're the best'. Because the empowered customer knows better and is cynical to the claims.

Your offering is more than just your product. A story brings your product to life, beyond the basic product or service, to something I want, as a customer. Something I can connect to, aspire to, relate to. Want me to stay in your hotel? What makes your hotel different to others? Why would I want to stay? Why would I choose you to supply my farmgate produce, to sell my house, to recruit my next leader? Bring your humanness, your history, your features, your staff to life in a story and watch me relate, connect and buy.

The story creates a deeper connection beyond the product alone, increases perceived value and delivers a lovely brag factor to boot. Customers connect with stories. Stories are memorable. Most importantly for your organisation – they are shareable. Do you have a compelling story around your business, or are you just showing up as facts and figures or features and benefits, like everybody else?

CUSTOMERS CONNECT WITH STORIES.

SELLING MORE THAN AIR – A CASE IN POINT

Take the air guitar story from 2004 where an air guitar was sold on eBay for the brilliant sum of $5.50. The seller told prospective buyers, 'You are bidding on an original air guitar from the 80s. This one was used once at a Bon Jovi concert in '89 for about three hours. I've taken it out a few times since, generally after about six beers and a couple of fruity shots.'* The bids started at $1, quickly jumping to $3, before peaking at $5.50. Even though the seller pointed out that by buying an air guitar, the customers were buying absolutely nothing, the bids came through regardless. Incidentally, the highest bidder was given a certified letter of authenticity.

* www.music-news.com/news/UK/1465/Read

#4 Purpose driven purchasing

There's a lot on the customer agenda these days. We're consuming media at a global scale, giving us a much broader awareness and empathy to social issues. When deciding to transact with an organisation, customers are now looking beyond just the product or offering. They're examining what the organisation stands for.

Humans are primarily a tribe or pack animal, with customers looking to align their choices with the tribe they belong to. If down to only a few choices, customers are increasingly choosing the organisation that is delivering to a higher purpose. It connects the customers' choice (be it new shoes or electricity) with the idea that their purchase is also contributing to society – a social good.

In our work with Surf Life Saving Clubs, we've seen this firsthand. Who's noticed that the cost of meals at your local Surf Club is now on par with decent restaurants? Our clients found that as their prices increased, their patronage began to drop off. The perceived value of the transaction had become less attractive. Surf Clubs used to be known for cheap meals, right?

By amplifying and communicating the fact that the customers' meal purchase directly helped the club to buy equipment to saves lives on the local beach (the social good), we shifted the value proposition and reversed the declining trend. It became a competitive advantage over neighbouring restaurants with no social good or conscience beyond profit.

There's also a lot of new ventures that have spawned out of the focus on purpose. In the highly competitive toilet paper market, Who Gives a Crap have led the way. Their purpose is to help build toilets and improve sanitation in the developing world. Who Gives A Crap prove that when it comes to purpose, it really doesn't matter what your product is. And it works! Their model donates 50% of their profits towards their higher purpose and they've proved that giving back and being profitable don't have to be mutually exclusive. To date, they've donated over $11m to charitable causes.

> For businesses, the game is changing. Consumers used to place value on the intersection of price and quality, but now increasingly, consumers are looking for products that can do good.
>
> *Simon Griffiths, CEO at Who Gives A Crap*

Who would have thought 'swipe for good' would catch on like this?

In your organisation, are you clear on your greater purpose and how you can leverage it to form a stronger bond with your customers?

#5 Personalisation

There's so much personal data and information held by organisations these days – more than ever before. Yet, how many times do you get a 'To the resident' or 'Dear Sir/Madam' in communications from organisations? As a customer, it is frustrating and a great example of dehumanisation. Like, when you need to complete a form from a company you've been with for 20 years – and NOTHING is prefilled for you. It's so much fun looking for that account number that means nothing to you, but everything to them!

As customers – it's all about me – and we expect you as businesses to know it. In the good old days, people knew people. They knew what they liked and disliked. Not that long ago, you could walk into your local newsagent and be welcomed by name. Proven through many research campaigns, your own name is still in the top five of the best things you like to hear! Somewhere along the way, it was lost – but the Customer-led Revolution wants it back.

Technology has enabled a whole new level of personalisation. It can make things easy, like one-click purchasing or help remind you, like your annual pest inspection. It's not like, 'Hey Peter and Sueanne, come and buy this' – it's more sophisticated. It's about knowing who I am as a customer and person-alising my experience with you, down to the products you present to me. (p185) We talk more about personalisation and what you can do later in the book.

Reflect back on how your organisation is operating today. Ask yourself, 'Are we really personalising the experience for our customers, or just paying lip service to it?'

THE NEED TO GET AHEAD OF THE GAME

Chances are if you're reading this book, you're already aware of the need to get ahead of the game. Customers are expecting more and if you don't deliver, they'll go elsewhere, creating churn, or even costing you through avoidable contact and complaints. Neither situation is ideal.

The good news is your competitors are in the same situation. Unlike the temporary benefits of traditional competitive advantages that can be easily copied, being a truly customer-led organisation – as only you do it – is difficult to replicate quickly. In this game, the first mover who invests wisely gets the upper hand.

It requires a shift in mindset. From inside-out to outside-in. By looking inside your organisation and doing what you've always done, to truly looking outside – understanding who your customers are, how you're performing in their eyes and making sure your whole organisation is aligned around them.

SELF-ASSESSMENT AND REFLECTION

Think about your organisation today within the context of the five trends. Are you on it, or a little off? Give yourself the super-scientific rating out of five stars for each trend, then jot down a few notes on some initial things you might be able to do. For those who like pristine books, you can also download the worksheet by joining us at customerframe.com/revolution.

#1 Paradox of choice	☆ ☆ ☆ ☆ ☆
#2 Customer has the knowledge	☆ ☆ ☆ ☆ ☆
#3 Stories over stuff	☆ ☆ ☆ ☆ ☆
#4 Purpose-driven purchasing	☆ ☆ ☆ ☆ ☆
#5 Personalisation	☆ ☆ ☆ ☆ ☆

Then, let's move on to get clear on what we really mean by 'customer'. We might assume we're talking about the same thing, but we'd like to share our view which may change your perspective as it has for many of our clients.

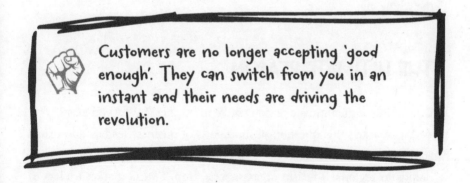

Customers are no longer accepting 'good enough'. They can switch from you in an instant and their needs are driving the revolution.

Chapter 3

THE CUSTOMER IS THE BOSS – LIKE IT OR NOT

When we strip back the complexity of the modern organisation, the genius of it all comes back to a simple idea. **Every organisation, in any sector, has customers to serve**. What we don't have is a common, shared and understood definition or an empathy for how important customers are to the whole gig.

THE ULTIMATE REASON

Do you know the ultimate reason you're in business? Why you exist?

We've asked this question of thousands of business leaders and teams across the world over the course of our careers. From global recruitment brands to regional Tourism organisations, from FMCG market leaders to government associations, we've heard it all.

The responses people give won't surprise you. There's your typical financially motivated responses – to make money, to turn a profit, to keep stakeholders and the board happy. Then there's the more lifestyle and emotionally-motivated responses – so I can have the lifestyle I want, to set me up for the future, to create a legacy, to set my kids up for the future, to do good in the world.

The answers are varied and interesting, yet not unexpected. What **is** unexpected is that rarely do people respond that the customer is the ultimate reason they're in business.

It's easy for us to come from a space of self. What do I want from being in business or from my role? What's in it for me? So when we consider these responses, is it any wonder that we've lost sight of the reason our businesses exist? Is it any wonder that we've lost sight of our customer?

Think back to when you started out in your career. It doesn't matter what industry or role you were in. Chances are, you were briefed to the nth degree about the systems and processes and rules and guidelines that you needed to follow, plus the targets and goals and achievements you needed to strive for. But how many of you were briefed deeply about your customer – the ultimate reason you're even in the role in the first place? Not just, 'Yeah, we have them' – but really briefed about who they are, what they need and what they expect.

NO CUSTOMER, NO BUSINESS

The truth is – without customers, we have nothing.

No income, no profit and loss, no product, no service, no job. Without customers, there is no need for any of these things – not a customer services line or a lunchtime huddle or incentives or suppliers. No need for a CEO, a CCO, a Board, not even a Maureen in Accounts.

Sad really, when you think about it. Or is it? We tend to think it's pretty exciting, actually. Because when it comes down to it, it's the businesses and organisations that look to the customer first, that are the ones who succeed.

When we gathered insights from a range of CCOs, CEOs and CX leaders from across Australia, more than three-quarters mentioned that one of the key challenges for business these days is the lack of focus on the customer by senior leadership. Distracted or obsessed with the bottom line, competitor activity or their own self-interest, leaders can drop the customer ball entirely, which doesn't go unnoticed by their middle management and wider team.

'BUT WE DON'T <u>HAVE</u> CUSTOMERS'

We've met countless numbers of clients who tell us they don't have customers. Usually it's their back-office functions – those that aren't necessarily face-to-face with customers – who tell us this. Or, they say, 'We have nothing to do with customers'. Another red flag!

They'll see Gary in Accounts as a colleague, not a customer. Or Mr Williams who stocks their products as just the distributor. In a government sense, they might see Mr Jones as a resident of their council, not a customer. Or Ms Smith who wants to invest several million dollars building a commercial premises in the region as a developer, not a customer.

It's all in the mindset and the vernacular used. The way we see people is the way we treat them, be they customers or team members.

> If you are not taking care of your customers, your competitor will.
> *Bob Hooey, Author, Sales Coach and Keynote Speaker*

We love the following story about Mike. An integral part of the team who had been doing his job completely disconnected from the customer. Why? Because his mindset and culture said, 'You don't have to worry about the customer, you have nothing to do with them.' But Mike realised he LOVED the fact that he was intrinsically linked with the customer. It gave him a new purpose and a human element to his role, beyond statistics and tick sheets.

This Jan Carlzon quote, borrowed from one of our favourite clients, says it all –

> If you're not serving a customer directly, then you should be
> serving someone who does.

YOU THINK YOU'RE ALL OVER CUSTOMER...

We were running one of our lauded Customer-led Accelerator Programs with a big-ticket client who had a large government contract coming up in the next 12 months. They were desperate to up their game and while the MD thought they were super customer-focused, she invited us in for a sense-check.

From our Initial Diagnostic, where we interviewed a couple of key staff across the business, we presented our one-page diagnostic of what we thought was going on. The MD was so taken by the findings – even though she was aware of a good chunk of them – that she booked a Customer-led Accelerator session with her senior staff the very next week.

We started the workshop, asking each individual to introduce themselves, tell us their department and why they're in the session today. The first cab off the rank was Mike (name changed to protect identities) who we had spotted from the get-go. He sat at the end of the table, arms crossed, head down, shoulders slumped – 'I'm Mike, I work in IT. I don't even know why I'm here, I have nothing to do with the customer'.

Ah, Mike... We smiled knowingly, welcomed him and moved on.

As we moved through our process, we started to see a bit of a change in Mike. His shoulders relaxed, he began to engage in the conversation, in fact he became quite animated and very competitive in some of the activities. Mike was coming alive in front of our eyes. So much so, that when we closed the session, Mike stayed back and cornered us about how much he loved the workshop, how he realised he DID have a lot to do with the customer and how excited he was about the future. Some 40 minutes later, we were asked to leave the boardroom as the next meeting was due to start.

HOW YOU 'LABEL' CUSTOMERS DRIVES BEHAVIOUR

If you're wondering where your customer sits in your organisation today, try this trick. Ask your staff what they call customers. And we're not looking for the polite answers, we're looking for the truth.

We once worked with an organisation whose disconnect with their customers was next level. As part of our Customer Strategy Transformation process, we not only ask the customers about their experience and perceptions of the organisation, but the team's too.

With this particular client who had a sizable staff, we ran several internal customer sessions with the team. We needed 100% honesty – a true sense check of what was going on within the organisation that reflected to the outside and impacted the customer experience.

We decided to keep the different areas of the organisation separate from each other, so the team showed up to their session with comrades and friends, people they knew and trusted (and of course, some they didn't). As well as external facing teams, we had internal facing teams (who unsurprisingly, didn't know why they were called to talk about the customer because they didn't 'deal with them' or 'have anything to do with them'). This also kept the subject matter pure as we could talk directly to their remits, their deliverables, their challenges.

The 'What do you call customers?' section of the session started out as you'd expect. Polite references to where they lived or where they came from, what customer group they might belong to, whether it be businesses or locals, tourists or service providers... all very polite. Until we started digging a little more. 'Yeah, and what else do you call them?' we asked. More polite responses but slightly less polite. We pushed again, 'What do you call them when you're talking to each other about them?' Ohhhh... Okay...

'Annoying. Frustrating. Painful. Stupid. Pains in the butt. @ssholes, even!' And further: 'Demanding, needy, don't listen, entitled, abusive, it's their way or the highway...'

Ah, the truth comes out.

Now, it's easy to judge these people as bad or terrible employees or blame them for the disconnect. But it's not their fault. This is culture at its core. This is the truth, the reality, hiding under the surface.

Is there any wonder their customers are feeling disconnected? Mistreated? Misunderstood?

Chances are, the staff and team members in these workshops are also feeling exactly the same way. And when we dug deeper, that was exactly how they were feeling. Disconnected from the leadership and the rest of the organisation. Unappreciated. Unloved. Taken for granted. Invisible. Fascinating stuff.

THE DEFINITION OF CUSTOMER

Do a Google search on the definition of customer and you'll get yourself a paltry six-plus billion results. And we think they're missing the mark.

We have our own definition of customer at Customer Frame. A customer is a patron – one who purchases or receives an offering from an organisation, or intends to do so.

What's the most important part of this definition? There are two things. The first is 'one', meaning a person. Not a business or an organisation. A person. A real person that makes the decisions and/or enjoys the benefits (tip: they may be different people!).

The second is the 'intends to do so'. So many of us forget about the customers that we don't see, the ones who 'bounce'. The ones that may come to our front door (literally and figuratively) but who turn away for one reason or another. **A customer isn't just someone who spends money or transacts with us, it's anyone who might spend money or transact with us – that's the secret.**

> A CUSTOMER IS A PATRON – ONE WHO PURCHASES OR RECEIVES AN OFFERING FROM AN ORGANISATION, OR INTENDS TO DO SO.

We often refer to websites as the 'store window' for your business. A customer comes along, peers in to check you out and decides whether they'll step in or not. Some may open the door (or click through to your site), take another quick look around and decide whether they'll take another step inside. At any point, they can change their mind, turn on their heels and walk out (or click back out to their Google search).

If you're too busy out the back working on something for an existing customer (even if they're not the right ones for you) or stacking shelves (like doing admin), then you're missing all those potential customers who are peering into your business, in the hope of engaging and seeking your expertise and help in solving their problem.

By changing the way you look at your business and your customers, you can fundamentally change just how many customers 'walk through your door' and engage with you – be it an enquiry or a sale.

WATERBOTTLE-GATE: TOO BUSY STACKING SHELVES, LITERALLY

We undertook an Experience Review for a major retail client who wanted to improve their customer experience and as a result, their sales figures. Let's just say, our first red flag appeared when, only moments into the experience review, we stood 10 steps away from a staff member who was too busy stacking the shelves with water bottles to help their customers who were clearly lost, frustrated and in a rush. Where did the customers go? They bounced out the door. What did the staff member do? Kept stacking the shelves, of course!

THERE'S TWO TYPES OF CUSTOMERS

Now that we have a clearer view of the definition of customer and an awareness of those we tend to miss – those who *may* purchase from us – let's look at the two main types of customers that exist.

Ultimate versus intermediate customers

First of all, we break down our customers into two main categories – ultimate and intermediate.

The *ultimate customer* either passes the products or services to the consumer or is the consumer themselves. They're the users of the offering. This is the group we typically think of when we think about customers. These can be B2B (business to business) or B2C (business to consumer), depending on the business you're in. As an aside, we think P2P (person to person) is better.

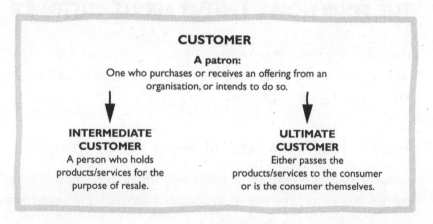

Figure 3: Customer definition and the two types of customer

The *intermediate customer* is a person who holds products or services for the purpose of resale. They're the distributors of the offering (for example, suppliers, wholesalers, merchants, dealers). These are the group that are most often forgotten, or worse still, treated as second-class citizens whose job it is to move our product or service on our behalf. They're also the group we believe often have the most latent or hidden potential.

There's also one other type of customer

Another overlooked customer type is the internal customer. While most of our focus lies on the customer external to our organisation, the internal customer can be as important, if not more so, particularly if they're directly serving external customers. Who are they? They're your staff, or team members as we'd prefer to call them.

An internal customer can be defined as anyone within an organisation that is dependent on anyone else within that organisation. So, yes, pretty much everyone!

The better we can treat our internal customers, the better our systems, processes and procedures can be followed and implemented, and the more efficient, effective and happy our team can be.

And what does a happy team deliver? Happy customers, of course!

THE FOUR NOBLE TRUTHS ABOUT CUSTOMER

There are a few truths or principles we live by at Customer Frame. They help our clients change their mindsets and their perspectives from an inside-out view, to an outside-in.

Truth 1: They're the boss, but they're not always right

In our definition of customer, we talk about them being the patron. Some may say that 'patron' just means 'customer' but dig a little deeper and you uncover something more meaningful.

For those who are familiar with English pubs (having lived and worked in London for 10 years, we are really quite familiar!), you'll know that customers of such establishments through the ages are referred to as patrons. By definition, a patron is a person who supports with money, gifts, efforts or endorsement, a cause, charity or institution, and whose social standing is improved as a result of the relationship.*

So if your team saw your customers not as simply someone who buys something from them, but as someone who supports your business or organisation, how different could your world be?

Now for those who are familiar with Spanish, you'll also know that 'patron' is not only a brand of our favourite tequila, but it translates to 'the boss' in English.

---

* galileo.rice.edu/lib/student_work/florence96/jessdave/patronage.html

Meaning, the customer is the boss, right?

During the 80s, the adage 'the customer is always right' was the catch-phrase for businesses across the world. It literally was the driving principle for every Customer Services team, plastered across kitchen pinboards and call centre message boards. But it is bullsh*t!

Let's put it another way. If the customer is the boss and the customer is always right, then does that mean the boss is always right?

No! The boss is **not** always right. Think about your illustrious careers, has the boss always been right? Heck no! Have you always been right in your role as the boss? Probably not. But, as the boss, you have people to help make you look good and succeed, right? That's the key.

Truth 2: Because they're not always right (and they don't know everything), you need to educate them

In fact, the boss needs to be educated in many respects. Remember the concept of 'managing upwards' in your early career? The boss can't know everything about everything. They rely on their team members to keep them educated and knowledgeable about the important things – like how the business is performing, what the market's doing, what moves competitors are making, how the new sales guy is working out. They employ people to manage that detail – they just need the summary.

The same is true for customers. Customers aren't always right and they need to be educated. They need to know what to expect from a business like yours, from a product or service like yours. Inform them and they'll have reasonable expectations, a reasonable level of knowledge and understanding and a reasonable level of connection with you and your business.

Don't do this and they'll make up their own stories and set their own expectations. That's when things go wrong.

That's when you get complaints, returns, bad reviews – because the customer believed one thing and you didn't educate them as to whether those beliefs were in fact realistic, true or achievable. We've seen this gap in many businesses. Customers don't necessarily know the specific remit of your organisation or what's realistic. It's your job to tell them.

Truth 3: Keep doing what you're doing and nothing will change

We love this quote from Henry Ford:

> If you always do what you've always done,
> you'll always get what you've always got.

It's similar to the definition of insanity – doing the same thing over and over again and expecting a different result. This is really common in business today. So many leaders in so many organisations are so afraid of changing what they're doing, for fear of what, we're not sure. Failure, probably. But the truth is, on many levels, they're destined for failure if they keep doing what they're doing.

At Customer Frame, we believe that the smallest change can make the biggest difference. That you don't need millions of dollars, a team of 100 or a magic wand to make things happen. You just need the will, some guts and your imagination.

Truth 4: You may not be as great as you think you are

By understanding where the customer sits within your organisation today, you can better understand your starting point and what you need to do. You can also identify sinkholes you never knew existed – like the fact that your teams don't know what each other's doing, or that they're all rowing their boats in different directions... it's fascinating how much you can learn by doing a simple diagnostic or health check of your operation.

Most of us would like to say that the customer sits at the heart of our business or is at least a key driver or component of our daily working lives. But in reality, by answering some simple questions, you can identify where your customer really sits. And just how important they are to you and to your team.

In this book, we'll help you ask questions of yourself you never thought of asking. We'll help you delve deep into ideas and concepts that may be familiar or completely unfamiliar. You'll likely know a bunch of this stuff, but whether it's in your consciousness on a daily basis is a different story.

DOES YOUR ORGANISATION TREAT CUSTOMERS WITH THE RESPECT THEY DESERVE?

Most of us would like to think we treat customers pretty well. That they're relatively happy with our service and product offerings. But are they really?

How does your team refer to your customers today? How long does it take to address customer issues or complaints? How many touch points does a customer have when they have an issue? How many good reviews do you have? What do people say about you in public forums?

By looking at your team's attitudes, mindsets and performance against feedback from your customers, you can begin to get a pretty good gauge of whether you afford your customers the respect they deserve.

Remember, they're the ultimate reason you're in business and without them, you have no business. But, is your organisation really ready for the Customer-led Revolution? Is it really skilled up for what is needed to not just survive but thrive? Let's find out.

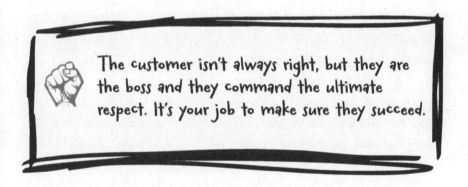

The customer isn't always right, but they are the boss and they command the ultimate respect. It's your job to make sure they succeed.

Chapter 4

IS YOUR ORGANISATION READY?

The Customer-led Revolution is here and its growing in strength. Success won't happen organically or by accident. It requires an intentional strategy to address and build up the customer capabilities you need to not just survive, but thrive in this next era of business.

It all starts with having a strategy and a plan.

Strategies and plans are nothing new and most definitely serve a purpose in driving the business forward to achieve your vision and goals. But when we focus solely on our strategies and plans, we tend to see the world only from our business perspective, putting the organisation's agenda ahead of everything else. This approach can see leaders and their teams lose sight of what's really important – the customer.

We call it an inside-out approach. An outdated way of doing business where all decisions are made with the interests of the business at the core. The antithesis of this is an 'outside-in' approach that puts the customer at the heart of strategy and decision-making.

HAVE YOU GOT THE RIGHT STRATEGY?

Most businesses and organisations have strategies, right?

There's your base-line business strategy of course, then your specific strategies, like your marketing strategy, sales strategy, comms strategy, finance strategy, HR strategy, perhaps an IT strategy… you get our drift. The size of the business or organisation would obviously impact whether you had a big-bang strategy or more of a business plan.

But where's your customer strategy?

If the customer is the ultimate reason you're in business, then why don't you have a strategy for them?

Many of you will say, 'We do have one! It's called our marketing strategy or our communications strategy.'

Not. The. Same. Thing. #sorrynotsorry

THE PROBLEM WITH MARKETING STRATEGIES

Marketing strategies and plans are all about telling our customers how wonderful we are, giving them all the reasons why they should choose us over others, buy our products and part with their hard-earned cash. Us, us, us.

Sure, we make our marketing really pretty and engaging and we hire marketing agencies and designers and web creatives and PR agencies and all the people to help us cut through the noise and stand out from our competition.

(Please know we're not poo-pooing marketing here – Sueanne is a die-hard marketer from way back!)

But it's all about telling. Tell, tell, tell.

Hey customer, let us tell you how wonderful we are. Let us tell you how our product or service is better than our competitor's. Let us tell you how our offering will enhance / improve / magically change your life.

There's a lot of tell, but very little listen. This is where you might say, 'Yeah but we do customer surveys, we DO listen!'

Again – Not. The. Same. Thing.

These days, customers want conversations with the businesses they interact with. Not all customers, mind, but most want to be heard, consulted, included, involved even, in the offerings they choose to spend their hard-earned cash on. They no longer want to be told.

THE PROBLEM: FUNCTIONAL STRATEGIES CAN CREATE SILOS

Ideally, your functional strategies would be aligned and bolted together to seamlessly deliver on your overall strategy. But the reality is, as you've probably evidenced yourself, this is often not the case.

Functional strategies create silos. Especially if they're not intrinsically linked with the overall business strategy.

Egos, motivations, personal agendas, resource snatches – you name it – get in the way. We've seen it in so many businesses – on the surface, function heads appear to be on the same page as the CEO or MD, but when it comes to the everyday, they are very much on their own course, running their own race.

It can happen inadvertently, even accidentally – but when it happens, it's tough to get said leader and their team back on track. Especially if they don't wholeheartedly agree with the CEO's intended course or even their destination.

As business leaders, you've seen this before, no doubt. Functional leaders – be it C-suite level, director level or even middle management – paying lip service to the strategy, then heading off and doing whatever they please in the day-to-day.

It's frustrating, it's demoralising and it's straight out wrong.

Yes, you pay your senior management the big bucks to be in the know, to be the experts in their field. Absolutely. But you also pay them the big bucks to lead with conviction and commitment to the common cause. To be your wing-people, your trusted 'right hand', your subs.

They simply have to be on the same page as you, the business leader, or there's trouble. Guaranteed. A common way this shows up in organisations is the 'not my job' scenario. This issue is particularly dangerous when those functional leaders don't believe that something is their – or their team's – job. And customer comes top of list in this situation. Try telling an IT or HR or Operations lead 10 years ago that customers had anything to do with them and watch them laugh it off. It's getting better these days, but we've still met a lot of function leaders who don't believe they have anything to do with the customer.

CUSTOMER TOUCHES ALL PARTS OF THE BUSINESS AND REQUIRES A STRATEGY

Why?

Because without a customer strategy, there is no common view of the customer, there is no shared ownership across the organisation or functions of the role your business has in fulfilling the customer's needs and wants.

When we don't look after our customer, when we don't give them a voice and a seat at our table, we create a barrier between the organisation and the customer. And much like the barriers that exist between the business functions or silos, self-interest and selfishness arise.

Without a customer strategy, the customer simply has no voice.

And without a voice, they can't tell you what they need. They can't help you improve your business's operations and offerings. They can't help you create new products or more profitable services. They can't help you weed out the bad stuff that upsets them and do more of the good things that they love about you.

That's why you need a customer strategy. Without a customer strategy, you have no roadmap for success.

WITHOUT A CUSTOMER STRATEGY, YOU HAVE NO ROADMAP FOR SUCCESS.

THE CUSTOMER WITH A SEAT AT YOUR TABLE: IT'S TIME!

We know customer is the ultimate reason we're in business. We know that without them, we'd have no business or organisation.

There's no doubt you've heard the term 'the customer must have a seat at your table'. Way beyond a nice catchphrase or concept, this is fundamental to being customer-led. There must be someone in your organisation who sits at your tables and represents the customer. We're not talking your Director of Sales or Marketing, or your Chief Technology Officer who has countless other responsibilities, competing priorities and balls to juggle. We're talking someone who is KPI'd on customer, who cares about where the customer sits in your organisation, who lives and breathes customer.

We're talking a customer champion. Someone who truly gives a toss about the outcomes for customer. Preferably not just because they're paid to, but because they truly care. Not someone who says they care or who has had 'customer' dropped into their existing title.

While not always possible, it makes a huge difference as it moves from box-ticking to heart-centred, purpose-driven and outcomes related.

The rise of the CCO

One way to give the customer a seat at your table is to have a Chief Customer Officer (CCO). No, this isn't the latest in the *Lord of the Rings* series, it is a movement happening across many organisations who want to get ahead of the Customer-led Revolution.

In Australia and throughout the world, the role of Chief Customer Officer (or equivalent names) are popping up in our org charts. Often, it is these people who are employed to be the glue between what the organisation wants to achieve and the operational reality of making it happen – it's a big job.

Many CCOs have come from Marketing or Operations backgrounds and in more mature markets like USA, UK and Europe, they've elevated from 'Heads of' type roles once responsible for customer. Yes – customer is now in the coveted C-suite. Tick that box! Job done, right? Ah, no.

It's important to note that this isn't just someone from the Customer Services function elevated to a higher position in the ranks. It is much wider and more symbolic.

The successful CCO

Like the customer strategy that they are charged to deliver, successful CCOs must be able to act cross-functionally to ensure the organisation can deliver on what the customer expects at every touch point, providing the experience that creates an advantage in this ever-competitive world we live in.

To be successful, CCOs need to have the skills to understand how the whole system of the organisation works, the tact and diplomacy to tell people their babies are ugly, while having the foresight and innovation to see opportunities others can't. Most of all, CCOs need to have support at all levels and recruit everyone in the organisation to the customer-led mission.

WHERE DOES YOUR CUSTOMER SIT?

The first thing to do on your journey to being customer-led is to look at where the customer sits in your organisation today. Where do customers sit in your overall business? Do customers feature in your cross-functional strategies? Do you have a dedicated customer strategy? How important are they – not how important you say they are or your team tell you they are, but actually when it comes to the crunch, what priority do they have?

Think of it this way – if you were on a sinking ship and you had to save your ideal customer or a bag of money, which one would you save?

IS IT INTENTIONAL OR ACCIDENTAL?

The next question to ask yourself is – is where your customer sits today, intentional or accidental? Do they have a firm place in your business because you gave them that seat at the table or gave them that voice? Or is it just sheer luck that customer feedback or the customer voice features in the right reports?

We will never stop barking on about accidental versus intentional. There's a big difference. And while you may be riding on the coat-tails of your 'accidental' actions, these will soon run out of steam and you'll either flick back to the way it's always been, or your team will be distracted by the next shiny object. Accident equals danger.

A GREAT TIP

Not sure where the customer sits in your organisation today?

Grab your latest organisational chart, take a long hard look at it and highlight where your customer sits and/or is represented across all of your functions. Block a meeting, sit quietly and think. Reflect. Highlight.

By doing this, the gaps in your organisation will soon become apparent. You'll already have a gut feel, but by doing these little things and asking yourself the big questions, you will soon uncover where some of the fundamental gaps lie in your business.

Remember, it's not about finger pointing, it's about identifying where we're letting the customer down and where we can improve, to grow, drive and build the business.

THE NEED FOR A CUSTOMER STRATEGY

Until now, there hasn't really been a 'playbook' to follow. Each situation requires its own nuanced approach. So how do you make it happen in your organisation?

There is one common reason that organisations fail to make traction – the absence of a customer strategy.

And, like anything in business, the things that are formalised and agreed get the budget and resources, and consequently, get the focus. This is where current efforts to become customer-led often fail. Leaders will put in a CCO or customer role, but give them very few resources (people and cash) to deliver on the complexity of what needs to be done. In these cases, small improvements are made to the customer experience, but they are not enduring or sustainable. They're not 'baked in' to the DNA of the organisation.

A customer strategy will help you move from a laundry list of ideas and opinions of what needs to change (an inside-out view) to an informed, coordinated and agreed focus for cross-organisational improvement and change (an outside-in view). And it needs an owner (a driver per se) with the right resources to make it happen.

Without a clear, coherent customer strategy, you will be caught in the waste and arguments of your organisation's squeakiest wheel while your competitors leap-frog you and get ahead of the game.

Now, before you go and open up a new blank Word document and start typing your next strategic masterpiece, let's get a couple of other concepts nailed down first. We know this revolution is coming. We know we need to get our organisation ready. We know we need a strategy. But, what is a customer-led organisation really about and what does it look like?

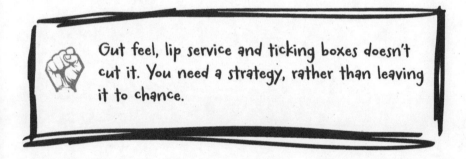

Gut feel, lip service and ticking boxes doesn't cut it. You need a strategy, rather than leaving it to chance.

Section 2

THE CUSTOMER-LED ORGANISATION

To achieve success in this new era of business, a new type of organisation is required. The challenge for leaders is letting go of those things that may have made you successful in the past, but that in the future, may be the things that hold you back.

In this section, we're going to guide you through our perspectives on what being customer-led is about, how it is different to ideas from the past and we'll shoot a couple of sacred cows in the process.

The journey ahead can be challenging and even confronting. However, we promise that when you come out the other side and see things in a new way, you will believe it is all worth it.

Chapter 5

WHAT IS BEING CUSTOMER-LED?

While the concept of customer has been around for a long time, the concept of creating a customer-led organisation is only relatively new. Some of the first roots were put in place during the 1990s by legends like Don Peppers, but the 'customer improvement thing' didn't really take hold until the early 2000s when buzz words like 'customer-centric' really came into their own.

ISN'T BEING CUSTOMER-LED THE SAME AS BEING CUSTOMER-CENTRIC?

The answer is no – they are very different.

Being centred around something brings a totally different energy to being led by something. However, the first is a stepping-stone to the second.

With customer-centric, you put the customer at the centre, at the heart, of everything you do. While the business sets the direction and priorities based on traditional KPIs and measures, there is an intentional focus on the customer. Your organisation actively invests in understanding who your customers are, what their needs are, monitoring what customers think (p23) (using our wider definition of customer) and ensuring that everyone from boardroom to back office is on the journey and rewarded for doing so. If you were on a journey to somewhere, your customer would be part of your pack, part of your group, following the direction you, as the leader, have charted. And this is great.

Being customer-led takes centric to the next level. When you're customer-led, the customer is elevated and respected as being the ultimate boss of your whole organisation. Everyone on the team is there to understand and serve their needs. It's more aspirational and active in approach, an ever-moving feast. It goes from being a consultative 'tick box' to being a true organisational competence – one that creates a momentum of its own. On your journey, the customer is out in front with your leaders, charting the way forward and the direction of the business, helping to decide priorities and actions, having a say on what you do, where you go and how you get there. *That's* customer-led.

WHAT DOES IT MEAN TO BE CUSTOMER-LED?

To be truly customer-led, you must first take stock and assemble yourself around the customer, putting them at the centre. But, like everything in this world, nothing is static. Customers are always moving and this is where the gold is in being customer-led. Yes, you need to assemble around them, but your organisation needs to have the agility to move with them, their changing preferences, expectations and needs.

It still has the customer at the heart, but it's a different way of doing business. It's a mindset. An approach. An ethos. It's intentional.

It's also very brave. Putting the customer in the driver's seat of your business is a big deal and not for the faint-hearted. And that's why not many businesses do it.

It takes the somewhat passive approach of being customer-centric and amps it right up, activating all manner of opportunities for growth and market domination that many customer-led world-leading organisations enjoy.

CUSTOMERS ARE ALWAYS MOVING – THIS IS WHERE THE GOLD IS IN BEING CUSTOMER-LED.

You have to have a great product, service and/or offering too, but it's those businesses that truly embrace the customer that stand out from the crowd.

It's not as simple as just calling up a few customers and asking them to come in for a meeting or for their feedback on a new product idea, but once you get the hang of being customer-led, it becomes second nature. And every little bit helps.

It helps you direct your business or organisation in line with what's important to your customers and their goals in life. By deepening your understanding of them as human beings, as thinking, feeling, knowing individuals, you can better relate to them, understand their issues and solve their pain points with maximum efficiency and effectiveness. No more wasted efforts chasing customers, they'll be knocking down your door!

We'll talk about this more in the Customer Profiles section, but let's put (p136) it this way – a deep and meaningful understanding of and relationship with your customer, beyond basic demographics and segmentation, will set you apart from your competitors in the hearts and minds of those customers you truly want. The ones who will buy more from you, more often, and tell everyone they know about you.

It's so important to understand not only the basic demographics – how old they are, where they live, how much they earn, their family structure and what they do for a job – but also what their goals are in life, what frustrates them and what gets in the way of achieving these goals. Then you can develop better products and services to cater for them, as well as deepen their connection to your brand and even more excitingly, improve the lifetime value of that customer.

WHY DOES THIS MATTER?

It matters because it's about a choice – a strategic choice, not some tactical lipstick on the operational pig or a bandaid solution. By outwardly stating a target to be customer-led, it positions the customer, the patron, as the boss. And – this is their rightful place.

It matters because it sets the tone for what is really driving the success of the organisation. It's not politics or personal gain – it's about the whole team working towards one goal. It helps to put aside the waste of internal squabbling and focus collective effort to generate growth and deliver on what really matters most.

It matters because it sets out whether you will be active in your pursuit or passive about it. It gives a clear signal to your people about the vibrancy and energy in your organisation and the mindset you expect. As an aside, customers also know and can easily see through veiled attempts at being customer-led when it is still about putting the business first. It helps you to be authentic in the mission.

BEING CUSTOMER-LED – GOOD FOR CUSTOMERS, GOOD FOR YOU

Being customer-led is a personal journey. You can't do it like anyone else because it's yours. It's how 'YOU DO' being customer-led. It's not about copying others, it's about being truly authentic in what makes you, you.

It's about finding your true north – that shared compass point around customer. Where you want to be as an organisation and who you want to be. It's then about bringing everyone on that journey – your customers included.

CUSTOMER-LED VERSUS THE OTHER 'LEDS'

Being customer-led isn't easy. Especially when as a business leader, you've probably been led by other things for so long. In fact, the 'leds' that may have ignited the start of your business (such as a product idea or a technology innovation), when trying to become customer-led now, can actually get in your way. So what are some of the other 'leds'?

There's product-led, where we are all about building the product to our own specifications and ideas, to sell on to anyone who'll buy it.

There's tech-led, where we're technology gurus and have designed a tool or system that will solve customer's problems, as long as the problems fit into our specifications and design.

There's sales-led, where we're all about selling as much of our product as we can, often-times less focused on the customer experience or longevity of the customer relationship.

There's ego-led, where the business exists purely for the purpose of the owner or senior leaders, driven by ego, self-interest and nepotism. This is not our favourite-led, truth be told – luckily we don't come across it very often.

FROM SERVICE MOMENTS TO EXPERIENCE: WHERE IT MATTERS

So how do we move towards becoming truly customer-led?

The diagram below will help you to grasp the difference between customer service and customer experience, and how each important element interrelates with the others.

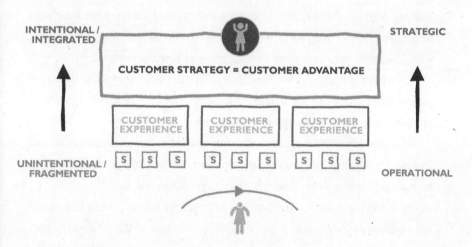

Figure 4: Customer service, customer experience to customer advantage

Moving from the bottom to the top of the previous diagram, customer service moments (S in the diagram) are the touch points we have with our customers, be they face-to-face, online, on the phone, in-store or live chat – each touch point is a service moment.

Each cluster of service moments or interactions a customer has with our business combines to create customer experiences, usually grouped together based on similar elements or even times within the customer journey.

As we move up the diagram, we see that customer experiences lead up to the top level, the intentional customer strategy that is based on a measured organisational capability. It is a form of advantage that directs everything from the source and creates consistency across everything you do. It creates the umbrella for the whole system.

Things can often go wrong when businesses and organisations focus too much on the individual service moments or interactions with the customer – or customer service as we like to call it. Fragmented, accidental and highly subjective to individual team members' behaviours and attitudes, this is where most businesses focus. This is where 'Customer Service training' 101 comes in.

When clients call us and ask if we do Customer Service training, we suggest they Google the top 10 customer service tips and save themselves thousands of dollars. It's just the bandaids at this level.

At Customer Frame, we flip the whole approach on its head. Instead of starting with the individual service moments at the base level, we believe in setting yourself a customer strategy first, an umbrella platform or approach, which informs your customer experience and customer service.

p33 Customer Strategy, as we read earlier in the book, charts the direction and strategic priorities for where customers sit in our business. It is strategic in its intent and is completely intentional.

The Customer Strategy then informs the customer experiences of our business, including the intentional emotion we want our customers to feel across their journey and through their interactions with us.

By knowing how we want our customers to feel and how individual interactions at the customer service level fit together at the customer experience level, we can better inform our customer service standards, intentions and outcomes.

From accidental (bottom to top in our diagram) to intentional (top to bottom), you can choose own adventure. Clever, hey?

THE NEED TO EMBRACE THE DIFFERENCE

If you take nothing else out of this book – take this.

Being a customer-led organisation is the next evolution of business. Being customer-led is about taking a courageous and active stance. It goes beyond just being 'centric' or 'focused' (and waaaay beyond 'customer service'). It brings your people together and aligned, energising them around a common vision that is more enduring than the average CEO's three-year tenure.

To be truly customer-led, first, leaders and customer catalysts must understand the difference and come to terms with the reality that they **are** different.

Secondly, the message needs to be taken wider, to get into the hearts and minds of the wider leadership and team. It brings new opportunities. For many, especially those at the front line, it will bring a sigh of relief and a huge release of positive energy. The many times we've heard, 'Finally I have a voice,' from front-line staff is astounding.

If you're not there already, get ready to jump on board the new 'led' era as we help you explore further how to become a truly customer-led organisation. More than just buzz words, there's commercial and cultural reasons why it is important to get ahead of the game.

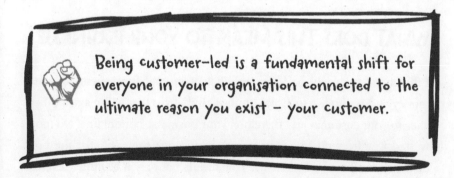

Being customer-led is a fundamental shift for everyone in your organisation connected to the ultimate reason you exist – your customer.

Chapter 6

WHY IS BEING CUSTOMER-LED SO IMPORTANT?

Being customer-led means walking side by side with your customer, so you can:

- traverse unscaled territory together, seeing the pitfalls and dangers ahead of time
- consult your customer on your initiatives, from product development to marketing campaigns, from pricing to innovation
- identify issues as they arise, not after they've done long-term or irreversible damage to your business.

WHAT DOES THIS MEAN TO YOUR BUSINESS?

Efficiency – you will be far more efficient in your investments of time, money and resources, focusing on those initiatives that will make a difference to your customer and therefore, your business's bottom line. No more wasted resources on things your customers don't want (or that the boss demands but hasn't researched). This means not only a healthier revenue stream, but a more profitable business overall.

CUSTOMER-LED CAPABILITY	=	EFFICIENCY	+	EFFECTIVENESS

Effectiveness – your team will be more effective in achieving your strategic objectives as they work on the right things at the right time. This will mean more engaged staff too, as they feel like the things they're doing are making a difference and they're achieving their KPIs. They'll feel more connected to the strategy, to the culture of the business and to each other. And to your customers.

REAL LIFE – REAL WORLD IMPACT OF CUSTOMER-LED

Being customer-led is more than just tweaking the edges to get the full impact of the advantage. We worked for a government client who was responsible for distributing support funding to the agricultural sector. Their role often meant the difference between their customers (primarily farmers) breaking even or going under completely. Pretty big stuff.

A vital part of this process was the application made by the customer for the funding. We're talking a 12-page application form, with a 128-page explanatory guide to go with it. If the customer misunderstood the form and got it wrong, it spelled disaster for them – at best, a wrong payment, at worst, no payment at all. Unpaid farmers were losing their livelihoods, and at times, their lives.

For the organisation, when the customer got it wrong, it meant reworking the application – unpicking it, fixing it and redoing it. The added complication was that each customer claim had a direct impact on the other ones. (If one was underpaid, it meant an adjacent one was overpaid, etc.). Imagine the snowball of work when it went off the rails.

When we started the customer-led journey work, around 40% of applications were being reworked.

The organisation took four to six weeks to resolve each failed application. When you have over 100,000 customers, that's 40,000 fixes! Inefficient for everyone involved – the resources required and the levels of frustration were off the chart (we're talking in the millions in costs!). Ineffective as there was a blockage between both organisation and customer getting what they needed – fast, accurate payments on time.

By taking a customer-led approach, the application process was revised and streamlined. We made it easy for customers to understand the application form and what they needed to do, then supplemented this with a range of support services (including online applications with instant verification). Reworking dropped from 40% down to under 5% within the first two years. The financial impact – huge. The social impact – immeasurable.

A COMPETITIVE ADVANTAGE THAT'S HARD TO REPLICATE

BY STEPPING INTO WHO YOU ARE AS A BUSINESS, EMBRACING YOUR VISION AND VALUES, AND BEING INTENTIONAL, YOU CAN CREATE A COMPETITIVE ADVANTAGE THAT IS HARD, IF NOT IMPOSSIBLE, TO REPLICATE.

By stepping into who you are as a business, embracing your vision and values, and being intentional, you can create a competitive advantage that is hard, if not impossible, to replicate.

That's the beauty of being customer-led. It's not about a product, or a service, or a commodity. It's about the combination of all these things. It's about an experience. In fact, you can have the exact same product or service as someone else, but if you wrap it up in an experience that's all your own, then it's **not** the same.

ADDRESSING THE CUSTOMER TRENDS

When you're customer-led, you take into consideration what's going on for your customers. Remember the five key customer trends we spoke about? (p11) These are the things that are happening for your customers, external to your business and out of your control. By being on top of these, you can better align your efforts, service and offerings with your customers.

THE CUSTOMER IS YOURS TO LOSE

We often talk about how the customer is yours to lose. If you have a customer who prefers to buy from a physical store or supplier, who comes to you for advice and interaction, you best serve that customer as well as you possibly can. Why? Because if you don't, they'll either find one of your competitors who will, or they'll move to an online purchase through pure frustration. Lose them to online, where things are often cheaper, quicker to be delivered and more seamless, and you've just lost yourself a customer for life. Once they've done it, they'll be more confident to do it again the next time. And the time after that. Don't give them a reason to go to a competitor company or channel – or chances are you'll lose them forever.

THE PROOF – STATISTICS OF SUCCESSFUL CUSTOMER-LED ORGANISATIONS

It's all well and good for us to harp on about being customer-led, how important it is and why you should do it, but by now we're guessing you'd like a bit of 'proof of concept'.

According to the Hubspot Annual State of Service in 2022 report, which surveyed 1400 service leaders in the United States, United Kingdom,

Canada and Australia, it has never been more difficult to be a customer service leader:

- Almost 90% of leaders report that customer expectations have increased to an all-time high.
- Most customer service leaders don't have the resources to adequately deliver on these expanded expectations with three of the top challenges being:
  - a lack of prioritisation: translating to inconsistency of customer care
  - too many tools: often adding more complexity than value
  - not enough time in the day: especially to address new opportunities and create organisational alignment.*
- 79% agreed that customers are smarter and more informed now than in the past.

However, the stats supporting being customer-led are also compelling:

- Companies that lead in customer experience outperform laggards by nearly 80%.
- 84% of companies that work to improve their customer experience report an increase in their revenue.
- 73% of companies with above-average customer experience perform better financially than their competitors.
- Brands with superior customer experience bring in 5.7 times more revenue than competitors that lag in customer experience.
- Customer-centric companies are 60% more profitable than companies that don't focus on customers.
- Companies that excel at customer experience have 1.5 times more engaged employees than less customer-focused companies.

---

* offers.hubspot.com/state-of-customer-service

From the customer viewpoint:

- 96% of customers say customer service is important in their choice of loyalty to a brand
- 73% of consumers say a good experience is key in influencing their brand loyalties
- 77% of consumers say inefficient customer experiences detract from their quality of life
- Loyal customers are five times more likely to purchase again and four more times more likely to refer a friend to the company.

As you can see from the statistics above, being customer-led and having a focus on your customer experience, works.

From where you are today to where you want to be, enjoying these same benefits and results, there is one core philosophy that needs to be in place and adopted by everyone in your organisation. Let's address the elephant in the room (boardroom even) and challenge the concept that 'customer service' is a stand-alone function, rather than an all-of-business responsibility. This limiting belief is one of the blockages to success.

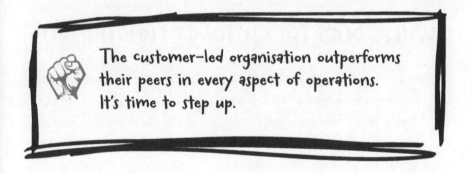

The customer-led organisation outperforms their peers in every aspect of operations. It's time to step up.

Chapter 7

CUSTOMER IS EVERYONE'S JOB

Customer is everyone's job – and the whole organisation needs to understand this key concept. Only then, will your organisation truly be customer-led.

WHERE DOES THE CUSTOMER FUNCTION SIT?

How and where we place 'customer' operations in our organisation is critically important to customer-led success.

For a lot of organisations, ownership of the customer sits with the Customer Services function. Sometimes they're positioned as a *support crew* alongside the Sales and Marketing function in commercial businesses or as *gatekeepers* to access services in government contexts. In most cases, they're generally a pretty long way down the food chain!

It's a tension that we see a lot in the organisations we work with – the 'us versus them' mentality. We'd have retired by now if we got a dollar for every time we heard complaints about one team against the other.

Funny thing though, when you step back – ultimately – everyone is on the same team. But we rarely see that in organisations running this traditional view.

WHERE'S IT AT FOR YOU?

Reflect on the structure of your organisation today. Where is the Customer Services function placed? How is it regarded – it is highly valued, or seen as the mop-up crew? How often does your leadership team spend time in the trenches, seeing customer interactions? Chances are, your Customer Services team are up for the revolution and ready for action!

It's at the coal face, where the vital interactions that can make or break an organisation's reputation actually take place. Take a Customer Service agent who goes rogue – for example, they side with a complaining customer, empathising with them about how bad the systems are or how crap the processes are or, even worse, bagging out their colleagues and team members. Often in protection mode, the agent sides with the customer to stand against the organisation to alleviate their own discomfort as the 'meat between the sandwich'. Instead of being empowered and having tools at hand to rectify a situation, the Customer Services team can be seen as the 'mop-up' department, whose role is to be the glue between broken processes, poor systems, average products, sub-standard solutions and the customer. And they feel it!

Of course, there are evolutions and mutations of this design. Sometimes marketing owns the customer, sometimes it's sales or some other equivalent function. The key question here is who **really should** own the customer?

THE REALITY: EVERYONE PLAYS A PART

Here's the rub. The customer is really everyone's job. Not only a job for Customer Services, or Marketing, or Sales… but for everyone.

Remember the famous quote from former SAS CEO Jan Carlzon which sums it up beautifully.

> If you're not serving the customer,
> your job is to be serving someone who is.

Team members who don't interact directly with the customer still impact the customer experience and need to be customer focused. Servicing their colleagues – their internal customers – to deliver the best customer experience is critical to the organisation's success. But it's more than just giving good service to each other internally. It is about connecting everyone to the ultimate reason your organisation exists in a way that compels them to do the right thing, without question.

THE CUSTOMER IS REALLY EVERYONE'S JOB.

ROCKETS AND MOP BUCKETS

It's here that we're reminded of the famous example of JFK visiting a NASA facility in the 1960s. The space race was on. USA versus USSR. Who would make it first?

JFK was walking through the corridors of the NASA facility and came across a janitor, going about his duties. He stopped and asked the man, 'What are you doing?' Now, the janitor could have stated the obvious – 'Cleaning the floor, Mr President.' But he didn't.

His response? 'I'm helping to put a man on the moon.' A true connectivity to purpose which propelled this janitor out of bed every day. This story puts into context that <u>everyone</u> plays a part in the organisation's success.

So, the question for you, our reader – how would your people respond to that question?

EVERYONE IN YOUR TEAM IS IN SALES

Your staff are also your advocates (or assassins). So, even when they're not at work, they're representing your organisation to customers (whether you like it or not). This is something that you can't directly control. However, by connecting them to the ultimate reason and engaging them on a deeper level, you can certainly influence them and the stories they tell.

THE IMPACT OF UNINTENDED CONSEQUENCES

We truly believe that no one ever shows up to work and says to themselves or others, 'I'm going to make it frustrating, annoying and difficult for customers today.' But somehow, in the complexity of organisational life, it just happens.

As a customer of a global financial services provider for some time now, we've experienced the perfect example of how unintended consequences flow through. Card schemes have a range of products, from basic no-frills offerings to uber-premium offerings with all the perks. At the low end, the card fee might be free while the premium offerings (like Platinum, Black, Advantage, etc.) come with a hefty 'membership fee'. What is your expectation as a customer of the service you get for each? Is it the same? Not likely. You're paying more for extra love and care the higher you go.

Then the clanger. The marketing team does a great job of schmoozing you with the premium offering and you sign up. Then, the behind the curtain functions take off. Next thing you know, you get your premium card in the mail… in exactly the same, boring, basic, bland card carrier you get for the free one. No bells, no whistles, just the basics. What happened? Well, the internal team who sends the cards out did their job (you received it, right?). Marketing did their job (they got you to sign up!). But, as a premium customer, you're left wondering, 'Is this all I'm worth? Is there really a difference between levels, because I can't see it!' You're less than impressed.

We've seen this a lot. Many of our clients have had major head-slap moments when they take a closer look at their customer experience and see the customer view, not just the functional view. This is why everyone in the organisation needs to own your customer. The unintended consequences happen and can only stop when everyone understands their part: essentially how they help put a man on the moon in your organisation.

HELP YOUR CUSTOMER TO HELP YOUR BUSINESS

A perfect example of the customer view is when we undertook a customer experience review for a major retailer. Positioned in a busy railway station location, customers dashed into the store on their way to work. Pressed for time, they'd often race around the store trying to locate their items while staff members were seldom to be found, oblivious to their stressed-out customers' pain. With more and more customers aborting mission, we suggested our client place a concierge at the store entry to help customers find what they needed in the shortest time possible. Not only did this help the customer and improve their satisfaction, it meant extra upselling opportunities with a 'Is there anything else we can help you find today?' enquiry. Footfall increased and even more importantly, daily revenue figures. What was once one of the worst performing stores in the group, turned around to become the benchmark for their peers.

The key is to reframe the way you see operations – from disconnected functional boxes to an integrated customer view. That is, an overall experience which is end-to-end. When customer truly becomes everyone's job, these disconnects magically disappear.

What happens on the inside of the organisation is reflected to the outside with customers. It is about moving from these moments being accidental to being intentional. And, in doing so, fundamentally shifting the dials towards stronger customer loyalty and advocacy, while energising your people to boot!

THE NEED TO SPREAD THE LOVE AND RALLY THE TROOPS

Customer is everyone's job – from boardroom to back office. Later in the book we'll give you some ideas on how to make this happen. But, right now, let's get the agenda straight. This is not an accidental thing. It requires a planned, intentional approach that reaches the various layers of your organisation in the right way.

You need to build a common knowledge base and level of capability around your customer. A structured approach, more than just bandaids. Going beyond individual opinion to shared insight that helps your people think, not just 'do'.

It's about thinking about the consequences of what you measure and the value you place on it. This links to how you reward your staff and the impact that targets and incentives can make.

It's about getting the right culture in place, which energises your people to go above and beyond. Providing them with principles or guides, not arduous rules, to act in the moment in a way that helps the customer and the organisation. It's about sharing a simple vision that includes the customer that directs everything they do – every decision or action – without confusion or waste.

If you take one thing from this book, it is that your organisation's success in the Customer-led Revolution requires one thing. It is a mindset shift towards 'the customer is everyone's job'. It might seem daunting at first, but there are many who have done it and reaped the rewards. It's our job to help you jump the experience curve and learn from their journeys to accelerate your own.

CUSTOMER OWNERSHIP IN ACTION

On a recent interstate flight, Sueanne was doing what she normally does – reading a business book. This particular time, she had a copy of Sir Richard Branson's autobiography in hand. Quite ironic really, since we were flying on a Virgin Australia flight.

Our hostie, Joel spied the book while offering us the standard options of tea, coffee or water. As he served us, he remarked, 'Oh, such a great book – have you read his other one as well?' After a few short moments of engaging conversation about how much they both loved the books, Joel wished us well and continued about his duties. Moments later, Joel returned with a glass of prosecco for us both. 'This one's on Richard – thanks for flying with us.'

At this moment, we felt as though Sir Richard himself was handing us this prosecco. Talk about empowering your staff to live and breathe your brand! And who do we solely fly with now? You can have one guess. Thanks, Joel, for embracing the concept that customer is everyone's business!

It seems so simple on the surface. So why isn't everyone doing it? Let's have a look at what is at play and some of the barriers that hold leaders back.

Everyone in your organisation, from boardroom to back office, is working for the customer – whether they like it or not.

Chapter 8

IF IT'S SO IMPORTANT, WHY ISN'T EVERYONE DOING IT?

Ah, we love this question so much!

If it's so cool, if it's so great, so powerful, profitable, ground-breaking, incredible, if it's all the things – then why are so few people doing it? Why isn't everyone doing it?

WHAT'S HOLDING THEM BACK?

When we spoke to a cross-section of CEOs, CCOs, business leaders and senior management in our book research phase, we asked this exact question – what's stopping businesses and organisations from becoming truly customer-led?

The answers were both interesting, not dissimilar to each other and in many ways, certainly not surprising – well, not to us.

> History, arrogance, bureaucracy, fear of test and learn. Too many
> people like to say that process stops companies from being
> customer-centric, but in fact good processes allow for it.

If you are able to use process to empower frontline staff, they can make decisions faster about how to help the customer.

Sommer Moore, Customer Experience Specialist, Boehringer Ingleheim

The fear of change and failure is a detrimental factor to being customer-centric. When technology and ideologies of the world change, the product should also pivot/adapt at the same rate of change. Being afraid to pivot at the right juncture could also lead to very unpleasant results.

Vivek Vasudevan, CCO, atisfy

There's corporate inertia around 'this has always worked / is working' as opposed to 'what's possible if we do something different?' Obviously there's expense, and there's complexity. Some organisations are so huge, like ocean liners – it takes forever to change direction or come to a stop.

Ben Alcock, Marketing Manager, Zepto

Organisations are inherently machines of self-preservation. They must survive to do battle with competitors and get their rightful share of a given market. This naturally makes them inwardly-focused. Marketing focuses on communicating features. Sales focuses on revenue. Engineering focuses on improvements. Operations focuses on efficiency gains. Once we understand this, the challenge is to change the paradigm: to become outwardly-focused. Many organisations pay lip service to this. Why? Because it requires a fundamental change of how a company operates and, also, leadership is often risk-averse. So, it's a rare thing. But the organisations that turn themselves 'outside-in' do reap a disproportionate share of the spoils.

Ron Ferdinand, CCO, ilume™

Mainly, a focus on short-term results over the long-term. In addition, data discipline is required to understand lifetime profitability of a firm's customers, which would inform the approach to customer experience for specific cohorts. Of course, a genuine commitment to 'thinking customer first', and a corresponding investment in CX, is more rare than common and this is key to embedding a customer-centric culture.

Chris Kenny, HO National Customer Experience, Stockland

THE ROADBLOCKS - THE BASIC ONES

There are so many roadblocks in business, it's hard to pick just one or two that could be standing in the way of customer-led success. And it's often the roadblocks we place in front of ourselves that do the most damage. Or worse still, the ones our fellow leaders put up to serve their own agendas, protect their own workload or avoid change for fear of how it might impact their remit.

Apathy

Apathy is a dangerous thing. While not showing up as an extreme or intentional action to take down your business, it's more an insidious, creeping disease that often starts in a number of places in an organisation and quickly spreads through the culture and into your performance.

When your team stops caring about how your business is performing or what impact they're having on the world, you're in trouble.

Entire teams and departments flicking the customer back to the Customer Services Department, not taking responsibility for their actions or their part in the customer experience, finger pointing and pleading ignorance are some of the ways apathy can show up in your organisation. And often, it creeps in quietly, makes itself comfortable, puts its feet up on your favourite coffee table and settles in, often without detection.

Lack of awareness

In our work and conversations with clever business leaders across the world, we've found that with the breadth and depth of their workload, it can be hard to keep abreast of what's going on, not only on the inside but on the outside of the organisation. Beyond spreadsheets and monthly reports where you can see how you've performed (we call it a lagging indi-cator – more on this later), there's little depth of knowledge in the why.

(p187)

CEOs constantly tell us of these niggling feelings or thoughts they have about the business performance, how they know something's not quite right but they can't put their finger on it. The figures show that perhaps business is okay but not particularly great, or that something's wreaking havoc on the monthly figures or YoY stats. But what?

Inside-out perspective

Viewing the world only from the inside looking out is a surefire way of limiting your potential for success. Call it standing in your glass house looking out, without ever stepping outside and taking a look at your business from the customer's perspective. It's a dangerous and limiting approach that many still take.

We find ourselves in business becoming precious about the products we build or the services we deliver. Historically, businesses were in the position of power when it came to transacting with customers, but those days are well and truly gone. No more 'you can have any colour you like as long as it's black' Henry Ford type approaches, the customer expects us to stand in their shoes and see the world from their view. We call it, outside-in. By stepping into our customer's shoes and seeing our business and the world as they do, we reveal threats and opportunities we may never have known about.

Blinkers on

Without the right people in leadership positions in our organisations, we can be left with a bunch of subject matter experts (from Finance to IT to Legal to Marketing) that are so intently focused on their own discipline, reporting and performance, that they refuse to take off the blinkers that keep them siloed and single-minded.

Keep your blinkers on and you'll find yourself left behind, or worse still, no longer in the race.

ROADBLOCKS - THE MEATIER ONES

So, that was the politically correct list of roadblocks or things that are holding leaders and organisations back today. Here's our meatier version of what's getting in the way.

Different ideas of what customer-led means

You'd be surprised how many leaders and teams don't actually understand what being customer-led really means. They might say they do and they might even believe they do, but many have not done the groundwork needed to be successful at it.

In fact, we find it quite common that the leader – be it the CEO, CCO or senior leader of say, Marketing or Customer – might know what being customer-led is, but their team doesn't.

What happens in these situations is that everyone thinks they're rowing towards the same destination, but in reality, they're not.

And without clarifying what being customer-led means, not only by a generic definition but what it means **in your organisation**, fragmentation, wasted effort and inevitable disillusionment will happen.

Get your team on the same page, get them to understand what being customer-led means and what it looks like for you, then get them doing that stuff. Oh, and don't forget to incentivise them and reward them for doing it too – no point telling them to do one thing then paying them to do another.

The 'not my job!' problem

The 'not my job' mindset takes apathy to the next level. Instead of just being uninterested in getting involved or lacking passion or energy for the purpose and goals of the organisation, these people actively avoid and hands-up-in-the-air-just-don't-care about their role in whatever initiative you are trying to get off the ground.

Fear of change

The fear of change in business is inevitable on many levels and it's unlikely you'll ever have a leadership team that doesn't have some degree of fear. It's natural, after all. But when the fear of change gets in the way of your success, of moving forward, of aligning with your customers and letting go of old habits and practices that no longer serve you, then it's a problem.

Fear of change is very closely linked to the culture of the organisation. Just think about how start-ups operate compared to mature businesses. Start-ups often have very entrepreneurial, risk-taking roots where teams are encouraged to take a chance on ideas in order to break ground. They try stuff, fail fast, pick themselves up and move on. The fear factor is generally low in these environments, for good reason and for great outcomes.

Although the start-up leaders were originally not averse to fear, as the start-up becomes a thriving profitable business, they can begin to avoid taking risks for fear of losing all they've built and shift from risk-takers to risk-avoiders. This culture permeates throughout the organisation with middle managers becoming fearful of taking risks that might lead to cancelled bonuses or restricted performance. Employees become fearful of making mistakes that cause the wrath of their managers. Change is seen as the biggest risk of all, for all.

Whether it's been deeply ingrained in your organisation for decades or a relatively new thing, fear of change can significantly impact your performance, the health and wellbeing of your team and the culture of your organisation.

Complexity

The more complex a business or organisation becomes, the trickier it can feel to make the changes you need to become truly customer-led. But we promise you, it's not impossible.

The complexity can lie in a number of different areas – the way your business is structured, your leadership team, your product lines or service offerings. It could be your technology that's complex, your financial processes or your training. Or it could be all of the above.

That's not to mention factors like numerous stakeholders, market uncertainty or new regulations impacting your operations. The list is endless, let's face it. And when things get complicated, us humans don't really cope. We like things to be relatively simple, straightforward. Who loves to untangle a laptop cord that's been in your work bag all week? Or untangle a bunch of clothes hangers that have been stored in a box? Don't get us started on paper clips!

But there's a difference between complexity and complicated, according to beinformed.com.

Complicatedness is something we create ourselves, including all the systems, processes and exceptions organisations have created. Over the years, businesses have stacked complicated systems and processes, but it has rarely given them greater control. Instead, all of these layers have led to less control, inefficient operations and a growing distance from the customer.

When it comes to complexity, while it's logical and natural for organisations to try to reduce it, complexity cannot be reduced. In fact, it's a dangerous and often counterproductive approach as it leads to oversimplified processes, systems and controls that are disconnected from reality. Organisations can achieve a competitive advantage through a different competence: embracing complexity.*

Bandaid solutions

Ah, bandaid solutions. Commonly used in businesses and organisations across the world, bandaid solutions have become the best friend of the leader or worker who wants a quick win on the surface, who wants to tick a box and move on...

---

* www.beinformed.com/blog/how-complexity-influences-your-organization/

We found this interesting quote from Malcolm Gladwell –

> The BandAid solution is actually the best kind of solution because
> it involves solving a problem with the minimum amount of effort
> and time and cost.

We absolutely agree – for small things like finding a solution to a customer's problem on the spot or taping up a loose cord on the office floor, bandaid solutions are the best.

But, the bandaid solution, when used in the wrong context or situation, is one of the main reasons businesses find themselves in trouble. Call them quick fixes, stopgaps, makeshifts, remedies, cure-alls – the terms are countless but they mean the same thing. Quick, let's find a solution that covers our butts now, we'll worry about the future later!

One of our favourite Local Government clients told us about the mess his IT and customer record system was in, when we spoke with him about the challenges he was facing in his organisation. Disastrous, the system had been 'bandaided' by IT and CRM 'experts' for years, resulting in such a complete mess of tools and processes, none of which could talk to each other and none that formed the basis of the customer relationship system they actually needed to service their customers. It was, in fact, his biggest challenge and the hardest one to fix.

If you use bandaids for big issues, please stop. Or at least consider the ramifications first. It's the brave business leaders, the ones committed to true change to become customer-led, who say NO when their teams suggest another quick fix. Granted, there are times when you need to take quick and firm action to fix a problem, but building your solutions, systems and processes – be it IT, financial or customer service – on these quick fixes, is a recipe for disaster. Oh, and if you already have an organisation built on bandaids, don't worry – there are things you can do and we're here to help.

Expense

'It's too expensive.' 'That'll cost a fortune!' 'Who has the budget to do THAT?' We've heard it all before. We've felt it all before.

The pain of attributing cost to something that we can't see can be hard, and it can certainly be hard to justify to boards or stakeholders or even management and teams.

We all want the quick return. To invest money in the things that will show up the quickest, that we can see, that we can feel and touch, that we can add to our KPIs and our list of achievements this month.

Being more customer-led doesn't fit into that category of put some money in here, see it improve there – like marketing spend, where you invest one month and by the next day, week or month, you've seen greater traffic, more sales, higher revenue. It doesn't work like that unfortunately.

But cost will always be one of the excuses used to talk yourself out of investing in being more customer-led.

We've had potential clients over the years who've laboured over whether to invest in a process with us, often asking for quotes and then on receipt, aborting mission. Even with clear, distinct and tangible benefits of investing in becoming more customer-led, business leaders, despite having had the initiative and drive to ask the question and get the quote, can't see it in themselves to put their hands in their pockets.

And that's okay. But please don't use cost as an excuse. You just have to look at what other organisations have achieved in switching their focus to customer, and the argument goes out the window.

But this is the way we've always done it – aka things are working fine right now

In most organisations, you'll find at least a handful of people who refuse to change anything because 'if it ain't broke, don't fix it'.

Why change things up if they're seemingly working okay? Why? Because if you look a little deeper than the bandaids and the monthly figures, you'll know that things aren't really okay.

Customers are changing, competitors are changing, the world is changing. Those businesses that continue to do what they've always done because it's always worked, will find themselves left behind. This attitude and approach can only take you so far. In the meantime, your competitors – both direct and indirect – are changing things up, taking risks, shaking up their worlds, challenging their staff, hunting down their competitors and frankly, not staying still.

For example, your monthly figures might be looking okay but your customer complaints seem to be increasing. Ah, must be because customer expectations are going up, nothing to do with you guys. It'll settle down again soon.

Or it could be seasonality, or a competitor has just run a massive campaign, or someone has a promo on and the prices have dropped temporarily, or it could be that Siobhan from Sales just left and well, she was our best sales person ever...

Excuses. Reasons. Look hard enough and you'll be able to make a list a page long of the reasons why things are happening in your organisation. Add mercury retrograde to it and your list is complete!

Or, you can stop, take the signs for what they are, and make a change.

You'll know in your gut whether things are okay or not. You'll know whether the things you've always done truly are the right things or whether you've been mulling over it for a while and think a few tweaks (or a huge overhaul) are in order.

CUSTOMERS ARE CHANGING, COMPETITORS ARE CHANGING, THE WORLD IS CHANGING.

Those that make the bravest decisions, make the greatest impact and movement forward.

Short-term thinking

This has got to be one of the biggest killers of success in our experience.

Even if you, the CEO or senior business leader have longer-term visions and aspirations, if your leadership team are all about the monthly figures, latest CSAT results and the number of likes on social media, then you've got yourself a problem.

Most businesses who find themselves on Struggle Street have this issue. The unrelenting focus on the short term without any – or very little – focus or attention on the medium to longer term. This is a slippery slope as the leaders – and therefore the rest of the team – shift their focus away from outside the organisation (customer, competitors, market) to what's happening on the inside (monthly P&L, efficiency numbers, internal reports).

By shifting the focus up towards the horizon, you and your team can have a better view of the landscape you're heading towards, the black spots and potholes you might encounter and even more importantly, the direction your customer is going.

No one wants to end up at a barren island when there's a tropical oasis with profit, customer connection and happy staff nearby.

LOOKING AT WHAT'S WORKING RATHER THAN WHAT'S POSSIBLE

We've given you quite a list of the black holes we've observed.

The fundamental difference between leaders who embrace being customer-led and the change this requires and those that don't – is this:

The leaders who are happy where they are look at what's working and focus on doing more of the same.

The leaders who want more, who want to improve, grow and thrive look at what's possible, beyond what's working and what they're doing today.

Which leader are you?

ASSESSING THE ROADBLOCKS

So, there you have it, the roadblocks to success that we have seen in our extensive work with clients all over the world. From small businesses to large corporations, no one is immune.

So what now?

Whether you're acutely aware that one or a few or all of these exist in your own business or organisation, or whether you think you're all over it, the important thing is not in the naming or blaming but in the awareness.

The need for a broader awareness of the gaps

Chances are, as a leader in your organisation, you have at least some level of awareness of the roadblocks and gaps that exist.

The need is for a broader awareness of those gaps, of those challenges that are holding you back. Beyond you or your senior leadership team (which is where many of the gaps and blockages actually exist), the entire business needs to be on the same page, with a level of awareness and accountability. And the willingness to change, of course.

Coming to terms with not being perfect, and having the tough conversations

As we mentioned, it's not about naming and shaming certain parts of the organisation or certain leaders or teams.

It's about accepting that no one is perfect, that perfection itself does not exist and that the power is in working together to overcome the obstacles, eradicate the bad habits, and rewrite the culture of the organisation. It's about giving things a try and accepting when they don't work out. It's about throwing out shame and blame and embracing change.

Tough conversations are just that, tough. But framing up change and improvement as a whole of organisation effort, rather than one person's, leader's or team's responsibility, can go a long way to getting everyone on the same page and engaged in the process.

Overcoming pride, egos and finger pointing to true collaboration

We've seen the whole gammit of players in our half day Customer-led Accelerator Program* with senior leaders and middle managers – from the arm-cross-ers, the don't-make-eye-contact-ers, the why-am-I-here-ers, the here-we-go-again-ers – to the I'm-so-excited-to-be-here-ers and the let's-get-going-ers.

All you need to do is look around the table in one of our sessions to identify who's who in the zoo and the roles they play in achieving – or not achieving – the company's goals and objectives. It's fascinating.

---

* Check out the end of this book for more info on our Customer-led Accelerator Program – it's a ground-breaking exercise that will change the way you look at your business and your leaders, in half a day!

It's often the egos, the pride and the finger pointing that goes on at different levels of the organisation that create the pain in the first place, or at least much of the pain.

By bringing your team together in one room, in a place where they can share their ideas, their thoughts and their views about what's going well and not so well in your organisation, we find these egos and attitudes soon take a backseat.

A backseat to what? To the customer. To the good of the organisation. To the reconnection with why they work for you in the first place. To the desire to make a change, to achieve, to create.

It's a beautiful thing and something that you **can** achieve. And you will achieve it, we promise.

Now, some of those things appear insurmountable, but they're not. You may feel like this customer-led thing is one for the 'too hard basket'. But, what happens if your organisation doesn't make the leap to becoming customer-led? Let's see.

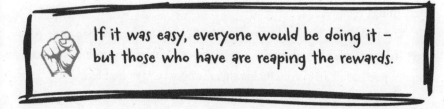

If it was easy, everyone would be doing it – but those who have are reaping the rewards.

Chapter 9

WHAT HAPPENS IF I DON'T?

So, by now we're thinking you're 100% on board with this whole customer-led 'thing', right?

The people we believed would read this book are people like you. You get that customer is important – even crucial – to your success, you just might need some help convincing those around you of that fact.

Revolution is here – things are changing whether you or the people around you like it or not. Customers are taking charge and they won't suffer fools lightly. Nor will they suffer bad service, impersonal service, being disregarded, being hard-sold to, or anything like that. You simply have to change if you're going to survive.

Your competition is doing it – even if you don't see or hear that they are doing something, it doesn't mean it's not happening. And even more importantly, it's the businesses that you don't even see as your competitors that are driving the stakes up, the standards higher, the customer expectations skybound. No longer do customers only compare like-for-like products or services, they compare everybody they encounter. You have to keep up or get ahead, if you're going to survive.

> **YOU SIMPLY HAVE TO KEEP UP OR GET AHEAD, IF YOU'RE GOING TO SURVIVE.**

Customers aren't just comparing like products anymore. They're comparing their customer experiences.

When you start really looking at why you're not where you want to be, why you're not achieving your goals or making sales or keeping your staff or whatever else is important to you, red flags will soon raise their little red heads. Ignore them at your peril. Remember it's not about who's right or wrong, finger pointing or blaming, it's about embracing what's working, changing what's not and moving onwards and upwards. Yes, it really is that simple.

THERE'S NOT A LOT OF CHOICE IN THE MATTER

The reality is this – you don't really have a choice as to whether you jump on the customer bandwagon or not. We don't mean to be harsh, but it's true.

In fact, those businesses that continue to ignore their customers, push them to the side or continue to be business-centric, will suffer. It may only be a red flag or two here and there for now, but those issues, gaps and performance slips will get worse.

> CUSTOMERS AREN'T JUST COMPARING LIKE PRODUCTS ANYMORE. THEY'RE COMPARING THEIR CUSTOMER EXPERIENCES.

Let's take a look at three cases where once market leaders lost sight of the customer to their ultimate demise.

BLOCKBUSTER

We know this is a common example to use, but let's talk Blockbuster for a moment. Once a global leader in video rentals and valued at $5 billion, Blockbuster went bankrupt in 2010.

There are many stories and reasons touted for why they failed, from their lack of technology nous to leadership issues to their business model. The truth is, a major factor in their demise was their lack of understanding of their customer. (Their reliance on late fees – read: their reliance on penalising their customers – was astounding!)

Customer needs were changing, technology was changing, competition was changing. Blockbuster was so busy being the market leader, smashing goals and raking in the money, they didn't notice their customers and competition emerging and evolving around them. They forgot that customers were the ultimate reason they were in business in the first place. And they suffered for it.

On the surface, they may have had good customer service but ultimately, they treated their customer interactions as transactions. They failed to build a connection with customers and meet their emerging needs. Nor did they bring them into the heart of their decision-making to set them up for the next phase of business, the future. With retail sites everywhere, they had huge capital investment. Meanwhile, their ninja competitor Netflix (who, did you know, actually proposed a partnership with them in 2000?) had far lower costs in their mail-order model, allowing them to offer their customers far greater variety. Instead of charging to rent videos, Netflix offered subscriptions, which made late fees unnecessary. In fact, instead of being on the company's timeline, customers could choose how long they wanted to hold on to the video before returning it for a new one.

Blockbuster soon cottoned on to what was going on and tried to change their course, but a series of leadership decisions and a growing competitor stopped them.

Perhaps if they knew their customers and their needs better, they could have evolved – it would have meant some tough conversations about the sacred cows internally but if they were customer-led, chances are that Blockbuster might have been the Netflix of today.

BLACKBERRY

Blackberry, once a market leader in portable devices and valued at $55 billion US, reported a $4.4 billion loss and a 56% revenue decline in 2009. They believe it wasn't that they didn't listen to their customers, it's just that they 'knew better' than their customers when it came to what they needed in a smart phone.

'The problem wasn't that we stopped listening to customers,' said one former insider. 'We believed we knew better what customers needed long term than they did.'*

Interesting reflection and yet, kind of the same thing as not listening, no?

---

* www.theglobeandmail.com/report-on-business/the-inside-story-of-why-blackberry-is-failing/article14563602/

BORDERS

An international book and music retailer founded by two entrepreneurial brothers at university, Borders had locations across the world and in 2006, recorded $600 million in sales of CD and DVDs alone (17% of their total revenue). They went bankrupt in 2011. The reason? Not only did they fail to monitor and adapt to shifts in customer preferences, their leadership team were not on the same page.

'We were all working hard towards a different outcome,' President Mike Edwards said. '[B]ut the headwinds we have been facing for quite some time, including the rapidly changing book industry, e-reader revolution and turbulent economy, have brought us to where we are now.'*

---

* slate.com/business/2011/07/borders-bankruptcy-done-in-by-its-own-stupidity-not-the-internet.html

IGNORE THE CUSTOMER-LED REVOLUTION AT YOUR PERIL

As we can see, even globally successful businesses aren't immune to failure. By taking their eye off the 'customer' ball, things can go very wrong, very quickly.

When businesses ignore their customer and keep doing what they've always done, or worse still, think they know better than their customer, one or all of these things can happen:

- **They become irrelevant to their customers** – so focused on their own products, services and offerings, they lose sight of what the customer wants and continue to focus on themselves. Until the customer doesn't care anymore and they become irrelevant. Remember the quote from the Blackberry exec above?
- **They lose market share** – at first, they might blame it on the economy or on a new competitor, perhaps even ignore it altogether while they busy themselves selling harder or making their staff work longer hours. Until their market share slide becomes something they can no longer ignore and they realise the customer has gone elsewhere.
- **They begin to lose staff** – so focused on driving revenue, protecting personal interests and saving face, they lose sight of who their staff are and how important they are. They ride them hard, question their integrity and blame them for the issues. Until the staff become so fed up, they move on to another business or worse still, a competitor.
- **Their profitability suffers** – when things go wrong, businesses tend to throw good money after bad, flailing and trying hard to recover the business they once had. Marketing, sales, promotions, investment, a brand-new IT system, incentives, sales, price reductions, new staff, a new business coach, a 'save-all' training program for their staff – they throw money at whatever they think will save the ship. Except it doesn't save the ship and they're still not focusing on the ultimate reason they're in business – the customer.

- **They have lower efficiencies** – when business leaders start to panic about falling numbers or poor performance, they tend to lean on their staff and team. By putting pressure on the frontline staff and their supporters in departments like IT, HR, Finance, Legal or Website Development, everyone begins to suffer. Calm, efficient, considered efforts fall ill to desperate measures to sell, sell, sell. Efficiencies fall, costs go up and the culture and people suffer as a consequence. Oh, and the senior leaders are so focused on the financials, they tend to miss that this is all happening, until it's too late.

- **Their brand reputation suffers** – so caught up in 'all the things', they forget one crucial thing – their brand reputation. While all of this is going on 'behind the scenes' (in our view, there is no such thing these days), the customer is likely having a few WTF moments, having noticed their service / product quality / price / delivery dates / staff attitudes / communication change over time. Take it from us, customers notice.

And when things like the above happen, people talk. Staff and customers. And they talk and talk and talk. Not just to 10 friends but to thousands of people. This is where the business's reputation can really suffer, sometimes irreversibly. We love this quote from Warren Buffett:

> It takes 20 years to build a reputation and five minutes to ruin it.
> If you think about that, you'll do things differently.*

Short-term, reactive thinking and actions can ruin a business.

The need to take action

Okay, so by now, surely you're convinced that taking action is crucial.

You may be asking yourselves, why are they still talking about this? We're not convincing you that customer is important, we know that you know that. But we ARE convincing you that it's time to stop talking about it / thinking about it / dreaming about it, and JUST. DO. IT.

---

* repairbadreputation.com/quotes-about-reputation/

Now is the time to take action, in fact there has never been a better time. Okay, maybe yesterday or last week, but we can't go back there, so let's stick with the achievable!

Let's highlight, find and nail those red flags before they get too big, too hard and too disastrous for us to tame. You've got this, and we've got you. Let's continue to share some wisdom from our experience and set you up for success.

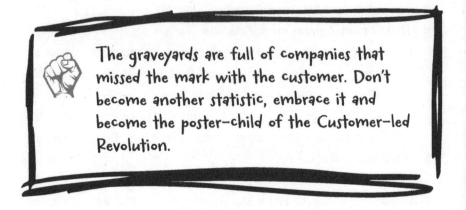

The graveyards are full of companies that missed the mark with the customer. Don't become another statistic, embrace it and become the poster-child of the Customer-led Revolution.

Chapter 10

BEFORE YOU SET OFF ON YOUR JOURNEY

Even though becoming customer-led is a relatively new concept in business, there's an opportunity to learn from our experience, averting making the same mistakes and jumping the experience curve. To set you up for success, we wanted to share some things you need to have in your kit bag before you set out on this journey.

MOVING FORWARD, WHICH PATH WILL YOU TAKE?

You've seen what success looks like and the benefits it will bring. You've seen examples of those who have done it. You've also had an insight into what happens if you don't get onboard. Every chapter until now has led to this moment.

It's this part of the book where you have to make a choice. Remember in the *Matrix* films, Neo was presented with the blue pill and the red pill. If you take the blue pill, everything just goes back to the way it was. Everything you've seen so far didn't happen. There's no Customer-led Revolution coming. You can just go about your seemingly merry way.

But, as the courageous leader you are, you decide to take the red pill. In taking the red pill, you can no longer unsee or unlearn these things. As a result, you can't go back to the way things were, because you now know.

This is that same point. Don't worry – Samuel L Jackson isn't going to come and kick your ass if you decide 'this is too much'.

However, in making the decision to keep reading, you're going for the red pill of becoming truly customer-led. There will be naysayers. There will be blockers. But, you will know better.

It's time to enter the matrix… okay, maybe not that dramatic, but you get our drift!

THE INGREDIENTS FOR SUCCESS

Let's take a look at what you'll need for the journey ahead (now that you've taken the red pill).

In all of our work to date, we've identified five ingredients that make or break a campaign to transform into being a customer-led organisation. Some of these aren't specific to just making a customer-led change and may apply to other things you might want to make happen. But – they're consistently present when we examine those businesses that are a success or a failure.

Courageous leadership

Your customer-led journey won't go anywhere without a courageous leader driving it and clearing the path for reinvention. It. Just. Won't. Start. It requires someone (even better a small group) with the mettle to challenge the status quo, to stand alone at times, to swim against the tide… or whatever analogy comes to mind! In most situations, you'll challenge the core foundations of the existing organisation. You'll find scorpions under rocks, like 'we've been doing it that way since…' and 'there's nothing wrong with that'. We've heard it all. It takes the right leader to see beyond all that, envision the future and, most importantly, recruit others to join the expedition to a better future.

Shared vision

Unless you know where you're rowing to, you'll all end up in different places. Consistently, we see successful organisations have a clear, compelling and repeatable vision for where they're going. The best ones start by engaging the wider team early, not just a single person coming up with a snappy slogan-style vision that is just MAAP (motherhood and apple pie). It's got to mean something and resonate with people at all levels, giving them clear direction for where the ship is heading. This clarity helps jettison those who aren't up for the journey too!

Team on board

With the first two ingredients on the shelf, it's about recruiting and getting the team onboard. Early – not after the fact. Making them part of the change. The old saying 'it takes a village to raise a child' is just as applicable here. To get this baby growing, you need to spread the word and get a core SWAT team of change-makers on your team. This is not about having a meeting or recruiting your Customer Services team. It's actively persuading, engaging and getting commitment from key functional leaders to sign on to the customer-led journey. With this wide scope pegged out, you can then move to the next ingredient for success.

Framework to lead them on the journey

This is where you need to provide some certainty and detail of the journey ahead. Without this, it could just look like a pipedream to those around you. So, you've recruited your band of merry change-makers and they're at the ready. They've signed on to the vision of where you're going. Where's the map to get you from where you are to where you need to be? To communicate the journey, you need a framework, a structure, to clearly lay out the rationale for how to move forward. That's when you, the smart courageous leader, will be ready with the answer, having taken the red pill and having this book in your hot little hands as a guide.

A CAUTIONARY TALE - IT'S NOT A TICK BOX EXERCISE

Here's the bad news from those who have the battle scars to prove it. If you're starting this journey to just 'tick a box' it's destined to fail. The veneer is easily seen through by your colleagues, the familiar wave of complacency washes over and the campaign is notched up to 'don't worry, this new fad will pass and we can get back to business as usual'.

It's also not going to reach success if becoming a customer-led organisation is only one department's problem. Countless times we have witnessed finger pointing between functional teams, each passing the responsibility (and dropping the ball) or directing 'that customer stuff' to be dealt with by the Customer Services team. By all means, it requires a senior leader to drive the initiative, but to be effective, the change has to be made the breadth and depth of the organisation.

While good PR can come from it, becoming customer-led shouldn't just be a public relations exercise. The risk here is that it becomes a bit 'lipstick on a pig' (no offence to the pig!) – and this can be dangerous. By outwardly stating you are customer-led, it raises customer expectations that you MUST be able to deliver on. Without the ingredients for success in place, delivery falls short of expectation for customers, losing trust and possibly doing the exact opposite of what you set out to achieve. By all means, once you have your ducks in a row, then turn on the PR machine. But, not before you're ready with the backbone to support it.

THE NEED TO: MAKE A CHOICE

Now that you know what you need and what to watch out for, it really is time to make a choice. Becoming customer-led can't be left to good fortune or accident. This is a conscious, intentional choice. By being intentional at this moment, everything you're about to read can be put into motion straight away.

Our framework has been tried and tested across many sectors, industries and organisations of all shapes and sizes. And, most importantly, it gets results. In the rest of this book, we'll be taking you through nine elements of the framework, sharing our insights, perspectives and experience for you to take action. While some of what we cover might seem familiar, the beauty of it lies in the power that it releases when combined with our intentional roadmap.

If you haven't taken the pill – now is the time. (Let's hope you chose the right one!)

BEING CUSTOMER-LED FEELS LIKE A BIG JOB

Being customer-led might feel like a big job, too big even. Depending on the size of your business or organisation, it can definitely seem like a mammoth effort. And quite simply, many of us just don't know where to start.

Well, trust us. You've started. By picking up this book, you're already on the journey.

In our line of work, we meet a lot of people. We can instantly recognise the people who think they've got it all figured out, who are sitting in one of our workshops or meetings with their arms crossed and a bored look on their face. 'I already know this stuff. What can you possibly teach me? You don't know a thing about (insert industry here).'

And there's those people who attend our online programs where we'll work across an industry or region, to step up the capability of an entire contingent, for example, a tourism region. There's those that show up every single week for the live (tutorial) sessions, keen to learn and share and collaborate with their industry peers, keen to see the world in a different way and build on their existing knowledge. And there's those who never show up. They're also the ones who are the first to complain, the first to say that the regional tourism body does nothing for them or that their industry colleagues are 'lucky' because they have more business or are doing better than them.

It's not about luck. It's about admitting that you don't know everything about everything, and that by building your knowledge, by widening your exposure to other's experiences, you can learn and grow and thrive.

There's no point telling your team, 'We need to be more customer-led'. They simply won't know what that means. You need to show them what this looks like. And then, when they do the stuff you want them to do, when they step into being customer-led, it helps to celebrate them and showcase to the wider team, what good looks like in your own organisation. How do **you** do good?

PEOPLE HAVE DONE IT AND TO GREAT SUCCESS

Everywhere you look these days, there's proof that focusing on your customers, getting to know them better and aligning your business around them, is a winning strategy.

And it's not impossible or out of reach. We promise.

It's not – if we stop giving reasons for why it won't work. If we stop doing the 'buts' and the 'if onlys' or the 'yeah but they have more budget / sites / people than we do'…

One of the challenges we see for business leaders in visualising their success and embracing the potential and possibility is this – there are many examples of successful customer-led organisations and brands and businesses, but they tend to be large, with big budgets, big teams and sometimes, even a celebrity entrepreneur head figure leading the charge (here's looking at you, Richard).

In our research, we also found it hard to find examples from Australia as most of them are based in the US or UK/Europe, who, let's be fair, have very different ways of doing business to the Aussies – well, the Americans at the very least.

We're asking you to trust us. We're going to show you lots of examples of successful businesses throughout this book, to inspire and educate and excite you. We may use a few of the big ones as examples, but we've made a big effort to look for the little ones too – because it's more likely you'll be able to do the things they do before you embrace the latest multi-million-dollar initiative of Sir Richard Branson!

IT DOESN'T HAPPEN BY ACCIDENT

To go on this journey requires intention. Nothing will happen by accident. Well, at least not at the beginning. You have to start your little fires within your organisation to get things moving, to get your team engaged, to create the change you need to succeed.

We harp on about this all the time. Because if you let things happen by accident, then you're not in charge. You're leaving it to luck, to hope, to the universe perhaps. You're leaving it to anyone but yourselves. If you lead with intent, with a view and a vision and a purpose of what and where and who you want to be in the world, then you're on track.

Make it intentional, not accidental.

THE NEED TO OVERCOME THE BARRIERS

The challenge may seem daunting, but we can assure you, you're not charting completely new territory. Yes, you may be charting new territory for your own business or even in your career, but there are experts to coach you (hello!) and peers to learn from.

But remember, one size does not fit all and we are not advocating that it does. Trust us, we know that you have your own nuances and challenges in your business and we respect that – just don't let that be your story that stops you making a change. The 'yes but no one else has this challenge…' story will only serve to take you down and stop you achieving your goals.

MAKE IT INTENTIONAL, NOT ACCIDENTAL.

One size does not fit all. Got it.

But you do need a roadmap or a playbook for your business that you can follow, based on those experts and those examples we mentioned, to help you get where you want to go.

This is that playbook. This is that roadmap. Whatever vehicle you feel you're travelling in, be it an old banged-up Holden or the latest Merc, this book will serve to show you the way – your way.

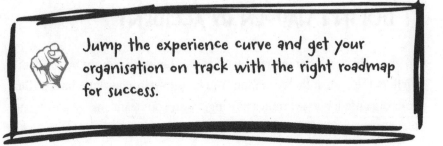

Jump the experience curve and get your organisation on track with the right roadmap for success.

THE CUSTOMER STRATEGY FRAMEWORK™ – YOUR ROADMAP TO SUCCESS

The revolution is coming. This is a given. We need a new type of organisation and operation to meet the demands and needs in the next era of business. This is known.

What's missing is the game plan and the guidance to move from where you are today, to where you want to be. In this section, we're going to explore the need to rethink the way strategies are connected in our organisations, pose some questions that can stump even the most customer-obsessed leaders and lay out a tangible, practical and actionable roadmap to get your organisation started on the journey to becoming truly customer-led.

It means being honest with yourself about where your organisation is at today, shifting thinking away from tactical solutions to looking at what's missing and how to close the gaps.

Chapter 11

CLOSE THE GAP BETWEEN STRATEGY AND OPERATIONS

We recently surveyed a range of business leaders and while all of them could rattle off their long list of strategies, less than three per cent had an identifiable, dedicated customer strategy. When you think about it, this is crazy considering customers are the ultimate reason any organisation or business exists.

STRATEGY IS A CRUCIAL BUSINESS TOOL

> Strategy is about what you do <u>and</u> what you don't do.
> *Costas Markides*

Strategy is the game plan chosen from a range of options. This isn't a book about broad strategy or even business vision – we figure you already know how each of these business elements work together. This is about your customer strategy, the one that's missing from the armoury of business.

But let's have a quick chat about vision and strategy to set the scene.

Strategies are important, right? Of course they are. They chart our way forward towards our vision, our destination, 'the island we're rowing to', as we like to say at Customer Frame.

Without a strategy, your organisation can appear rudderless. Your entire team can lack direction, seemingly rowing in different directions. Truth is, they're probably really trying hard to get somewhere, it's just that that 'somewhere' isn't known. Your business vision is unclear. There isn't a common destination and vision that they share. But they're still trying.

Most businesses have an overarching business strategy, and then (when done well), functional strategies and plans that support the wider business strategy and vision.

SO, WHAT IS A CUSTOMER STRATEGY?

A customer strategy is just like your average business or HR or IT strategy. Except, it's not.

A customer strategy's purpose is to help organisational leaders and teams put the customer at the heart of your business or organisation. It is the strategy that you create, adopt and deploy to build the necessary organisational capabilities to be a truly customer-led entity. These capabilities are the foundation for everything you do – product development, marketing, sales, service, support functions, everything.

> A CUSTOMER STRATEGY'S PURPOSE IS TO HELP LEADERS AND TEAMS TO PUT THE CUSTOMER AT THE HEART OF YOUR BUSINESS OR ORGANISATION.

Supporting your corporate strategy, it sets a destination, a place you want to be in the future in relation to your customer. It supports and informs your plan, laying out your roadmap to reach that destination, that 'customer-led nirvana', if you like.

WHAT'S THE DIFFERENCE?

The difference between a customer strategy and say, a HR or IT strategy is that the customer strategy must sit across **the entire organisation**, not just one specific department. With a HR strategy, for example, the HR Director is in charge of HR's strategic priorities, plans and KPIs, which primarily charts the priorities and actions of the HR team specifically.

The customer strategy, on the other hand, spans the entire organisation. It makes the customer everyone's business. Ideally the customer strategy would be headed by a Customer Director or CCO, but depending on the size of business, this might not be possible. It's one of the few strategies that is truly owned by everyone in the organisation.

SOMEONE NEEDS TO OWN THE CUSTOMER

Are you a small business with less than 40 employees? Then it's likely a CCO or Customer Director is an unreasonable request for you. But that doesn't mean someone shouldn't own the customer strategy. No matter how large or small you are, if you have customers, you should have someone waving their flag, representing them and steering the business towards them.

For those of you who have a team of 40 employees or more, you have no excuse. If the customer doesn't have a seat at your leadership table, then it's time they did. Why is 40 the magic number? In our experience, this is the number where the level of internal complexity starts to drift away from being close to the customer and those earlier chasms between customers, staff and leadership begin to appear.

Your customer strategy, much like any other strategy, provides a clear roadmap, has a set of consistent guiding principles or rules that define the actions your team should take (and shouldn't take) and the things they should prioritise to achieve your organisational goals.

The difference? Most of your strategies, such as your operational strategy or IT strategy, will likely be focused on operational contingencies, cost reduction, efficiencies and the like, probably with very little reference to customer. These strategies come from an operational viewpoint, an inside-out view.

The customer strategy flips this whole perspective on its head. The customer strategy incorporates all the operational and strategic priorities and considerations, but with the customer's desired outcomes, unmet needs, pain points and drivers at the heart. By bringing all the functions together to explore new solutions and ways of doing things, it brings the customer to every conversation and changes hearts, mindsets and ultimately, the world. It's an outside-in view.

Instead of pushing out to the world what you do as a business and selling it as it is, you stop and listen to what the world needs from you, then align your products, services and offerings with that. This then becomes part of your story and completes the circle.

Your customer strategy is more about your customer than it is about you. It's about putting them first. It's about what they need, not what you sell. Try to sit down and write a customer strategy that starts with your products or services or a story about you, and you're automatically off-track.

WHAT IT'S NOT

Your customer strategy is not a corporate strategy about which customers you're going to go after or not go after. That's what your marketing strategy should cover. It's not your customer service strategy or a set of rules that your staff should follow, like pick up the phone within five rings. It's working out what your organisation needs to focus on with the resources available – no one has an open cheque book after all.

It's sits neatly between your corporate strategy and your operational or functional strategies – it closes the gap, it's the glue between them.

YOUR CUSTOMER STRATEGY IS MORE ABOUT YOUR CUSTOMER, THAN IT IS ABOUT YOU.

London Business School Strategy Professor Costas Markides simplifies strategy beautifully into three areas – 'WHO, WHAT and HOW'. In paraphrasing his view, your strategic position is the combination of WHO (who are you targeting?), WHAT (what products or solutions are you offering?) and HOW (how you are delivering them?).

Your customer strategy, then, helps you build the capability to delve into the WHO, the WHAT and the HOW by beginning to define the answers and longer-term capabilities needed to make it a success. Your operational strategies simply plug in to support this delivery, creating the functional and technical expertise and action to make it happen.

WHO SHOULD OWN THE CUSTOMER STRATEGY?

So you've got it – a customer strategy is imperative for success.

You know that the CEO generally owns the overarching business strategy, while the functional leaders own their functional strategies that underpin the organisational one.

But who should own this customer strategy we keep harping on about?

We believe it should the CEO. Yes, that's right. No, not the Customer Services Manager or the Marketing Director. The CEO.

Okay, maybe the CEO and the C-suite, so the CEO has a team to support them.

Why? Because the CEO and the C-suite have the widest view of the organisation. They also have the widest impact, and in most cases, the widest experience too.

By having your top people on the customer strategy, you can ensure that the organisation, the team, can be steered in the right direction from the top. Think of the CEO as the captain leading their fleet of boats on the journey towards your organisation's vision. Ahead of the others, the CEO charts the way, steers the course and keeps the senior leaders (captains of their own boats) focused and motivated, all the while with their focus on their agreed destination. We expand on this analogy later. (p246)

That's exactly what they need to do with customers. Keep the focus, keep the heart, keep the faith.

It's for this reason we believe the CEO is the person ultimately responsible for the customer strategy, using it to set that true north point to guide the whole organisation.

Without this customer strategy, led and managed by the leaders within the organisation, functions will pull against each other. They will demand resources for competing objectives, bicker and fight in their quest to get what's rightfully theirs (remembering they're probably not really even thinking about the customer, but more about their KPIs or their own personal agendas or the latest cool thing they could do).

The result of a rudderless, leaderless customer strategy? Or worse still, one that's been 'lumped' with Customer Services or Marketing? Or even worse still, one that's been lumped with someone who doesn't even care or want the responsibility? Friction, tension, incompatible and inconsistent customer experiences and an undermined, unlikely-to-be-achieved, strategy. Lipstick on a pig. Potential damage to your organisational reputation.

We're not saying you can't enlist these business leaders in your quest. Even highlight the hotspots around your business of customer love that you could tap into. But it has to come from you, the leader. It has to come from the top.

IF IT DOESN'T COME FROM THE TOP, IT WON'T HAPPEN

We can't tell you how many times we have been approached by someone (usually middle management level) in a business or organisation who has heard about us, loves what we do and really wants to work with us.

We chat about their issues, we head nod vigorously as we've heard much of it before, they ask for a quote to help 'fix' the problem, we provide it, then it goes nowhere.

Ouch. For anyone who's ever prepared a quote before, you know how much time it takes. You know how much blood, sweat and tears go into understanding the organisation, creating the best solution for them, documenting it in a way that aligns with your brand, then often, presenting in person or via video conference. It's a lot of time. And in our case, not just time but heart, soul, thinking time, and a genuine desire to provide the best solution.

So, what's the problem?

Two things.

First off, these lovely individuals are simply too junior in the organisation to get the quote signed off. And this is where it gets tough. They're often in exactly the right place to notice what's going on and what needs to be done, but they don't have the sign-off authority or seniority to get it happening.

They try to push it up the levels to the 'right' person, who they have to convince to a) pay attention and listen, b) reallocate resources to support the project without truly knowing enough about it and c) put self-interest, ego, agenda or promises they've made to someone else aside to prioritise this new initiative. Tough gig.

The second issue – they think they know what's wrong and they think they know what they need but in reality, they often don't. We have had so many people call us and ask for us to provide a quote for say, a customer journey mapping process. When we dig deeper in our initial conversations, we realise that they actually don't know who their customers are (so how can they map their journey?). The issue is often far wider and far deeper than what appears on the surface.

UNLESS IT'S DOCUMENTED, IT'S NOT REAL

You can have all the will in the world, all the greatest intentions, but friends, if it's not documented, if it's not written down somewhere, then it just ain't real. Without documentation and formalisation, there's too much of a risk that the intent will be lost. Your plans, your ideas, your commitments, be it C-suite level or senior management or below – it simply must be documented.

And shared. For your senior leaders and your team to take things seriously, it needs to be documented, affirmed, intentional.

DIY – DO IT YOURSELF! OR DRIVE IT YOURSELF!

Within our Customer-led Accelerator Program, we take our clients through a diagnostic process, where we get them to score themselves on how they're performing in certain areas of the business. **They** highlight and tell us what the problems are. **They** work through the problems with us in the process and then **they** come up with the priority projects – what's most important, what's least important, what might have the biggest impact, what projects need whose support in the organisation. It's fascinating. And a lot of fun.

And that's where you get the most impact. When you work through the framework and truly understand what's going on – what's working, what's not working, where the gaps are.

Completely opposite to your standard consulting framework, where you pay a consultant a shag-load of money to diagnose your business problems (usually based on a few meetings and a good look over your financials) and give you recommendations that may or may not be achievable, relevant or aligned with your values.

Which leads us neatly into one of the main concepts of leading the Customer-led Revolution. That is, to reframe the customer to be an all-of-organisation capability.

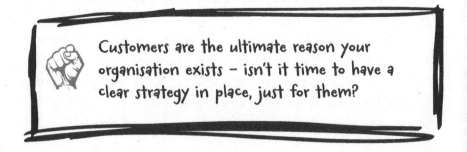

Customers are the ultimate reason your organisation exists – isn't it time to have a clear strategy in place, just for them?

Chapter 12

CUSTOMER IS AN ORGANISATIONAL CAPABILITY

A customer strategy can take many different forms. The key to leading the Customer-led Revolution is to create your customer strategy so that it progressively builds your organisation's capability around your customers.

CUSTOMER IS NOT A FUNCTION, IT'S A DISCIPLINE

Let's get one thing very clear. Customer is not a function and shouldn't sit as yet another 'department' on your organisational chart. Yes, customer services is a function, but we're focusing on making customer and the ownership of customer an organisational discipline. Not put in a box, but a discipline that can be built and strengthened over time.

While it may look a bit like business process reengineering, which certainly has a place in finding new efficiencies – being customer-led goes much, much deeper. It goes beyond the simple confines of 'Customer Service 101'.

(p54)

It is a fundamental shift in thinking. We've covered in previous chapters that the customer is everyone's job and that you're either serving a customer or serving someone who is. Becoming truly customer-led is about baking this thinking into the DNA of your organisation. No matter where you take a sample or a cut-through section of your organisation, you would see the same consistent level of customer-led orientation.

It's not about setting up another department or function to serve the customer. It is about engineering the whole organisation to serve the customer. This way, your team connects to why they do what they do and to the ultimate reason they're here. Your customer.

WHY SHOULD IT BE A CAPABILITY?

Think of your organisation as a person. What capabilities does this person have? If you're Porsche, you might have exceptional sports car design capability, production capability, marketing capability and so on. As a Council, you might have great compliance process capability, community consultation capability and so on.

Yes – by all means you need to have the functional and technical capability to deliver on the basic customer proposition. However, we propose that there is also room from boardroom to back office for what we call 'customer capability' – to ensure that you have the nous and knowledge of your customer at the heart of everything you do.

> NO MATTER WHERE YOU TAKE A SAMPLE OR A CUT-THROUGH SECTION OF YOUR ORGANISATION, YOU WOULD SEE THE SAME CONSISTENT LEVEL OF CUSTOMER-LED ORIENTATION.

And, the great thing about a capability is that it is something you can learn and build, to set you apart from competitors, make you more efficient, more effective and ultimately, more successful. Like any capability (like learning to ride a horse or be a burlesque dancer) you need to be working on the right capabilities to achieve your goals. And for our KPI driven folk, capability can be measured, tracked and improved. Measurement also means accountability. Phew – you can even get the bean counters on board by reorienting towards this view!

By reframing 'customer' to be an organisation capability, it also by default, engages the whole organisation. It is something that the whole team can get behind. The number of organisations that we've seen without a clear purpose or clarity on customers is astounding. The amount of waste that is created by people pulling in different directions, internal squabbling and just plain getting it wrong for the customer. Waste like this is a hidden cost. With the whole organisation view, you can seek to build capability in weaker areas and reinforce your strengths – with everyone playing their part. No longer just one person. It is the collective organisation focused on being better, stronger and more successful.

A NEED TO ASSESS YOUR CUSTOMER CAPABILITY

So, like any capability or skill, there are levels of proficiency and deficiency in your organisation's customer capability. Think of it like an iceberg. Some issues are easily seen – like a higher number of customer complaints, negative reviews, decreasing profitability or revenue declines. But, they can also be hidden, under the surface.

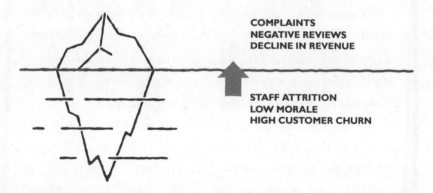

Figure 5: The iceberg – the seen and unseen issues that indicate a problem

Things like increased staff attrition, low staff engagement, high customer churn, low morale – these are all symptoms of a much deeper and more complex problem and are often hidden under the surface.

The great news – like personal skills, you can measure your organisation's customer capability. By getting a benchmark of where you are today, you can begin to systematically break down this complex problem into more manageable pieces.

However, it can't just be opinion-based or informed by some loosely constructed survey. We've seen this lead to even larger problems. What works is to use a standard approach that engages everybody at all levels – and that is what this book will give you. A common frame for everyone to look through and examine the issues together. This allows you to gauge where you are, but also measure your progress over time. Your organisation is made up of a range of smaller capabilities (not functions) that are the drivers of your overall success.

NO ONE LIKES A BAD REPORT CARD

The biggest hurdle at this point is to be honest, real and authentic in gaining this 'bench strength' view of customer capability. No one likes a bad report card, of course, but an assessment is of little use unless you get to the heart of the issues.

It's about shining a light on that elephant in the room, shooting the sacred cows or any other analogy you choose to use. Leave no stone unturned and challenge the current status quo. There are always roadblocks or diversions in place to cover up the gaps. Some of these could be intentional or simply inherited and never challenged.

As the leader of your Customer-led Revolution, it is your role to remove the anxiety and fear that may exist around bringing the customer in to the heart of your operation. It's about helping everyone on the journey to realise that only by working together and sharing the challenge can it be overcome.

NOT A TICK-BOX – BEING CUSTOMER-LED IS A JOURNEY THROUGH LEVELS OF MATURITY

We often see organisations operating under a compliance mindset. That is, getting the rubber stamp of reaching a particular standard, then moving on. It is either on or off, yes or no, have or have not. Being customer-led is not a binary destination. It is an evolution, a journey through various stages of development as the organisation builds its capability and strength in becoming truly customer-led.

In fact, there are five levels of customer-led maturity that organisations work through.

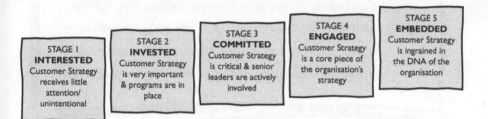

Figure 6: The five stages of customer-led maturity

By understanding where you are on the scale, you can begin to focus the whole organisation around the customer. Each stage represents a different set of activities and focus required – all helping to put the customer at the heart of everything you do. It also provides a stepped vision that can be shared, benchmarked and linked back to your customer improvement initiatives.

There is in fact another stage – Stage 0. That is for the organisation that is not yet on the journey at all. In one of our early engagements back in 2010, we benchmarked a quasi-government organisation in the UK. The organisation was a vital link between government and the business community who was struggling with internal inefficiencies. When we asked the senior leadership team, they expected to come in somewhere around Stage 2 – Invested. Imagine the surprise when their initial score didn't make the scale! Fast forward 18 months and, with focused customer-led programs in place, the organisation had leapfrogged to Stage 3 – Committed. But without knowing where they were, or the roadmap of where to go, they'd have remained stuck with their inherent inefficiency and believing they were somewhere else on the scale entirely.

So, how do you work it out? Do you wonder where your organisation would sit? What are the areas where you're doing well? This is not a service review or experience audit – it's about engaging at a more strategic level and addressing the questions that really drive your performance. And it starts by taking it back to three simple, strategic questions.

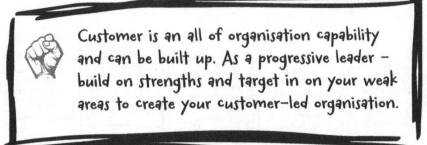

Customer is an all of organisation capability and can be built up. As a progressive leader – build on strengths and target in on your weak areas to create your customer-led organisation.

Chapter 13

THE THREE STRATEGIC QUESTIONS

We know the struggle. We've talked about the struggle.

There is hope. By putting the customer at the heart of everything you do and giving your senior leadership and wider team purpose, you can make the changes you need to make to become truly customer-led.

You may find yourself rudderless at this time, unable to chart a formidable and compelling way forward for your organisation and your team. You have the drive, the will and the skill, but you may not have the tools you need to make it happen.

We're about to show you that it is possible. With a simple, powerful framework through which to see your business, you will identify what's working, what's not working, and the actions you need to take to make the biggest difference to your business.

ASKING THE RIGHT QUESTIONS

First things first, it's about asking the right questions.

Countless clients we have taken through our process – if not all of them – have said to us, 'I never thought about it that way.' When they say that, we know we've nailed it.

Whether it's a one-on-one client consulting project or a workshop of senior leaders from a range of businesses, this framework and this thinking change lives.

The key – asking the **right questions**.

Once you start asking the right questions, you start to unearth the things that are holding you back, the things that you're doing well and the gaps you need to fill.

It's not easy, don't get us wrong. Questions often have answers we don't want to hear. Your senior leaders, middle management and your team may not like it.

But it's only by asking the powerful questions that you get the answers you need to make change. To make meaningful, long-lasting, ground-breaking, competitor-busting, market-leading change.

> IT'S ABOUT SEEING THE WORLD NOT AS YOURSELF BUT AS YOUR CUSTOMER. BECAUSE THE WAY THEY SEE THINGS IS THE WAY THINGS ARE.

It's about changing your view. From inside-out to outside-in. It's about seeing the world not as yourself but as your customer. Because the way they see things is the way things are. It's that simple. It doesn't matter what you think or do or believe, your customer's perception is your customer's – and in turn, your business's – reality.

Did you know that 70% of buying experiences are based on how the customer **feels** they're being treated?* Fascinating, right?

As we always say in Customer Frame, once you see the world from your customer's view, you can never unsee it.

So, what are the right questions?

Based on our combined 50 plus years of experience, we've been exposed to a huge range of different business environments, markets, countries,

---

* www.helpscout.com/75-customer-service-facts-quotes-statistics/

leadership styles, organisational challenges and team cultures. You name it, we've probably seen it.

It may seem impossible to think that we could have a framework or an approach that could apply to all of these different styles and situations. But trust us, it's possible. And we do.

In our Customer Strategy Framework™, on which this book is based, we ask three strategic overarching questions that help begin to chart your roadmap to success:

- KNOW – Do you know who your customers are and what's important to them?
- TRACK – Do you track your organisation's performance from the customer's view?
- ALIGN – Do you align your organisation to the customer?

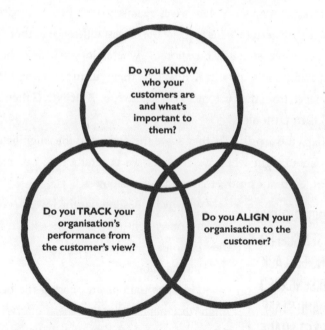

Figure 7: The three core questions of being customer-led

Pretty simple – yet powerful – questions, right?

Read over them again. Go on. Look, if you're anything like us, you probably skimmed over them, answered, 'Pffft, yeah of course,' and moved on.

But have you ever really asked yourself these questions? We'd hazard a guess that you probably haven't. At least not in the context of each other. Perhaps one or two in isolation, but we doubt you've got the trifecta before.

And that's okay, because most people haven't. But what matters now is asking these three questions of yourself and your team, together.

A FASCINATING INSIGHT

An interesting thing happens when we ask these questions of our clients and audiences.

p115 Using our Customer Strategy Framework™ (which you'll hear about later), we use the three strategic questions to gauge their performance in the nine key areas an organisation needs to be strong in to be truly customer-led. As part of the process, they score themselves against world's best practice to figure out where they need to focus to make the biggest difference in **their** business.

Of our three strategic questions – where do you think the highest scores usually show up – in KNOWING their customer, TRACKING their performance from the customer's perspective, or ALIGNING their business around their customers?

Perhaps unsurprisingly, they score the highest in the Align field, which sounds about right when we consider we generally base our marketing, sales, PR, even our product, around our customers.

IS IT ANY WONDER THEN, THAT BUSINESSES SUFFER FROM INEFFICIENCIES, LACK OF DIRECTION, DISENGAGED CUSTOMERS AND STAFF, FLAILING MARKET SHARE AND REVENUES, WHEN IT'S QUITE POSSIBLE THAT THE EFFORTS THEY'RE MAKING ARE ACTUALLY ALIGNED TO THE WRONG THINGS?

And which question has the lowest score?

This one might surprise you – it's in Knowing their customer.

Wait, hang on.

So, if organisations are scoring the best in the Align discipline (aligning their efforts to their customers), yet they score the worst in the Know discipline (knowing who their customers are), then who or what are they actually aligning to?

We told you it was fascinating. Well, fascinating, but also a bit scary. Is it any wonder then, that businesses suffer from inefficiencies, lack of direction, disengaged customers and staff, flailing market share and revenues, when it's quite possible that the efforts they're making are actually aligned to the wrong things?

We'll talk more about this in the coming chapters but keep this in mind as we take you through the framework.

ASK THE TOUGH QUESTIONS OF YOURSELF AND OTHERS

Have you ever heard the old adage that people on average think they're above average? In our experience, this is very true (no offence to the people we've worked with or met in the past!). It's just human nature.

And that's what's so powerful about asking the tough questions, not only of yourself, but of your senior leaders and even your middle management.

Why? Because your self-reflection only gives you a sample of one. There's also no one to argue with you or give you a different viewpoint.

When you get a bunch of clever people – yourself and your leadership team – in a room and ask these questions, you'll find you get some incredibly diverse answers. And some very insightful ones.

You might think, ugh I don't WANT more questions and answers, I just need to get the job done and keep this business going. Trust us, pausing and taking the time could be the difference between you on a hamster wheel, and you sipping a cocktail under a palm tree.

THE JOY OF SELF-REALISATION: A QUICK STORY

We worked with a client who was a major contractor to a government department in Queensland. We knew the MD and knowing their contract was soon coming up for renewal, we suggested a quick health check of the business.

The MD was confident that they were super customer-focused and that we wouldn't find anything, but she welcomed us anyway. We were a fairly new business at that stage and she was interested to learn more about our offering.

We took the MD through our Initial Diagnostic process, where we spent an hour with the CEO/MD and then one or two of the key people charged with customer in the organisation. On one page, we gave her our findings – a quick view of what was happening in the business, our perceived roadblocks to success and some next steps they might take to overcome those roadblocks. We also gave her a traffic light system view of our nine-box framework – green for great, orange for okay and red for non-existent or pretty bad.

When we talked her through the diagnostic, she was flabbergasted. 'Oh my goodness. You have taken everything that has been in my head for the past two years, all the niggling worries and to-do's, and put them on a page. There's nothing necessarily new here, but my God, it's brought together everything I've been thinking I should do something about, but never gotten around to.'

One of the recommendations was for her to run her senior leadership team through our Customer-led Accelerator Program. A half day diagnostic workshop where leaders from all the key areas of the business work through our Customer Strategy Framework™. They 'score' themselves against the nine key capabilities, share their findings, then agree as a cohort, where the major gaps are and what actions need to be taken.

Our MD immediately booked in the half day session with her senior leaders, which we held within weeks of the initial diagnostic.

At the end of the session with the senior leaders, the MD came to us and said, 'That was incredible. I need you to come back next week and do this with my middle managers'.

Cutting to the chase, by asking some key, strategic questions of her team at the crucial levels of senior and middle management, we uncovered all the things that had been holding them back for years. Not only that, they walked away with a consistent strategic view of where they wanted to be, how important customer was to their business, where the gaps were in their current efforts and how they each – in their own disciplines and departments – could contribute to achieving the goals they'd set in the workshop.

One of the key outcomes of their Accelerator workshop was the need to better understand the customer journey. Always action-based, our full day workshop saw them map out the entire customer journey, assess where they were doing well and not so well, and the actions they needed to take to improve. We also highlighted the crucial stages where they were either losing business, missing out on revenue and profit, or simply, pissing off the customer.

They walked away with 134 actions.

Most businesses would be overwhelmed, feeling we'd just given them more to do than before. Not this amazing MD and her team.

Fast forward to their 12-month health checkup and not only had they done 97% of the actions they'd set in their customer journey workshop, but they'd blown their +2% YoY revenue target out of the water, achieving 7% growth since we'd seen them the year before. This might not seem like massive growth but in a mature market with a very specific (discretionary) product, this is outstanding. A better way to think about it is that by being customer-led, they delivered over a 300% increase on their expected growth.

Incredible. One of our proudest moments and a big real- isation for Customer Frame – we had to work with brave CEOs and leaders within organisations, who embraced not only the process, but the outcomes and the challenges.

Our client went on to win the next three-year contract too, securing the future of the business and the livelihoods of the team for the coming years. Winning!

THERE'S MORE TO IT THAN YOU THINK

As you'll see in the coming chapters, there's more to each of these strategic questions than meets the eye.

We promise you, by asking yourself these questions and taking the time to ponder and answer them, engaging your team and really getting under the skin of your business, you can uncover some of the fundamental issues that are not only holding you back, but that could be destroying the value in your business.

Three key strategic questions – simple, powerful, life-changing. And they direct the areas of customer capability you need to build to help your organisation step up to being truly customer-led.

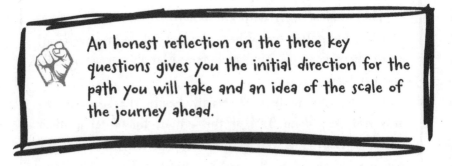

An honest reflection on the three key questions gives you the initial direction for the path you will take and an idea of the scale of the journey ahead.

Chapter 14

YOUR ROADMAP FOR SUCCESS: THE CUSTOMER STRATEGY FRAMEWORK™

Like any journey you go on, you'll drift aimlessly unless you have a roadmap to direct your thinking and efforts. In this chapter, we'll introduce our Framework which will help you to chart the course for your organisation and enjoy the success that it brings.

HIGH PERFORMING BUSINESSES START WITH CUSTOMER

In our experience working in and studying organisations of all shapes and sizes, across a variety of industries, in Australia and across Europe, we noticed a consistent difference between the high performers and the not so successful. There was a clear demarcation between those that had customer woven deep into their DNA and those who were trying to make it happen, but it wasn't embedded into their organisation.

The high performers were the ones that consistently invested in understanding who their customers were, measured their performance from their customer's perspective and made sure that everyone from boardroom to back office was aligned around the customer. It was a shared, collective approach to bringing the customer into the heart of the business, with everyone understanding how their part played a role in success.

It was clear that this was more than just customer service bandaids, but an intentional series of capabilities that provided true competitive advantage.

In 2015, we began a process to codify this difference and identify the elements that made these organisations successful. As every business is different, a top 10 cookie-cutter list of quick fixes simply didn't cut it (pun intended). What works in one, may not work in another.

When we zoomed out, we realised it was a whole of organisation problem that appeared to be quite complex, and the larger the business, the greater the complexity.

THE NEED FOR A COMMON FRAMEWORK

In working and speaking with customer-led transformation leaders from Australia and around the world, we noticed that the majority of them didn't have a set approach – they had to create a bespoke solution specific to their business, which took a lot of time and money. After all, there's no playbook, no 'customer school' to learn the function of customer like there is for finance or marketing or IT.

THE HIGH PERFORMING ORGANISATIONS WERE THE ONES THAT CONSISTENTLY INVESTED IN UNDERSTANDING WHO THEIR CUSTOMERS WERE, MEASURED THEIR PERFORMANCE FROM THEIR CUSTOMER'S PERSPECTIVE AND MADE SURE THAT EVERYONE FROM BOARDROOM TO BACK OFFICE WAS ALIGNED AROUND THE CUSTOMER.

We found that this in itself was one of the biggest barriers to getting traction for action. It takes time to diagnose the issues, pull it all together and work out what to do. Sometimes, as we've evidenced, it gets too complex too quickly, scaring your colleagues and stifling progress before you get started. The knowing-doing gap kicks in and the strategy gets shelved along with the other 'we tried that before' items. But the revolution is here and the faster you can get going, the better off your organisation will be.

The Customer Strategy Framework™ was designed to put structure around the problem. It provides a common language for courageous leaders to take into their organisations and bring everyone on the journey. Simple, yet powerful. A way to engage everyone, at every level, so they can instantly understand.

As a strategic compass, it can help you do three things:

1. FIND – as a diagnostic tool, you can find the issues residing in your organisation in a way that cuts across the limitations of functional silos
2. FOCUS – instead of trying to tackle everything head on, it helps you hone in on what matters most for your organisation
3. FIX – it provides the roadmap to taking collective action to put in the right foundations, fix the issues and take the organisation up a level.

INTRODUCING THE CUSTOMER STRATEGY FRAMEWORK™: YOUR KEY TO BECOMING A CUSTOMER-LED ORGANISATION

The Customer Strategy Framework™ outlines the nine core competencies of high performing organisations, the nine key areas you need to be strong in to be truly customer-led. It helps you, the courageous customer-led leader, in three ways:

1. It provides a simple structure to break down the complex problem of becoming a customer-led organisation.
2. It helps you to focus in on where the gaps are for your organisation (not just a generic list).
3. It lays out the roadmap and is your compass for where to go next.

Each of the nine elements can be measured and when combined together, provide an accurate gauge of how customer-led your organisation is today. By building capability in each of the nine frames, you move closer to putting the customer at the heart of everything you do.

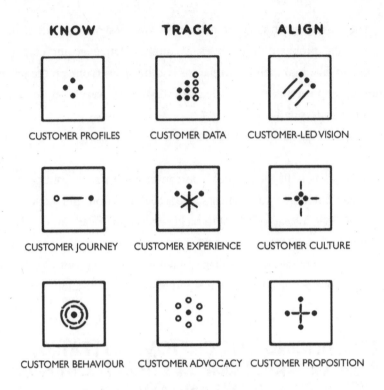

KNOW   **TRACK**   **ALIGN**

CUSTOMER PROFILES   CUSTOMER DATA   CUSTOMER-LED VISION

CUSTOMER JOURNEY   CUSTOMER EXPERIENCE   CUSTOMER CULTURE

CUSTOMER BEHAVIOUR   CUSTOMER ADVOCACY   CUSTOMER PROPOSITION

Figure 8: The Customer Strategy Framework™

It's a framework that applies to organisations of every shape and size. Any sector, any industry. As a management tool, the strategic questions that it sets out to resolve are:

- how do you stack up today and where are the gaps?
- where are you on the journey to being truly customer-led?
- what do you need to improve for the greatest impact?

The Framework becomes the roadmap of your strategy to become a customer-led organisation. It moves away from opinion and political agendas and helps unify the whole team around your customer – the ultimate reason you exist.

THE SEVEN DWARFS PROBLEM

What the? What have the seven dwarfs got to do with anything?

We want you to see how many you can name. Don't Google it. Don't ask Siri. Don't phone a friend. Go – how many can you name?

Chances are, having done this a few times around the world (our German friends for some reason REALLY love it!) you will be somewhere near the average of 4.3 dwarfs. If you got more than that, good for you – remember to bring it up at your next performance review.

So what do the seven dwarfs have to do with this? It's hard to remember seven things you've known all your life. So, how the heck would you be expected to remember the nine elements in the Customer Strategy Framework™?

THE FRAMEWORK IN DEPTH

The Framework is a three by three grid, with three capabilities each set within three disciplines. Within the Framework:

- the first vertical, KNOW, examines the capabilities relating to knowing your customer – who they are, what makes them tick and what's important to them
- the second, TRACK, looks at the capabilities relating to measuring your performance through their eyes – customer data and how you use it, how your customer experience stacks up and the level of loyalty and advocacy you have across your customer base
- the third vertical, ALIGN, measures how well your organisation is aligned – from your vision and values, the elements that drive a culture of valuing the customer and ensuring what you say you provide lines up with reality.

ENABLING A WIDER VIEW OF THE CHALLENGE YOU'RE FACING

The Framework is a catalyst for change that gives you a wider view of the landscape ahead. This is elephant-sized big. So, how do you eat an elephant?

Firstly, it helps you see the width and breadth of the problem. This is bigger than just 'customer service' or the failings of a function keeping those dreaded customers out. It helps break down each capability into actionable areas that you can target and improve.

Secondly, it removes some of the complexity of the problem you face. As you're looking at the Framework you might feel that some of the areas may seem complicated. We promise, the way we see them and share them with you – you'll see they're not. We certainly cover some complex topics, but in a real and actionable way.

Chances are, you don't need to focus heavily on everything all at the same time. You will only need three main focus areas, with specific actions to level up your organisation and move it up the customer capability maturity scale.

Thirdly, even before we get you into some of the specific detail over the following chapters, you can already begin to get an idea, just from this section, of what you might need to do. This is the wider view. The reframe of where you are today to help you depict where you want to be and the possible path to get there.

So, how do you eat an elephant?

You start with the feet, of course, so it can't run away.

And, those feet are the three key disciplines that are the pillars of successful, high performing customer-led organisations. Hope you've got a big appetite.

 The Customer Strategy Framework™ is your compass for where you are today, what you need to focus on and the roadmap for how to make it happen.

Chapter 15

THE THREE DISCIPLINES TO MASTER

We touched on the three key strategic questions every business leader should ask themselves. It's important you understand the disciplines that (p107) underlie these questions to really get under the skin of your business. Let's go into a bit more detail here before we dig right down into the Customer Strategy Framework™.

We've covered a few core concepts so far in the book. Let's revisit:

- customer is the ultimate reason you're in business
- customer should be at the heart of everything you do
- by putting customer at the heart, you will have a more efficient, effective and thereby, profitable business and a stronger, more engaged team
- change isn't easy and you need some help to make it happen
- you need a framework, a roadmap for success that helps you chart where you are today, where you want to be and how you can get there, identifying your gaps and strengths along the way.

THE CUSTOMER STRATEGY FRAMEWORK™

In the previous chapter, we introduced you to our Customer Strategy Framework™, our roadmap to making the process of becoming customer-led – or in some cases, **more** customer-led than you are today – as easy as possible. With structure comes support, with support comes peace of mind, and with peace of mind comes confidence.

We believe this Framework will give you the confidence you need to change your view and accelerate forward towards your goals, towards your true north. It's the key to becoming more customer-led and enjoying the success that entails. And it's not as difficult or mammoth as it might seem.

THE THREE KEY DISCIPLINES AND WHY THEY'RE IMPORTANT

Underlying the Customer Strategy Framework™ are three key disciplines. You'll recognise these as they relate to our three key strategic questions (p107) every business should ask themselves.

> WITH STRUCTURE COMES SUPPORT, WITH SUPPORT COMES PEACE OF MIND, AND WITH PEACE OF MIND COMES CONFIDENCE.

Each key discipline has three capabilities within it. These three areas are what give the meat to the bones of the Framework and meaning to the disciplines. Before we get into the Framework though, let's talk you through the three key disciplines.

KNOW

Do you know who your customers are and what's important to them?

Knowing who your customers are is fundamental to business success. If you don't know who your customers are, then who are you developing your products and services for? Who are you tailoring your offering to? Who are you picturing as you develop your marketing and sales strategy or your communications calendar?

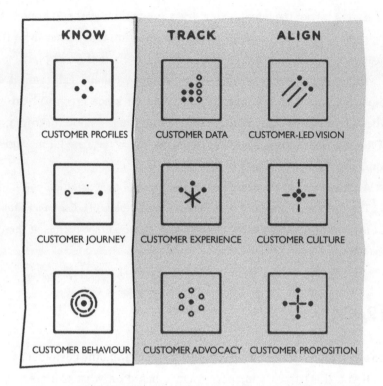

Figure 9: KNOW and the three capabilities

So often we meet business leaders and teams who simply do not know who their customers are. When we first started out in this field, we were gobsmacked by this fact. But in truth, we'd been working in organisations for years who didn't have a firm handle on their customers, so why should we have been surprised?

> We've completely forgotten about our customer!
> *Resort owner, Great Ocean Road Region*
> *(Customer-led Accelerator Program)*

Many business leaders we meet are struggling. This is a pretty obvious thing to say, right? Everyone is struggling with something. But these are usually really clever people, who have a love and passion for their product, a strong drive to succeed and the nous to make it happen.

Except it's not happening. Or at least, not in the way they'd hoped. And the reason, in many cases, is because they've simply forgotten who their customers are. Or they didn't know who they were in the first place.

Things have changed. While as a customer, I don't really care if you know the colour of my undies (that could be kinda creepy), I **do** care whether you know me. Whether you know what's important to me, my needs and wants, my goals and frustrations. Know me, care for me and I'm yours, maybe forever. Don't and, well…

As busy business leaders, we can lose sight of the customer.

The three capabilities that sit in the KNOW discipline are: Customer Profiles, Customer Journey and Customer Behaviour. You'll learn more about these in p136 *Section 4.*

TRACK

Do you track your organisation's performance from the customer's view?

If you don't track your performance based on what matters to your customer and use their feedback, then how do you know how you're really going? Beyond your profit and loss statements and monthly invoice reports, how do you really know? How will you identify the red flags before they become an issue?

It's common in today's business environment – as it has been customary for as long as we can remember – to track your performance based purely on numbers. Profit and loss, balance sheets, top-line revenue, unit sales, operational KPIs – essentially what's contributing to your bottom line and what's not. So you might throw in a customer survey here and there or your HR staff engagement survey, but in reality, it still all comes down to the numbers.

> THE PROBLEM WITH NUMBERS AND FINANCIAL REPORTS IS THAT THEY TELL YOU WHERE YOU'VE *BEEN*. SURE, THEY MIGHT GIVE YOU AN INDICATION OF WHERE YOU MIGHT GO IN THE FUTURE, BUT FOCUSING ON YOUR PAST PERFORMANCE IS LIKE DRIVING FORWARDS WITH THE WINDSCREEN BLACKED OUT, ONLY USING THE REAR VISION MIRROR TO SEE WHERE YOU'VE BEEN, NOT WHERE YOU'RE GOING.

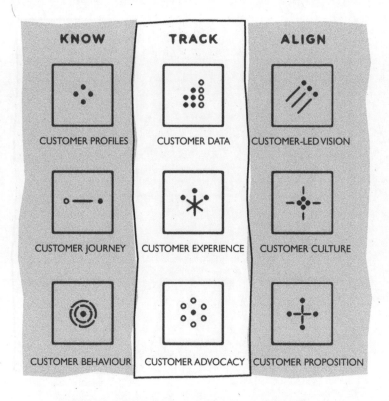

Figure 10: TRACK and the three capabilities

The problem with numbers and financial reports is that they tell you where you've *been*. Sure, they might give you an indication of where you might go in the future, but focusing on your past performance is like driving forwards with the windscreen blacked out, only using the rear vision mirror to see where you've been, not where you're going.

Things have certainly changed in this regard. No longer can you rely only on your financials to make robust, informed, educated, intelligent decisions. There are so many other factors that need to be considered if you're going to thrive in your business and your market, smash your competitors and be a long-term, profitable, not-to-be-messed-with entity.

The three capabilities that sit in the TRACK discipline are: Customer Data, Customer Experience and Customer Advocacy. You'll learn more about these in Section 5.

p194

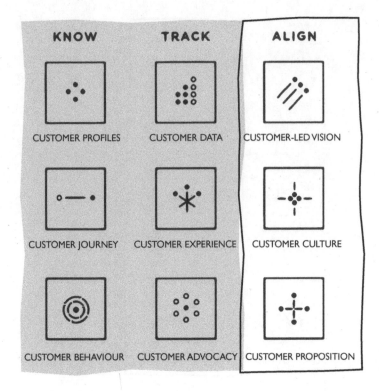

Figure 11: ALIGN and the three capabilities

ALIGN

Do you align your organisation to the customer?

Aligning your team and your business efforts to your customer is a non-negotiable these days if you want to survive and thrive in business. If you're not aligning yourself to your customer, then what's informing the decisions you make in your business? What are the drivers behind those decisions? How do you know if you're on the right track or not?

It's common for businesses to lose focus, find they're achieving less than optimal results, then realise they've been focusing on the wrong things all along. Disengaged staff, loose visions and strategies and confused customers can all be symptoms of a misaligned organisation.

We've met some businesses in our time that do Align really well. In fact, there are countless examples online of brands all over the world doing it well. Clear visions, amazing internal cultures, laser focused customer propositions, Problem is, we tend to only hear about the big guys, the ones with a celebrity entrepreneur at the helm or a multi-billion-dollar budget attached. It's hard to see yourself in these examples, it's hard to relate.

We mentioned in Chapter 13 the countless times we've run our Customer- (p108) led Accelerator Program with clients where they've scored the highest scores in the Align discipline and the lowest in Know. Meaning they're making big efforts to do the right thing for their customers, they're just likely doing the wrong things, since they don't truly know who their customers are or what they need or want from them. So much effort, so little traction or impact. No wonder business leaders and teams are frustrated and why resource wastage and inefficiencies are the bain of our businesses today.

The three capabilities that sit in the Align discipline are: Customer-led Vision, Customer Culture and Customer Proposition. You'll learn more about these in Section 6. (p255)

A NEED TO GET A MORE GRANULAR DIAGNOSIS

Now you know a bit more about the Framework, it's time to move forward with diagnosing where you are today, compare it with where you want to be in the future, and identify what you need to do to get there.

By asking a series of questions from each of the nine areas, assessing where you are and considering best practice, we help you understand where you are today and why your performance might not be where you want it to be.

This helps you to understand the actions you need to take and prioritise, in order to achieve your goals.

The first of these pillars is about having the capabilities across your organisation to truly know who your customers are, what they need from you and what makes them tick. Let's get into KNOW.

Three disciplines – KNOW, TRACK and ALIGN – are the vertical pillars of truly customer-led organisations. Each has a series of customer capabilities you can target to make your organisation stronger, more resilient and ready for the Customer-led Revolution.

Section 4

KNOW

Welcome to the first discipline of the Customer Strategy Framework™: KNOW.

In order to be truly customer-led, it's imperative that you truly know who your customers are, what makes them tick and what ticks them off (among other things). Beyond basic demographics of where they live and what job they do, it's about really getting to know your customer in order to deliver on their needs and begin to create a customer connection that will serve your business for the long term.

So, here's the strategic question we want you to keep top of mind for this section: Do you know who your customers are and what's important to them?

Chapter 16

SO, YOU THINK YOU KNOW YOUR CUSTOMERS BUT DO YOU?

When we ask business leaders if they know who their customers are, their first reaction is 'OF COURSE WE DO!'

Truly knowing your customer – beyond the basic demographics of where they live, their family structure and how much they earn a year – is a powerful tool in business. And one that is not often embraced or adopted, not to its full value.

Many business leaders we meet tell us they know their customers. But when we dig a little deeper, we soon realise that they know their customer **through the lens of their own business**, their own measures. They may know how the customer buys their product, how many they buy, how often, how much they spend – but that's **not** really knowing your customer at all.

We'd go so far as to say that this is a very narrow view of the customer. Yes, this information is valuable when it comes to tracking sales cycles and inventory management and staffing needs. But it only gives you a view of the customer in relation to **your** business. What about the rest of their lives? They exist separately to your business, a fact many business leaders forget.

What does 'knowing' your customer really mean?

Knowing who your customer is and the clusters of customers you serve as a business can be the difference between an efficient, effective, profitable business and a flailing one. After all, it's the customer who buys your offering. It's the customer who puts their hands in their pockets and spends their hard-earned cash on purchasing from you. It's them who choose you over competitors, over other options. So knowing them makes sense.

They're people who likely behave and make decisions differently from you. Knowing them is about creating a new level of empathy for who they are and what they need, right across your organisation.

Clustering them into groups so you can better serve them makes even more sense. We can't tend to each individual customer at a strategic level, it's simply not possible. But by grouping like-minded or similar customers together, we can better understand their needs, what makes them tick and as a result, serve them better.

But it's not enough for senior leaders to know who the customer is. It's about this knowledge of the customer being shared across the breadth and depth of the organisation. It's about every team member having an acute awareness and understanding of who the customer is and what they need from the business and from their role. We're not talking just the frontline staff either, we're talking everyone. It is crucial that every single team member understands how their role impacts the customer and their experience of the business. Without this relevance and awareness, team members will be disconnected – not only from the vision and purpose of the business, but from the customer.

In fact, if you know your customer but your team don't, then it's NOT an organisational capability at all.

Knowledge is power. There is no point in the senior leadership team having all this information, intel and insight into customers and the business, if it's not shared with the whole team.

Many business leaders fail to realise that by sharing this customer intel along with business performance insights, they are arming their teams with the tools they need to succeed. To drive true capability, you have to share your knowledge and bring your team on the journey to success. Arm them with these essentials and they will grow and thrive. Keep this information from them and watch them wither.

THERE'S KNOWLEDGE, THEN THERE'S INTELLIGENCE

Let's be fair, you can have endless knowledge, data and insights at your fingertips, but unless you're using it, it's fairly worthless as a business asset. This is the difference between knowledge and intelligence. You can know stuff but not use it. In fact, it only becomes intelligent when you apply it to your business or life situation.

So many business leaders we've met sit on one side of the fence or the other. They either have no data or intel at all and are basing all their business decisions on gut feel or instinct, or they have so much data and intel that they don't know what to do with it – still basing their business decisions on gut feel or instinct.

BEYOND GUT FEEL/INTERNAL STATS LOOK AT YOUR KNOWLEDGE OF CUSTOMER IN A NEW WAY

Moving beyond data overwhelm, gut feel and your internal sales stats and performance measures, we're going to challenge you to look at the knowledge of your customer in a new way. A way that will help you grow your business, make better decisions, get ahead of the competition and thrive in whatever big plans you have for the future.

> THERE'S A DIFFERENCE BETWEEN KNOWING WHO YOUR CUSTOMER IS, AND KNOWING YOUR CUSTOMER.

There's a difference between knowing who your customer **is**, and **knowing** your customer.

FACELESS DATA IS JUST THAT

We do a lot of work in Tourism, an industry known for having healthy marketing budgets and lots of customer persona and visitor information. Industry bodies invest heavily in research and have some of the best data intelligence at their fingertips. The issue is – beyond the demographic data, persona names and pretty photos, we've found that people on the ground – the business owners and industry leaders – don't necessarily know how to use the data.

We once worked with a region on a customer journey project. The project purpose was to identify the journey a visitor would go on in researching, planning, booking and taking a holiday to the region.

As a key project input, we outlined our need for access to clear customer profiles, which we were assured were available. But when we requested the profile detail at the relevant stage, the clear customer profiles emerged as a series of tricky number and letter combinations on a market research portal. Far from clear profiles of specific customers, we were faced with psychographic, attitudinal and behavioural data for the wider population, broken into over 50 unique personas and grouped into communities.

It was when we had to dig through loose guidelines of 'Look at the 100s community, particularly 101, 102, 110, the 300s community and some of the younger 400s' that we hit trouble. Far from having a clear mental picture of who we were targeting, we were drowning in a sea of data instead.

Learning: having access to a bunch of data does not mean you have clear customer profiles!

The need to build your organisation's capabilities (KNOW)

A common mistake we see business leaders make is assuming they know their customer. Sure, they might have some good stats about buying behaviours and spending patterns, perhaps even some 'personas' they've had done. But that's often as far as it goes.

Instead of treating this knowledge as a business asset, a powerful tool to drive profitability and growth, a living, breathing thing; they treat it as a box that needs to be ticked. Left static and unattended, unused and saved in a file somewhere, it loses its power and impact.

Let's take a look at how we can know our customers better and what good looks like.

THE THREE CAPABILITIES OF KNOW

The three capabilities of KNOW are Customer Profiles, Customer Journey and Customer Behaviour. By building your business capability in these three areas, you'll find yourself making more efficient, effective, powerful, impactful decisions, with a team that is focused, motivated and firing on all cylinders. Sounds good, right?

Let's touch on the three KNOW capabilities quickly before we launch into them in more depth in the coming chapters.

KNOW Customer Capability	Context	Overview
  CUSTOMER PROFILES	Clarity + focus	**The main question:** Who are your core customers and how much do you really know about them? **The outcome:** An in-depth understanding of your customer base is crucial to becoming truly customer-led and differentiating yourself from competitors. Beyond market segmentation, it's about bringing to life who they really are and what they want to achieve.
  CUSTOMER JOURNEY	Empathy + opportunity	**The main question:** Do you know the journey a customer travels in seeking an offering like yours? **The outcome:** Mapping the customer's purchase process (from research to post-purchase) against your internal processes is a valuable tool and highlights the areas that will deliver the greatest value.

KNOW Customer Capability	Context	Overview
CUSTOMER BEHAVIOUR	Understanding + foundations	**The main question:** Do you understand customer behaviour and how it applies to your organisation? **The outcome:** Understanding what makes customers tick and the drivers behind their buying process helps you make informed choices that create greater engagement and connection. By examining trends in customer behaviour and the nuances of the customer environment, you build a strong foundation for effective decision making.

These three capabilities enable your organisation to build the empathy to truly know your customer – how they think, the journey they're on and who they really are.

We'll cover these in more detail in the coming chapters with examples and stories to bring them to life and get you thinking about how you can level up your organisation today.

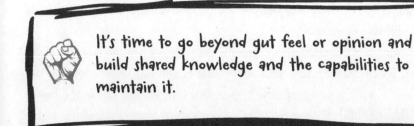

It's time to go beyond gut feel or opinion and build shared knowledge and the capabilities to maintain it.

Chapter 17

CUSTOMER PROFILES: DITCH THE DEMOGRAPHICS AND BRING BACK THE HUMAN

The strategic question we're setting out to answer is:

Who are your core customers and how much do you really know about them?

We love this topic.

It's one of those areas of business that people think they're all over, that they know a lot about, but when they dig a little deeper, they realise just how much they DON'T know.

Most of us have a gut feel about who our customers are. How couldn't we, with the way businesses and customers interact, how the world and the customer has evolved over the past 30 or so years and the tech and tools available to us today?

What's so great about this capability is the depth you can go to, to really know your customer. You can know a little or you can know a lot, and the deeper you go and the more you know, the better the relationship with your customer, and the better your business.

> **WE CALL IT GOING BEYOND DEMOGRAPHICS TO BRING BACK THE HUMAN.**

We call it going beyond demographics to bring back the human.

WHO IS YOUR CUSTOMER?

We ask this question of all business owners and leaders we meet. We get all manner of responses, ranging from the vague (common) to the very specific (impressive but not so common).

When we ask this question in our workshops, the answer is almost always the same – EVERYONE!

'Everyone? Really? Absolutely everyone?' we repeat. 'Yes!' they say. 'Everyone!' 'Anyone with a wallet' is another popular response.

IS IT REALLY EVERYONE?

Look, we get it. As human beings, we don't like to miss out. FOMO (fear of missing out) is really a 'thing'.

We think that if we ignore a particular customer group, it will be the death of our business. The more customers, the better, right? Who wouldn't want everyone as a customer?

Truth is, us! And you! The reality is this – not everyone is your customer. If you're everything to everyone, then you're nothing to no one. It's true. You cannot possibly be everyone's cup of tea. Your products and services cannot fulfil everyone's needs, wants and desires. It's just not possible (and we don't say that statement very often!).

SCARCITY TO PROSPERITY

In tough times – think pandemics, natural disasters, recessions and the like – it's natural to move towards 'any customer is a good customer' as we try to keep our businesses afloat. But that's not a sustainable approach moving forward and one best avoided or moved away from as quickly as possible.

There's customers you want, and there's customers you don't. Smart business owners and leaders know this. While lots of businesses chase down anyone with a wallet and a pulse, it's the clever ones who know that aligning themselves with the customers that will most value their offering, is the best business strategy of all.

By working out and then focusing on the customers you want, you find yourself running or leading a more efficient, effective, profitable business. One that has strong customer connections with the right customers, while leaving the rest for your competitors to deal with.

So, what's the answer?

INTRODUCING CUSTOMER PROFILES – THE KEY TO UNLOCKING CUSTOMERS

Customer Profiles, or personas, as many know them, are simply a snapshot or representation of your customers. Each profile represents a group of customers, clusters of like-minded individuals. At Customer Frame, we believe you should have between five and eight profiles for your business – any more and you're likely getting too granular (and could do with making larger clusters), any less and you're likely being too generic (and need to make smaller clusters).

In fact, one profile should take up no more than 20% of your customer base. One of our clients had a profile that represented over 50% of their customer base. At that size, it's too broad and generic to be useful and they wondered why they weren't getting traction with this audience. There's no 'perfect number' – ultimately, it's about finding the right balance, and in this sense, every business is different.

In our world, there are 13 key elements that make up a great Customer Profile:
1. Name (this is so important, right down to how you spell their name)
2. Image (every element is specific, from their clothing to their facial expression)
3. Summary (the highlights you'd use to describe them to someone)

4. The facts (as close to demographics as you'll get)
5. Goals (what do they want in life?)
6. Frustrations (what stops them achieving their goals?)
7. Behaviours (how do they behave in their lives, how do they do what they do?)
8. Interests (what are they into, their interests, loves, past-times?)
9. Common objections (what objections might they have about a product/service like yours?)
10. Watering holes (where do they hang out, who and what influences them and their decisions?)
11. Common themes (what messaging might you use to address their goals/frustrations to cut through to them?)
12. Day in the life (what does their day look like from wake to sleep?)
13. Quotes (what might you hear them say?).

PERSONA VERSUS PROFILE

There are varying views on whether persona and profile are the same thing, but there are subtle differences. A persona is a primarily fictitious character that represents your ideal customers, whereas a profile is based on real insight and data from real customers. In our Framework, the Customer Profile capability sits somewhere in between the two – all the psychology, emotion and drivers of personas, rooted in a deeper understanding of who your customers are and who they should be. It's the best of both worlds.

Meet Alex, our example profile

Check out Alex, a Customer Profile we built for and in conjunction with the wonderful team at Daylesford Macedon Tourism in Victoria.

While we can (and probably will) write a book on how to build effective Customer Profiles, you can certainly use this as an instant strategic guide. If you have existing profiles for your organisation already, can you tick off all 13 elements? If not, it's worth filling in the gaps to complete the picture.

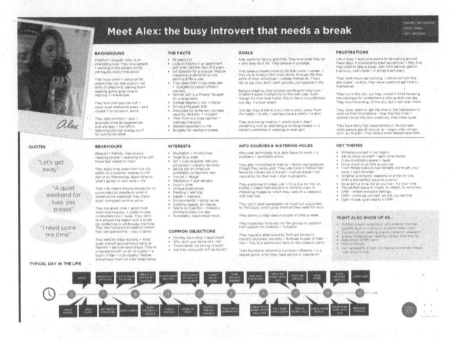

Figure 12: An example of a complete Customer Profile

WHY IS IT SO IMPORTANT?

What happens when you have the wrong customers?

Well, a better question might be, how do you <u>know</u> if you have the wrong customers?

When you have the wrong customers, you'll know. Trust us, you will.

High customer complaints, a high rate of returned goods, bad reviews, harried staff, diminishing returns, higher number of touch points with complaining customers, loss of or damage to reputation, lower productivity, constantly reduced prices, falling revenues, higher customer turnover (constantly needing to replace lost customers) – these are just some of the symptoms.

And on the people side, for you and your staff (an impact often overlooked) – higher stress, constant worry, consistently on high alert, upset team members, increased staff sick leave (higher staff absences), losing staff to competitors, a damaged culture, lower productivity, leading to an ailing business.

HOW THEY CAN WORK?

We've built ourselves a bit of a reputation in the Tourism industry, particularly in the southern states of Australia, for writing Customer Profiles. You name a world-class destination in Victoria and chances are, we've developed their Customer Profiles. The magic comes in not only working closely with industry players (who know customers best), but aligning those profiles with the destination sub-regions to help local tourism boards and business owners understand who they should be targeting (and the complementary products and regions they should be working with).

Take the Great Ocean Road Regional Tourism team, for example, who took their new deeper understanding of their customers and built an innovative marketing campaign never before seen in the region. They matched the sub-regions with specific target customers, right down to the talent used in the ads, the products portrayed and the core emotive messages. Gone was the generic destination campaign of old, they matched their unique offerings with their customer needs and reaped the benefits – the campaign results were outstanding. How's that for targeted communications?

 ## CUSTOMER PROFILES: GET CLARITY AND FOCUS

Now we understand the importance of Customer Profiles and what makes up a good one, let's take a deeper look at our Customer Strategy Framework™ and the guiding capability of Customer Profiles.

We see Customer Profiles as one of the foundation elements of a truly customer-led organisation and that's why it's the top left of our Framework. For without understanding who your customers are, your TRACK and ALIGN efforts are less useful and relevant.

We've set up this section (and all the sections in the coming chapters) to make it as easy as possible for you to read and understand the concept, ask yourself the core question and familiarise yourself with the five ingredients or drivers for success.

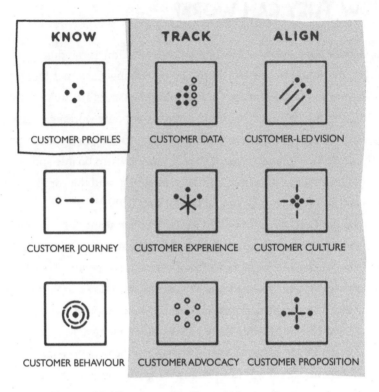

Figure 13: Customer Profiles within the Framework

The core question

Who are your core customers and how much do you really know about them?

Why does it matter

An in-depth understanding of your customer base is crucial to becoming truly customer-led and differentiating yourself from competitors. Beyond market segmentation, it's about bringing to life who they really are and what they want to achieve.

THE FIVE DRIVERS/INGREDIENTS FOR SUCCESS

There are five key drivers or ingredients you need in this capability for success. Let's take a look. As you read the statement, ponder your answer – what's your gut feel? Read over the best practice and explanation to see what good really looks like. Then, go back and consider again how strong you are in this area. What gaps and opportunities emerge?

#1. You have research into why a customer uses an offering like yours

Best practice: Key drivers of customer usage are identified and inform operational delivery and market communications.

Do you know why a customer uses your product? Or a product or service like yours?

This is tricky, but worth the consideration. We've had clients in the past who thought that they didn't have competitors because their product was unique. Perhaps it was a patented idea. Or a one-off contract.

We worked with an organisation that had a government contract for a product no one else was allowed to build or distribute. 'We don't have have competitors,' they told us in one of our sessions. Okay...

So, no one else MAKES the same product as you, but that doesn't mean that you don't have competitors. In mapping out their Customer Journey, (p186) which we'll touch on later, we quickly helped them realise that it's actually NOT about their product. It's about the customer and the needs and wants they are trying to fulfil with a product or service like theirs.

So this product no one else could build, when viewed from the customer perspective, DID indeed have competitors – LOTS of competitors. For the customer who was looking to treat themselves to a 40th birthday present, they could buy this product – or – they could buy a Chanel handbag. Or a shopping weekend away with girlfriends. Or a custom-made piece of jewellery...

By understanding how and why your customer uses or buys a product like yours, you can better understand your competitors, the challenges you face in helping your customer decide to choose you, and more importantly, help you improve your operational delivery and marketing communications to support their customer experience.

#2. You have clear demographic and psychographic insights to define your customer base

Best practice: Proactive primary and secondary research provides factual and tangible information to help drive key decisions from strategy through to operations.

So we're not talking millions or even hundreds or tens of thousands of dollars spent here. Whenever people talk about research, all we see are dollar signs and all we hear is the ching ching of the cash register. It's a myth that you need to spend huge amounts of money to gain any real advantage from research.

There are so many resources available these days to help inform your business decisions. You don't have to do it yourself. Just by knowing where to look and which sources are the most trustworthy, you can build a robust and valuable picture of your customers. These insights will, coupled with your business nous and inside knowledge of your customers, help you build demographic and psychographic intel.

Notice here we talk about psychographics, not just demographics. As is everything with Customer Frame, this is completely intentional. Why? Because demographics aren't enough. Demographics are research elements, numbers, words, statuses.

Psychographics are all about the heart. What makes people tick? What do they think, like, loathe? Why do they feel the way they do? Why do they do the things they do? This is where the richness comes in. It puts the meat on the bones, you might say. If you have demographics and no psychographics today, we gently suggest you dig a little deeper.

#3. You have clearly defined Customer Profiles for your main 5–8 typical customer groups

Best practice: Clearly defined Customer Profiles drive innovation, operational delivery and organisation design, creating a deeper, longer lasting connection with customers.

We've talked about demographics versus Customer Profiles, so this one won't be a surprise to you. Demographics definitely have a place, don't get us wrong. But it's when businesses rely solely on them that things start to get dicey. It's when they say, 'Sure we know our customers, they're 35–50-year-old women who live in capital cities and earn $125k a year'.

Riiight. When's the last time you saw a 35–50-year-old woman walking down the street? Neverrr.

Demographics can lead us to treating everyone the same, putting bunches of people in buckets that can actually be irrelevant, outdated, or simply, wrong. Demographics are a support, they're not the leading lady. Customer Profiles are.

When you have clearly defined Customer Profiles – actual 'people' you can relate to, understand and connect with – your innovations, operations and even the way you run your business, will change. By truly getting to know your customers beyond how much they earn or where they live (yawn), you can create that long-lasting connection with your customers that we all crave.

#4. You have documented what is important to each of your customer groups

Best practice: Customer needs, wants and pain points are clearly understood and the organisation builds products and services to deliver the most important aspects for each customer group.

Beyond knowing who your customers are, knowing what's important to them is #nextlevel. By understanding what they need, what they want and what their pain points are, you can better align your offering to them.

It's what we call turning the view from you to the customer. Gone are the days where we sell the products we want to sell and people just buy them. A big part of the Customer-led Revolution is this – the customer is boss. They'll tell you what they'd like, thanks very much. And if you don't listen, address and fulfil what's important to them, they'll simply go somewhere else.

#5. You have 'a day in the life' mapped out for each of your customer groups

Best practice: 'The customer day' is used to tailor customer contact, support and pre-emptive service strategies with a view to providing the best experience possible.

We love a good day in the life. When we run our Customer Profile sessions with our clients, it's this element they're most surprised by. They've simply never thought about it.

But knowing or even mapping out your customer's day as you think it might run, is a powerful tool in driving efficiency and effectiveness in your business. We're not advocating stalking your customer or employing any drone or long-range video equipment to track what they're up to. But we are advocating for putting yourself in their shoes and stepping into their day.

By doing so, you can figure out when the best times are to contact them. When they'll read an email and when they'll skip past it. When they'll see a social media post and when it will be completely lost at the bottom of their feed. When to ask them for feedback and when it's just too bloody much for them.

Take the time to think about what's going on for your customer in their day-to-day (remember, you're not the only thing in their lives, there's quite a few other things going on) and we promise, your customer will thank you and your efforts will be more effective.

SELF-ASSESSMENT: HOW DO YOU STACK UP?

Now that you're familiar with the five key ingredients for success and what best practice looks like, it's time to do a self-assessment.

To get an initial benchmark, check out the statements below and circle the one that best matches your current situation. Mark yourself on the harder side, there's no gold stars here, just learnings and opportunities.

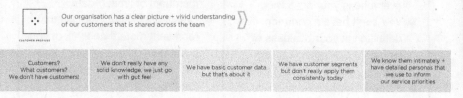

This quick assessment is a simplified version of our full-blown Customer-led Accelerator Program. But, straight away, this gives you an initial idea of how you stack up.

Share it with colleagues and see what they think. It's a great way to open up the conversation on customer. What answers do you think you'd get if you asked your senior leadership team? Are you aligned or are you on completely different planets?

Refer to the section 'How to use this book' for tips on who to ask in your organisation, how and why.

RED FLAGS AND ROADBLOCKS

Let's look at some of the red flags and potential roadblocks for Customer Profiles.

Red flags	Potential roadblocks
■ You seem to be chasing any customer with a wallet – everyone is your customer. ■ You don't have a common definition in your business of who your customer is today and who you want in the future. ■ You think you know your customer but you're really just using your transaction data or gut feel and opinion without any solid grounding.	■ Building profiles in isolation with only customer-facing team members or limited data. ■ Creating individual profiles that represent more than 20% of your business – if it's any larger than this, it needs to be broken down further. ■ Thinking that fictitious personas are enough – the profile set needs to be authentic, real, well-considered, truly representative and complete.

WHEN YOUR ORGANISATION BUILDS THIS CAPABILITY

Take a moment now to fast forward to a future moment in time where your organisation has a full set of quality Customer Profiles. These profiles are shared across all teams and functions and are directing their operational and strategic decisions.

Team members are having efficient conversations about specific Customer Profiles, prioritising their tasks and efforts according to their needs. Your **people** are feeling more connected to the ultimate reason you exist and have more purpose and connection with what they do and who they do it for. Your **marketing** is more effective as it's hitting customers right in their needs. Your **product development** is bang on as it solves customer's pain. And your **financial performance** has improved as you've become a more efficient and effective organisation overall. Is this a better business than you have today?

*

With the cornerstone of Customer Profiles in place, let's now take this KNOW discipline even further as we help you step into your customer's shoes to find even greater levels of empathy and new opportunities.

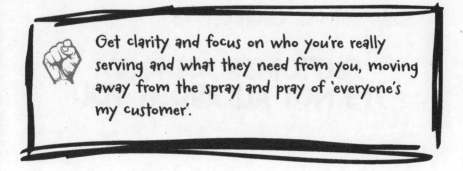

Get clarity and focus on who you're really serving and what they need from you, moving away from the spray and pray of 'everyone's my customer'.

Chapter 18

CUSTOMER JOURNEY: IT'S NOT ALL ABOUT YOU

The strategic question we're setting out to answer is:

Do you know the journey a customer travels in seeking an offering like yours?

If we could give one superpower to every organisation, it would be the capability to map out their main customer journeys against their existing business processes. As we guide you through this chapter, you'll see that it is much more than process mapping. It brings the level of customer empathy up a few notches. It helps you find gaps you never knew existed. It helps engage people from right across your organisation so they can begin to see how they play a part in your overall success.

CUSTOMERS ARE ON A JOURNEY AND YOU'RE ONLY PART OF IT

As a customer, you don't just wake up one day and decide – I'm going to buy x product or service! For pretty much any transaction that takes place, the journey that leads up to that moment and the journey after that moment is much longer and more complex, depending on the product of course (no one puts that much thought into toothpaste, do they?).

And, here's the rub. Your organisation is only a part of the wider Customer Journey. Sure, you may play a big role, but ultimately you don't control it. If there's one thing we've seen consistently in high-performing, customer-led organisations – it's that they know where they stand with their customer and what they need to do to serve them.

The customer owns the Customer Journey. Your organisation owns the customer experience.

This 'ah-ha' moment is huge. The only thing that you can control is the experience your organisation delivers to the customer. How well that supports their journey and whether they achieve their goals dictates the perception of how well you do what do you.

Those in the know put this in context and seek to understand what happens for the customer before and after they interact. By only looking at the moment a customer traverses through your front door (or homepage) and transacts, you're missing the opportunity to capture more customers (before) and retain them (after). In fact, looking only at the middle bit, it becomes more about 'customer service' which is why so many organisations are limiting their potential today.

In working with a variety of businesses and organisations across sectors, one of the first questions we ask is, 'Have you mapped out the Customer Journey?' In many cases we hear a resounding 'YES!' However, it is the **business processes** that are mapped out from the organisation's perspective – not from the customer's view. It's the internal view – they do this step, then do that step, then fill in that form. This is not the Customer Journey. It is good practice, of course, and a foundation of business process reengineering, but it is about you – not the customer.

WHAT IS A CUSTOMER JOURNEY MAP?

Following is a full Customer Journey Map, created in collaboration with our friends at Murray Regional Tourism. If you'd like to see it larger than a postage stamp, head to customerframe.com/revolution to download it and see it in greater detail. For now, take a moment to marvel at just how much could be going on for your customer that you've perhaps never thought about.

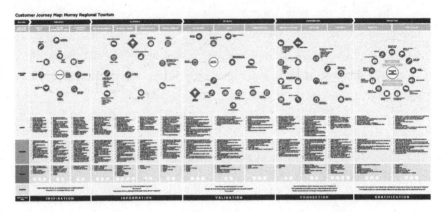

Figure 14: Customer Journey Map for Murray Regional Tourism

You will note on the map the steps, customer processes, the doing, thinking and feeling elements, with a range of actions based around the primary customer need at each stage.

This map, the first of its kind for a tourism destination, fundamentally changed the way the Murray Region industry empathised with customers. By visualising it and examining what the collective industry was doing to support customers, innovative step changes were introduced to shift their entire visitor servicing strategy and operations.

> THE CUSTOMER OWNS THE CUSTOMER JOURNEY. YOUR ORGANISATION OWNS THE CUSTOMER EXPERIENCE.

Now – this mapping example is big and complex. Yours doesn't have to be this detailed. The point is that by mapping out the Customer Journey your organisation will find hidden cost, unrealised revenue and new opportunities to create customer connection. You can start simple, or dive right in. As your organisation builds this capability, it will continue to make you stronger across everything you do.

(p340) In our full-day masterclass where we teach businesses how to build their own Customer Journey Map, our attendees tell us that this tool fundamentally changes their lives, the way they run their businesses, how they prioritise their actions and investments, and how they see the world in general. Powerful stuff.

WHAT'S REALLY GOING ON FOR YOUR CUSTOMER?

Understanding the Customer Journey means stepping into their shoes and working through the steps, processes and activities that they undertake. But it's more than that. We need to examine what they are doing, thinking and feeling through each step, as this has a significant bearing on what happens next.

When working on the Customer Journey, it's important to put all labels and content in the customer's language. Not in your internal language and certainly not in process or systems gobbledygook.

Let's break it down in the following matrix.

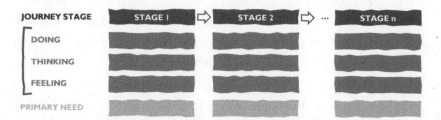

Figure 15: Customer Journey Map –
Stages, Processes and the Primary Need

Let's take a closer look at the core elements of the Customer Journey in the diagram above.

Journey stages

These are the high level stages that the customer goes through on their journey. It's rare to see more than four or five stages in total and the challenge is to keep them simple, yet specific, to the journey.

We love to grab the management consultant's tool of choice (the Post-It Note) to help ideate and make sense of these stages. What are the main stages you would go through in the process of buying a product or service like yours?

Here's a great example that we use to kickstart the thinking of something a bit closer to home. Let's tackle the joyous task of getting your car serviced. The overall stages could look something like:

Think of the journey your customer is on when your organisation gets involved. Have a go at mapping out the main stages. You know you've nailed it when there is at least one stage before and one stage after your organisation is involved.

Doing, thinking and feeling

This is where you really get inside the head (and heart) of your customer. These lenses each provide valuable insight that can lead to new opportunities – be it to sell more, be more efficient or build long-term advocacy. Or even rescue the customer or solve a problem.

So, what are they **physically doing**? We often present this in icons and pictures as a flow chart (see figure 14). It helps us to understand how complex things are and identify where we might be dropping the ball.

What are they **thinking**? We all have that inner voice chattering away. Your customer is no different in their journey. Conscious thoughts drive actions. So, have you got what you need in place to address their inner voices? If it gets too hard or uses too many brain calories, they'll bounce to an easier solution.

How are they **feeling**? Ah, the F word. Your customer's emotional state drives much of their thinking. How are they feeling at each step of their journey? If they're feeling confused, imagine if your organisation could show up as providing clarity. If they're worried, what if your business supported and guided them? If they're excited, how powerful could it be to build on that (and make sure you're delivering on it!)?

Let's return to our car servicing example. As you can see, new understanding and opportunities emerge as you begin to unpack it. Each touch point can start to be examined – Is this the best way? What other ways could we do it? How can we delight our customer in this moment?

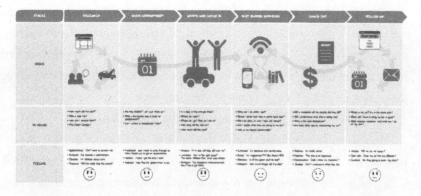

Figure 16: An example Journey Map – getting your car serviced*

If you're up for it, take your stages and flesh them out using the doing, thinking and feeling lenses. What opportunities or 'a-ha' moments arise? If you want to enrich it even further, ask a few colleagues to brainstorm it with you. You'll be glad you did!

Primary need

At each stage of the journey, customers have a need to be met. When you tap into this and deliver purposefully to it, you get ahead of the game. This is where the magic begins to unlock by building your organisation's capability around Customer Journey. Usually expressed as one word, it can fundamentally change the way you do what you do. Let's look at a new example.

When we look at the Customer Journey for travel, the first stage is the 'dreaming' stage, where customers are visioning what their holiday could be like. But what do they need? Let's try on two different needs and see what happens.

If we say their need is 'information', what comes to mind? You'd expect that it would be about getting them ALL the details about their options. This has been the case in tourism in the past. The ninja-starring of brochures and overwhelm of information can actually lead to inaction (remember the paradox of choice?).

---

* www.servicebridge.com/articles/customer-experience-in-service-businesses

The alternative outcome might be to say that customers need 'inspiration'. Now this would lead to a very different set of activities to deliver. Aspirational imagery, stories about what it feels like to visit the destination, inspirational messaging – all set to meet the need for inspiration and move the customer along their journey to choosing you.

Very different scenarios and very different outcomes.

This is the strategic question we're setting out to solve in your organisation. Are your customers' needs understood and are they being met? Chances are, by mapping out the journey and unearthing the underlying needs, you will find new opportunities for growth, efficiency and greater customer connection – even if you think you're nailing it today!

USING THE CUSTOMER JOURNEY TO FIND NEW OPPORTUNITIES

Now that we have the academic stuff out of the way, let's look at some purposeful ways you can use the Customer Journey to find new opportunities and make your organisation the poster-child in your sector.

The key to unlocking the Customer Journey is identifying the trigger. EVERY customer journey starts with a trigger. Without the trigger, there is no need for a customer to take action and start a journey.

Remember our client who didn't think they had competitors? With products ranging from $175 to $30,000, we posed this question to their senior team – what is the trigger for buying your product? Customers don't just wake up and think, 'I'm going to buy one of these today.' Our client found it hard to answer this question – at first. They'd never thought of the triggers. They thought people literally decided to buy their product and well, just did it! Not the case.

So what's the trigger? For our client, it could be a 40th birthday coming up, it could be a pay rise, it could be a need for social status… the list is endless. Why is this important? Because – it frames up who and what you're really up against in terms of competitors. It highlights traditional competitors and non-traditional ones – the ones you don't consciously think about, but that compete directly with you for a share of the customer's wallet.

You probably have competitors you haven't considered before. Thinking about the trigger opens up the competitive landscape. Imagine how many ways you could celebrate your own 40th birthday? Then, think about a work colleague. What options would be on their list? This is where a new TV and a holiday could end up as direct competition. How many tourism destinations realise that Harvey Norman is actually a competitor? How does this play out for your organisation? Everyone has competitors — even if you think you don't. Your Customer Journey Map will help you uncover competitors you'd never considered before.

Exploring the trigger event provides deep insight into your customer's state of mind. Not only that, it gives you a great anchor for acknowledging the customer's need and positioning your offering to meet those needs. That's when you begin to build loyalty and advocacy. This works across public sector as well as private sector. Think about the mundane task of registering your dog with your local Council — what could the trigger be? What opportunities exist to build customer empathy?

One of the most powerful outcomes of Customer Journey mapping is the new perspectives that it brings, touching every part of your organisation and what it delivers. As you unpack each element of what the customer is going through, then compare it to what you do today, there are always moments that go well and others that could use some updating.

YOUR CUSTOMER JOURNEY MAP WILL HELP YOU UNCOVER THE COMPETITORS YOU'D NEVER CONSIDERED BEFORE.

CUSTOMER JOURNEY: MAPPING OUT THE CUSTOMER JOURNEY TO DRIVE EMPATHY AND OPPORTUNITY

Now that we've covered the main elements, the opportunities and things to think about, let's have a look at how you can work out where you are on this capability through the lens of the Customer Strategy Framework™.

JOURNEY MAPS FIND GAPS

We were working with our client's team on this very process. When the team unpacked the journey, they found a raft of improvements, some small and some absolute clangers. The one we want to share is when they began to think about the end of their Customer's Journey. What we unearthed was that the customer who paid $3000 for their product got EXACTLY the same the same delivery experience as the customer who paid $175. The same carton, the same messaging, the same everything.*

Fast forward a few months, the team fundamentally changed the experience for the higher priced, premium product, leading to greater referral sales, customer loyalty and (most importantly) customer advocacy. New revenue opportunities also emerged, including an add-on fitting service for the premium product, which helped alleviate customer distress and drive incremental profit straight to the bottom line for the organisation.

And this was just one finding – imagine the power unleashed from the rest!

---

* Actually, this is not entirely true. The $3000 product came wrapped in a layer of bubble wrap! That's some expensive bubble wrap!

The core question

Do you know the journey a customer travels in seeking an offering like yours?

Why does it matter?

Mapping the customer's purchase process (from research to post-purchase) against your internal processes is a valuable tool and highlights the areas that will deliver the greatest value. You truly step into the customer's shoes, looking outside in, marrying up what you provide to support their journey, inside out.

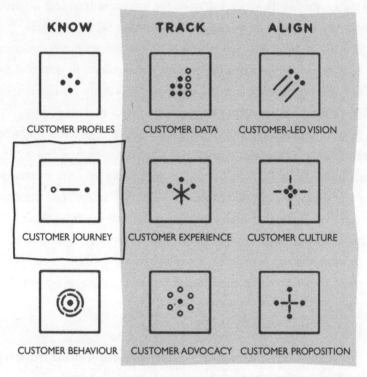

Figure 17: Customer Journey capability within the Framework

THE FIVE DRIVERS/INGREDIENTS FOR SUCCESS

There are five key drivers or ingredients you need in this capability for success. Let's take a look. As you read the statement, ponder your answer – what's your gut feel? Read over the best practice and explanation to see what good really looks like. Then, go back and consider again how strong you are in this area. What gaps and opportunities emerge?

#1. You have drawn the journey your customers travel when they seek an offering like yours

Best practice: A vivid picture of the Customer Journey for each Customer Profile is shared across the organisation and is used to inform key business decisions, from customer service to sales.

This one is fairly self-explanatory. If it's not written down, it's not real. Business process maps won't do (though they're useful to help find gaps). Unless your organisation has mapped out the primary Customer Journey and has shared it across departments or functions, there is definitely scope for huge improvement. The organisations we've helped have started by identifying the Customer Journeys for their top three customers. This is a little bit of the 80:20 rule, as it hits a large majority of your transactions with a smaller scale, targeted effort. As you build the skills and capabilities, you can then chase the smaller gains in a much more efficient way.

In most cases, your wider team can see the complexity of what is going on for customers. It is ALWAYS more complex than we assume. It brings with it a new appreciation and empathy between the organisation and your customer.

#2. You understand what customers are doing/thinking/ feeling at every step of the Customer Journey

Best practice: Customer activity at each journey step is analysed to find frustration points and new opportunities, driving new product development and customer-led improvement plans.

In working with the UK government agency who was responsible for (p49) payments to farmers, journey mapping opened up a new level of efficiency and effectiveness for both the customer and the organisation.

By mapping out the Customer Journey for their primary transaction load, we found that their application process for farmers to gain funding was cumbersome, causing all sorts of errors and waste. The journey revealed a need to validate the data in the application early, saving complex rework for the organisation and frustration for farmers, the primary customer. Fast forward 12 months, with an online application system developed to close the gap, the costly rework of more than 40% of all applications was reduced to less than 5%. What did this mean? For the organisation, a net saving of millions of pounds every year and most importantly, for their customers, the farmers – they were able to get on and do what they do best. All by building empathy through the Customer Journey Map.

#3. You have identified the touch points that matter most to your customers

Best practice: An intimate knowledge of customer touch points (which ones matter and which ones don't) is used to prioritise business efforts to directly improve the customer experience.

In every Customer Journey, there are critical moments. They might be decisions or actions. They might be moments that are emotionally import- ant to your customer and help build or destroy their relationship with you. There are also moments that you may be putting a great deal of effort into, that your customer simply doesn't care about.

You don't need to be going customer-love-crazy at every touch point. None of us have the time or the open cheque book (remember those?) to fund it. The task is to work out what really matters and what doesn't.

It's at these junctures that the magic happens. When you can fulfil a customer's needs or even surprise your customer (in a good way!) at a key touch point, you become memorable. This adds another thread to their connection with you, leading to greater advocacy which is only a good thing.

#4. You map the Customer Journey against internal process to identify delivery gaps

Best practice: Business processes are actively reviewed, refined and mapped against the Customer Journey, to meet the intended customer experience and fulfil customer promises.

Having the journey map is great and identifying the touch points goes a long way. But high-performing organisations take this one step further. They open up their business processes and lay them over the Customer

Journey to find the gaps. Find those areas that they can do differently. Find the activities that cost, but aren't valued by or cut through to the customer. Remember, part of understanding the journey is how the customer feels they're being treated. This is a perception that can be influenced to your advantage.

When we worked with the team at Murray Regional Tourism to map out their travel Customer Journey, then laid the industry delivery against it, we were able to highlight specific gaps that collectively the industry could rally together to resolve. Similarly, when our government contract client undertook this exercise, we worked out they were delivering some parts of the journey well, but left their customers in limbo between the sale and the delivery of the product. This resulted in confusion, angst and frustration for the customer in an otherwise positive experience, and generated avoidable contact and extra admin cost for the business.

#5. You actively use the Customer Journey to inform your strategy and operations

Best practice: Business strategy and plans are dynamic, with the customer at the heart of key decisions. Plans are built around the customer, rather than systems, processes or people.

While we like to think that customer is the be-all and end-all, they only make up one (vital) part of the broader strategy for an organisation. In high-performing organisations, the customer becomes part of the central strategy dashboard. Tools like the Kaplan and Norton balanced scorecard seek to bring the customer into this wider view.

What we've evidenced is that by mapping out the Customer Journey, you find areas for tactical improvement across your operations. However, you also find the bigger strategic gaps that require consideration at the management level. These are usually bigger ticket items, or even new business model options that might move away from the traditional or core approach you take today.

Many of the businesses we regard as 'disruptors' today simply looked at the Customer Journey, what customers needed and what's really important, then changed up one of three levers of strategic innovation – the who (customer), the what (offering) or the how (the way we do it).

On completing the mapping process, the CEO of Murray Regional Tourism placed the map directly on the wall beside his desk. An instant reminder of what needs to be done at both the tactical and operational level – without the need for some 100-page consultant's report!

SELF-ASSESSMENT: HOW DO YOU STACK UP?

Now that you're familiar with the five key ingredients for success and what best practice looks like, it's time to do a bit of self-assessment and ask yourself, how do we stack up?

To get an initial benchmark, check out the statements below and circle the one that best matches your current situation. Mark yourself on the harder side, there's no gold stars here, just learnings and opportunities.

This quick assessment is a simplified version of our full-blown Customer-led Accelerator Program. But, straight away, this gives you an initial idea of how you stack up.

Share it with colleagues and see what they think. It's a great way to open up the conversation on customer. What answers do you think you'd get if you asked your senior leadership team? Are you aligned or are you on completely different planets?

Refer to the section 'How to use this book' for tips on who to ask in your pxviii organisation, how and why.

RED FLAGS AND ROADBLOCKS

Let's look at some of the red flags and potential roadblocks for Customer Journey.

Red flags	Potential roadblocks
■ You are receiving a higher level of customer complaints than you'd like, perhaps at specific points in your delivery. ■ Your team seem to be focused heavily on sales but less so on customer care or customer retention after the sale. ■ Your team is focused on the moments from where your customer 'walks in the front door' to when they leave, with little regard for what happens before and after their interactions with you.	■ Using your business processes instead of truly mapping the Customer Journey from a customer's perspective. ■ Assuming all of your customer (profiles) have exactly the same journey (meaning you're missing out on some big opportunities to better serve them). ■ The team struggle with the wider Customer Journey beyond the traditional transaction and sales pipeline view, as they take an inside-out view, rather than the outside-in view of your customers (and the wider world).

WHEN YOUR ORGANISATION BUILDS THIS CAPABILITY

Take a moment now to fast forward to a future moment in time where your organisation has a deep understanding of your customer's journey. The journeys are mapped out, documented and presented for all to see. They are used to inform business process improvements and priorities, customer communications and customer care initiatives. You're finding new opportunities to solve customers' pain that directly contribute to your bottom line while building a stronger customer connection and greater advocacy. You've located and removed historical inefficiencies and are focusing on delivering things that customers value, not what you think they value. Your team are more engaged, more connected and are constantly looking for new ways to innovate. Is this the oganisation you want to create?

*

Now you know the journey a customer goes on to buy an offering like yours, let's go even deeper into the KNOW discipline, to unlock what's going on in your customer's mind with how they make decisions, choices and actions, and build up your capability on Customer Behaviour.

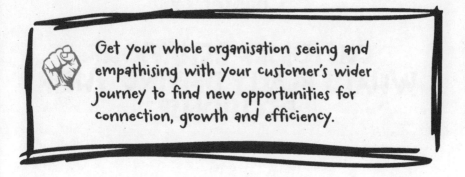

Get your whole organisation seeing and empathising with your customer's wider journey to find new opportunities for connection, growth and efficiency.

Chapter 19

CUSTOMER BEHAVIOUR: WHAT'S REALLY DRIVING THEIR DECISIONS?

The strategic question we're setting out to answer is:

Do you understand customer behaviour and how it applies to your organisation?

The human brain and the way we make decisions are complex beasts. In fact, there are many books on this topic from subject matter experts written over the years. What we know is that making decisions is not a simple on-off transaction. There's a lot to it, involving a human's history, current state of mind and urgency of the need, to name but a few.

This section is about what makes customers tick. What their inherent motivators are. What makes them make the decisions they do. What in their external environment impacts them, what internally is going on for them. What their internal psychology is. These are things you cannot control as a business, but you must know about in order to understand your customers better – why they do what they do and what you can do to better connect with them.

CUSTOMERS AVOID FEARS, AS WELL AS SEEK BENEFITS

As humans, we often think that we are motivated towards benefits or the upside. In fact, marketers try to convince us we want features and benefits. This is partly true, but misses the underlying psychological drivers at play that drive decision-making behaviours.

We've noticed there are five fears that customers have when engaging or making a decision.

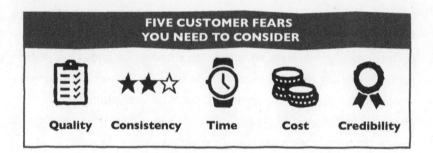

FIVE CUSTOMER FEARS YOU NEED TO CONSIDER

Quality   Consistency   Time   Cost   Credibility

Figure 18: The five customer fears

#1 Quality

Will this organisation (or product, service, offering) deliver the quality that I am expecting? Imagine you were buying a gift for a loved one. How would it feel for you if the quality wasn't up to scratch? You'd feel like a goose! Embarrassed. Let down. The same goes when you are procuring for work. Will this reflect poorly on me, the purchaser? Will I get a DCM (Don't Come Monday) as a result? *How can you put your customer at ease when it comes to the quality you offer?*

#2 Consistency

Will this organisation provide consistency every time? In our world, coffee is really (REALLY) important. When we need that fix in the morning, inconsistency has been a key driver for finding a new supplier of our caffeinated morning goodness. Imagine travelling for work and staying at the same hotel each time. Would you stay there again if the rooms weren't always at the same standard? You might put up with it for a while but you would likely switch if it continued. If you're a government agency that provides inconsistent answers to developers or investors, where do you think they would move their attention? *What can you do to alleviate this underlying customer fear facing your organisation?*

#3 Time

Will this take up my most valuable commodity – my time? We often don't think about this for customers, but time has become hugely important in our instant-gratification society. Beyond traditional things like waiting periods, time can show up in many different ways. It could be time going through arduous purchase processes. It could be time getting used to a new product. The list goes on. The question for you is this. *What time fears do your customers have when purchasing a product or service like yours?*

#4 Cost

Will this cost more than I expect? How many times have you had an initial quote for something, only for it to cost more at the end of the process? If you've ever purchased an expensive car, they seem to have an endless list of options. And, by the time you're finished adding a steering wheel and tyres, the thing is almost double the cost of where you started! Cost fears are huge. In a corporate environment, will I put myself on the line that the cost will be the cost? *What is the cost structure in your organisation – is it transparent or plus plus plus?*

#5 Credibility

Is the organisation or product the credible choice for what it provides? The old line 'no one ever got sacked by buying IBM' rings true here. Your credibility as an organisation is vitally important to your customer. If they choose you, their own credibility is put under the spotlight. This customer fear shows up when buying washing machines at home through to choosing transformation consultants – and everything in between. Testimonials help here, as do industry accreditations or case studies of your results. *What do you have in place to alleviate the credibility fear for your customers?*

CYNICISM AND THE NEED FOR AUTHENTICITY

As customers, we all want genuine feedback or insight when deciding on our purchases. With all the customer reviews, influencers, paid content and the like, it's harder to make sense of what's real and what's not these days. And so we can be distrusting and cynical about reviews and content. Are they real?

That said, social proof is important in the customer's decision-making process.

It's your role to be as authentic as possible in how you present your business or organisation to the world. Allowing customers to see who you are and what you stand for creates a greater, more genuine connection, meaning when they're ready, they'll be more likely to choose you.

CUSTOMER BEHAVIOUR: THE DRIVER BEHIND THEIR DECISIONS

Why is this important to you, the customer-led leader? Understanding what makes customers tick and the drivers behind their buying process helps you make informed choices that create greater engagement and connection. By examining trends in Customer Behaviour and the nuances of the customer environment, you build a strong foundation for effective decision-making.

When we break down the complexity, it helps to remind ourselves of some head-slap realities.

Businesses don't buy things. People in businesses do. We often think about customers being end consumers, like in a business-to-consumer (B2C) sense. In fact, we hear about business-to-business (B2B) quite a bit but the reality is that it is really P2P – people-to-people. A person within a business makes the decision. Yes, it might have a complex, multi-layered process, but they are still people who have needs, wants and desires like the rest of us.

So, now that we have that out of the way, let's get into some 101 about human psychology that applies to most situations you inevitably face in your organisation today.

People aren't always rational. Reflect for a moment. Have you ever been in a relationship with someone? Chances are, you probably have. Now, would you say that your partner always made rational decisions? Make sure they're not reading over your shoulder here! They don't. Depending on the situation, we have varying levels of functional (rational) and feeling (emotional) parts of our decision-making. In fact, there's many instances where the emotional justification is so strong that we look for rational facts to help prove the feelings-led business case!

> UNDERSTANDING WHAT MAKES CUSTOMERS TICK AND THE DRIVERS BEHIND THEIR BUYING PROCESS HELPS YOU MAKE INFORMED CHOICES THAT CREATE GREATER ENGAGEMENT AND CONNECTION.

As the customer-led leader, your role is to help your organisation understand the need for both sides of the decision-making process and intentionally design your experiences around it.

Customers have a pool of love. Not to get all soppy here, but every customer has a sentiment (or opinion if you will) towards your organisation and how well it performs. We'll be exploring some of the specific concepts in the next section, but for now, let's go with this. Every time a p184 customer has an interaction with you, the pool level either increases or decreases, depending on whether it's a positive or a negative experience. This pool of love and forgiveness is a foundation of customer management and ultimately, your sustainability and performance. What happens for a new customer who begins with a low level in the pool and something goes wrong? Ever jumped into an empty pool? Ouch!

By building up the level intentionally over time, you begin to build customer resilience. If one day, we happen to be human and make a mistake, there is enough in the pool for the customer to ride the wave. If it continues, the level will drop and you'll eventually need to prepare for plaster and crutches! In our chapter on customer experience, we'll provide (p209) some ideas on how you can build this level up.

Customers have needs and wants. This might sound obvious at first, but the two concepts are hugely different in terms of understanding Customer Behaviour. Marketers have for many decades been great at linking the want of a product to serve an unmet need. Take sports cars for example. Do you need a Porsche 911? (One author says yes!) But the reality is – no. The product is not the need in itself. It serves a need of the customer. What is the need? The need to be recognised. The need to feel fast. The need to feel successful. A need can be met through a range of different wants (products). To go one step further, people only buy things or transact with your organisation to serve their need. Your job is to make sure that your product is the one they want to serve that need. The current trend towards purpose-driven marketing is a great example. I can now buy toilet paper, from Who Gives a Crap, and every time I wipe, I feel like I am changing the world. It meets my need at a deeper level, to play my part in social change.

And another example – Harley Davidson doesn't sell motorbikes, it sells freedom.

CUSTOMER BEHAVIOUR – A ROBUST FOUNDATION BASED ON UNDERSTANDING

Now that we've covered off the main elements, the opportunities and things to think about, let's have a look at how you can work out where you are on this capability through the lens of the Customer Strategy Framework™.

The core question

Do you understand Customer Behaviour and how it applies to your organisation?

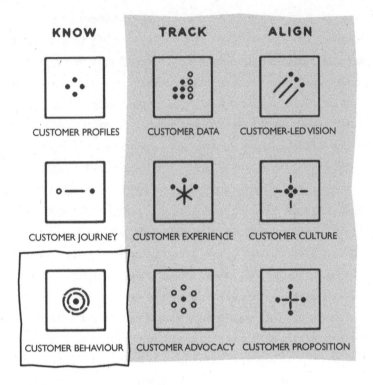

Figure 19: Customer Behaviour capability within the Framework

Why does it matter

Remember, businesses don't buy things – people do. By getting your team's head around the behaviour drivers and how they apply to your situation helps you build a new level of understanding, in addition to the technical aspects of what you do. So what do you need to consider? Let's examine the five drivers that help chart your success.

THE FIVE DRIVERS/INGREDIENTS FOR SUCCESS

There are five key drivers or ingredients you need in this capability for success. Let's take a look. As you read the statement, ponder your answer – what's your gut feel? Read over the best practice and explanation to see what good really looks like. Then, go back and consider again how strong you are in this area. What gaps and opportunities emerge?

#1 You proactively research and follow trends in Customer Behaviour, relevant to your industry

Best practice: Dedicated resources undertake desk research and trends analysis to help shape the organisation's understanding of the market for strategic decision-making.

Across every industry or sector, there is a wealth of information about trends. The task is to proactively seek it out and make sense of it. If you can't get it, even research from adjacent sectors can help. What can your organisation learn from others to apply forward? After all, truly unique, new ideas are a small fraction of innovative thinking.

We're not talking about spending hundreds of thousands of dollars on research. There are so many tools and resources available – many free – to help you. Start small and with the most pertinent data, so you don't overwhelm yourself. Check out customerframe.com/resources for some helpful tools to get you going.

#2 You understand why customers seek an offering like yours and what motivates them to do so

Best practice: Focus groups and customer panels reveal customer's underlying behaviours and attitudes, which are then used to shape management decisions, new product development and marketing initiatives.

Anecdotally talking about some customer feedback or chitter chatter is not a structured way of capturing this insight. Bringing your customers together in meaningful ways, however, does. You might think you know, but do you really know why they do what they do? Their fears? The best way is to ask them. But make sure it is coordinated and not just scattergun opinion. This doesn't have to be expensive, it can be as simple as basic customer surveys, or customer interviews, conversations between your Sales or BD teams with their clients, or an invitation to a customer focus group complete with tea and coffee and a chat.

#3 You know the key external influencers on Customer Behaviour, for an offering like yours

Best practice: The social, cultural, environmental and physical influences that impact customer decision-making and preference are regularly reviewed and actioned to shape and improve connection to customer.

Considering what customers are being exposed to and the things that are influencing their decision-making is crucial in the Customer-led Revolution. For example, online shopping and the ease of the process set by Amazon undoubtedly impacts customer expectation and behaviour across all their purchases and interactions. These external influences change behaviour. Market innovations, government changes, consumer confidence, technology improvements – all of these need to be scanned across your horizon and played out to see how they might impact your future operations. They might not be a direct impact. But like dominoes, things that hit your customers will eventually hit you too!

#4 You know the steps of the customer buying process and apply them in your organisation

Best practice: Product development and operational decisions are informed and driven by the customer buying process rather than by internal systems, processes and behaviours.

Related to Customer Journey mapping, understanding the customer buying process and the key steps helps you to make sure your operations reflect what they need. For example, winning military contracts have a complex set of steps, with multi-level approvals required. By understanding and empathising with the poor suckers who have to pull it all together on the client side could easily put your organisation on top of the pile.

#5 You regularly and actively monitor customers that are using an offering like yours

Best practice: A structured plan is in place for observing customers in competing environments, both online and offline, to inform business decisions and priorities.

Observing customers using your product or engaging in your services (and even services like yours) is always an eye-opener. Many innovations, that often save cost, are born out of these moments. It may sound simple, but as leaders, we often don't prioritise it or realise the power of doing it. There's so much great technology these days to help too. Online mouse tracking through to AI and video facial recognition… it's all there.

By looking at each of these five ideas, you begin to see how strong you are. Or, you begin to identify new opportunities to improve. Either way, getting under the hood of how your customers make decisions and their behavioural drivers will help you smooth out their journey. And, in doing so, your organisation starts to show up as 'getting them', establishing that deeper, personal connection.

SELF-ASSESSMENT: HOW DO YOU STACK UP?

Now that you're familiar with the five key ingredients for success and what best practice looks like, it's time to do a bit of self-assessment and ask yourself, how do we stack up?

To get an initial benchmark, check out the statements below and circle the one that best matches your current situation. Mark yourself on the harder side, there's no gold stars here, just learnings and opportunities.

We have a deep understanding of how our customers behave + the consumer trends affecting their lives

We don't need to know – we offer the services we offer + they can use them or not	Our customer-facing teams might know a bit, but it's not something we actively pursue	We have a pretty good understanding, but it's more accidental than intentional	We study our customers regularly to understand their problems + how we can solve them, in pockets of our organisation	100%! Our understanding of what makes our customers tick underpins our decisions + actions across our organisation

This quick assessment is a simplified version of our full-blown Customer-led Accelerator Program. But, straight away, this gives you an initial idea of how you stack up.

Share it with colleagues and see what they think. It's a great way to open up the conversation on customer. What answers do you think you'd get if you asked your senior leadership team? Are you aligned or are you on completely different planets? Refer to the section 'How to use this book' for pxviii tips on who to ask in your organisation, how and why.

RED FLAGS AND ROADBLOCKS

Let's look at some of the red flags and potential roadblocks for Customer Behaviour.

Red flags	Potential roadblocks
■ You feel like there's a lot of guesswork behind senior leadership and middle management decisions, rather than a solid understanding or appreciation of what makes customers tick. ■ You have higher customer attrition rates than you would like and observe competitors doing a better job of connecting with and retaining your ideal customers. ■ There's little internal discussion of customer behavioural trends and how they impact on your organisation and operations.	■ Underlying beliefs that customers make purely rational decisions when there is a significant emotional component that can't (and shouldn't) be ignored. ■ The wider team's apathy or resistance, or even arrogance, that they know what's going on for the customer and why they make their decisions, in turn limiting the potential for growth. ■ Having too much or too little customer insight to make valuable, informed decisions.

WHEN YOUR ORGANISATION BUILDS THIS CAPABILITY

Take a moment now to fast forward to a future moment in time where your organisation has developed and applied knowledge of Customer Behaviour in everything you do. The organisation is in tune with what's going on in your customer's mind (and life). Your team is engineering every part of your customer experience to address the customer trends and fears, giving you a truly sustainable competitive advantage. Your customers are close and the organisation is in constant dialogue with them to reveal their underlying behaviours and attitudes. Your organisation is ahead of the game and pre-empting what customers need even before they know they need it. You and your team are making confident, informed decisions that directly contribute to the bottom line. Does this sound like a good way to operate?

*

This rounds out the three capabilities that help you truly KNOW your customer – who they are, their journey and what makes them tick. We've shared a view of what your future organisation could look like with these three things in place. Now, let's take a look at the next discipline, TRACK.

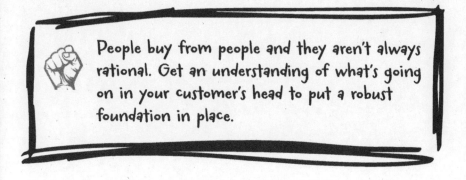

People buy from people and they aren't always rational. Get an understanding of what's going on in your customer's head to put a robust foundation in place.

Section 5

TRACK

Welcome to the second discipline of the Customer Strategy Framework™: TRACK.

The organisations that are smashing their goals through being customer-led have embraced the need to track their performance from their customers' view, not just through their internal traditional performance metrics. It's about changing the way you see customer data, how you gauge their experience of your organisation and truly understand how they feel about you beyond satisfaction alone.

So, here's the question: Do you track your performance from the customer's perspective?

Chapter 20

SO, YOU'RE TRACKING WELL, BUT ARE YOU REALLY?

Tracking your performance – beyond basic sales and transaction data – is a powerful tool in business. And one that often falls short of its full potential.

Many business leaders we meet tell us they're measuring all the important things – sales, revenue, cost per acquisition, marketing ROI, training budget returns and so on. But it's in the lost and forgotten data where the true magic lies.

What matters to your customer should matter to you.

There's a reason why we have a whole discipline dedicated to TRACK. And there's a reason why we don't call it research. By focusing in on this particular discipline, you come to realise that tracking your performance from your customer's perspective is much more valuable than a bunch of research and stats from a source far removed from your operation. We're not saying research isn't valuable, it's just not everything it's cracked up to be.

WHAT MATTERS TO YOUR CUSTOMER SHOULD MATTER TO YOU.

THE STORY OF THE KID'S ROOM AND THE FLASHLIGHT

As humans, we're attracted to measurement, numbers and meeting targets. The problem is that sometimes, we don't understand the behavioural outcomes from the choices we make. One of the best analogies we've come across over our years is by Bernard Marr, one of the leaders in data intelligence. We paraphrase his story here.

If you ask an eight-year-old to clean their room, you are often met with a groan. If they're smart (like our kids are), they might clarify the expectations of what deems a 'clean room'. Now, similar to some of the metrics we use in our organisations, what if we told our eight-year-old that we're going to turn off the light in his room, and we're only going to inspect the area that the flashlight can illuminate near his bedside table. What do you think would happen? Like most eight-year-olds who have better things to do, he'd push his stuff aside and make that area look as clean as possible. Flashlight inspection – pass. Turn on the light however, and it's a different story. We might not have the time or resources to analyse every part of the organisation's 'room', but the challenge you have as a leader is this. Are you only using one flashlight and is there mess lurking in the dark? That's where, as leaders, we need to be specific and selective about what we measure and what it means.

WHAT'S IMPORTANT TO YOUR CUSTOMERS?

By tracking your performance and delivery from your customer's perspective, you look at the world through their eyes. You find out what's important to them. This helps you understand what measures you should pay attention to.

Tip: the ones that are important to your customer are the ones you should be watching closely.

There's no point, for example, watching a measure that means nothing to the customer. Take a call centre operation. It might matter to you that you get people off the phone as soon as possible so you can take more calls, but the customer doesn't care about that – they care that you effectively and efficiently deal with their issue or request and sort it out. If that takes 10 minutes, so be it.

What they don't want to do is sit on hold for 10 minutes only to be told that you can't help them, or that they're flicked to a different department, or worse still, their call is cut off and they have to call back.

What's important to the customer is this: To have their problem solved as quickly and efficiently as possible, with the least amount of angst, waiting and frustration.

What's important to the business should be *not* the number of calls a day you take, but how many times one customer has to contact you to get their issue solved. It should be about having the right number of staff to service the call volumes, not stretching the existing staff so thin that you upset your customers. Because soon enough, you'll find you'll get less calls because you'll have less customers.

What's important to your customer should be what you measure yourselves on. Put your own KPIs or the interests of your senior leaders or ego-driven measures on the back-burner. Think customer first and you'll always win.

HOW DO THEY PERCEIVE YOUR BUSINESS? HOW DO THEY FEEL ABOUT YOU?

By paying attention and tracking your performance from the customer's perspective and based on what's important to them, you'll have more impact and influence over this very important topic.

How they feel about you

For years we've been told that customer satisfaction is the key metric in understanding how happy your customers are. This is true – to a point. But how they feel in one moment versus the next can change.

How they feel about your business overall – what we call their sentiment towards you – is something that ebbs and flows but that generally stays fairly static.

How they perceive you as a business and a brand, and how they feel about you are intrinsically linked. It informs how they talk about you, how they interact with you and whether they'll buy from you again.

Further, the sentiment of your current or past customers – thanks to things like reviews and ratings – will inform how new and potential customers perceive you.

In this section, we'll learn about how measuring how they feel about you can help make or break your business.

WHAT CUSTOMER MEASURES ARE USED AND SHARED ACROSS THE ORGANISATION?

So what customer measures do you currently use in your organisation, by whom and are they shared?

Often, the Customer Service team will run a feedback survey or NPS survey. The Sales team will have stats on sales figures, revenue per customer, perhaps repeat revenue. The Senior Leadership team will of course have P&Ls and various dashboards and metrics.

That's great. But how many of them are actually customer measures? Not business measures, but customer measures? Things that specifically link to customers, what's important to them and how they interact with your business.

It can help to make a list of the customer measures used in your business today. Then think about if and how they're shared across the organisation and whether it can be done better.

WHAT ARE THE CRITICAL MOMENTS THAT REALLY MATTER?

One of our favourite outcomes of the TRACK discipline is figuring out what the critical moments are in a customer's journey, the moments that matter the most to your customer.

It fascinates us just how many business and organisation leaders have no idea which are the most critical moments in their interactions with their customers and how to measure them. They often think they know, but when we dig deeper, they soon realise they don't.

Focusing on the wrong moments in a customer's journey can be lethal. Not only do you miss what matters most to customers and the opportunities this brings – for both new products and services, but also crucial service delivery and recovery – you waste resources focusing on the wrong moments.

HAVING ROBUST DATA IS THE FOUNDATION FOR PERSONALISATION

Personalisation is the next big thing in many customer experience conversations. Considering one of the five key trends is all around customers wanting everything to be about them, it's no surprise.

We believe that the foundation for personalisation isn't a big bank account – though that can help. It's robust data. Not necessarily lots of it, but good data. Data you can use to better understand your customer, what they need from you and what they value.

Personalisation isn't about sending an email with the correct name. It's way beyond that. It's about truly understanding your customer so that you can give them the very best experience possible. Your data – the stuff that often sits under your radar – is the key.

p21

FIND AND MEASURE WHAT MATTERS

Back to our client with the government contract. We worked with them on mapping their Customer Journey following their Customer-led Accelerator Program – it was one of the elements that we'd identified as lacking within their organisation.

Boy oh boy, did we find some gold in this process. Not only did we find major opportunities across the journey (and discovered they had competitors, which they didn't think they had!), we helped them realise that they had been focusing on all the wrong things in their customer's journey. The bits they thought were important, when we dug deeper, paled in significance to the parts of the journey they'd been ignoring, but were most important to the customer – the critical moments, we call them.

By identifying these critical moments, we helped the team find not only new service opportunities (to improve their NPS and satisfaction), but product development opportunities that drove directly to their margins and bottom line. Magic!

WHAT'S ON YOUR COCKPIT DASHBOARD?

In recent years, data has become a monster. All manner of experts have recommended tracking all manner of data points via all manner of tools and technology. What ends up happening is pure overwhelm. So much data, you simply don't know what to do with it.

Consider this cockpit of the Concorde – pretty straightforward, right? Just kidding. Overwhelming, for sure. Do the Concorde pilots use all of these measures all of the time to keep this precious piece of metal from hitting the ground? Of course not. In fact, they primarily use the elements, the dashboard, circled in the following image. Trying to monitor all the dials would surely end in disaster.

Figure 20: The complex cockpit of the Concorde,
showing what the pilot really focuses on

And that's what happens in business. Overwhelm. Too much data. Too many dials and measures that don't mean much or can be more of a hinder than a help.

FOCUSING ON THE WRONG MEASURES

Beyond having too many elements to focus on, a huge risk to business is focusing on the wrong measures, which can inadvertently and unintentionally drive the wrong behaviours in your business.

LEADING VERSUS LAGGING INDICATORS

We love this one. It's all about the data you use in your business. Traditionally, we've been told as business leaders to focus on the sales and revenue, and cost lines of the balance sheet.

MEASURES HAVE CONSEQUENCES

Sueanne used to work in a wholesale call centre, waaay back in the beginning of her career in Tourism. Incentivised on the number of calls per day, length of call and number of sales, the focus was to get as many sales as quickly as possible throughout the day. That meant getting rid of the customers who weren't making a booking, quick smart.

Being super competitive, Sueanne was top of the leaderboard each month, smashing her sales goals and call volumes. Boom.

While it meant good news for Sueanne who continually received kudos, incentive prizes and weekends away as rewards, the news for the customer wasn't so great.

For those customers who weren't making a new booking but simply changing dates or updating details, it meant they were processed at high speed, with little care and even less regard. As travel agents themselves, they may have been trying to solve big problems for their own customers, but that didn't mean much to the call centre team. They weren't a new sale. And in many cases, they actually took longer to process than a new sale, particularly if there was a problem to be solved.

Not only that, by underservicing them, they'd have to call back more often, meaning higher avoidable contact and problems for peers.

Sueanne and the call centre team were incentivised on the wrong things. By focusing only on driving new sales and maxing call volumes, they were treating their existing customers like numbers, like transactions, like second-rate citizens. They didn't realise it at the time, but they weren't incentivised or KPI'd on taking care of their customers, only creating new ones.

Focusing on the wrong measures can undermine all you are trying to achieve in your customer experience.

LOOKING OUTSIDE

How much time do you spend a month sitting in a room talking about **last month's** figures and **last quarter's** performance and **last year's** comparison? Like. A. Lot.

We call these lagging indicators. They look backwards. They tell us where we've been, not where we're going. While certainly useful, there's too much focus put on looking backwards.

It's a great way to help us justify our results, particularly if they're not as good as we'd hoped. Let's sit around and talk about all the reasons why we couldn't possibly have hit our target given this and that and this. Lagging indicators are useful for flagging areas for improvement, process and policy issues, even staff challenges. But they're not the be-all and end-all.

Leading indicators help us look forward. They're our sales forecasts, our future bookings, and externally, consumer confidence and market trends. They help us know what's coming and give us the focus for improvement and effort. By focusing on leading indicators instead of lagging ones, we can ready ourselves for what's coming, not wallow in what's been.

Looking outside and assuming it's costly and onerous

For some reason, data and customer insight has a bad name in business. Many people we speak with think that data means research. And research traditionally means looking outside the business and it means expensive.

We've met countless leaders and been part of many organisations where exorbitant amounts of money have been spent on market research, only to then sit on a shelf gathering dust.

When we talk about research and reviews in our projects, our clients always ask how much the research will cost.

The thing is, you don't have to spend lots of money on research, nor does it have to be onerous. By simply looking at what's available both inside your business and outside, you can build a pretty good picture.

Many external research sources are free or low cost. If you're in Tourism for example, the State Tourism Organisations and Regional Tourism Organisations, not to mention the National body, release extensive reports on visitor data and trends. Same goes for most industries and sectors. Use these as your first port of call when it comes to external data. Focus on the main, most reputable sources and remember, a Google search can also be fruitful (albeit a rabbit warren if you're not careful).

Sitting on a data goldmine

So often we look externally for intelligence and data to help inform our business decisions, when there's a goldmine of information right in front of our eyes. Let a team member spend a week reviewing, refining and making sense of your data – it'll not only help make better decisions, it'll uncover hidden issues, resource wastage and opportunities to inform your future actions and next steps.

Unused data is like carrying rocks in your backpack. It's heavy, resource inefficient and quite frankly, a waste of energy and time. Unpack your data backpack, take stock of what you've got, decide what you need and don't need, and go from there.

THE NEED TO BUILD YOUR ORGANISATION'S CAPABILITIES (TRACK)

A common mistake we see business leaders make is thinking that external research (which they often can't afford or don't know what to do with) is key to better business. Research and insight has become a lauded asset in business, while internal data has been the poor cousin.

Instead of using their data to inform their business decisions, new product development, experience improvements, pricing strategies and customer service plans, they abandon it for more glamorous solutions.

The three capabilities of TRACK: Customer Data, Customer Experience and Customer Advocacy

Let's touch on the three TRACK capabilities before we delve into them in more depth in the coming chapters.

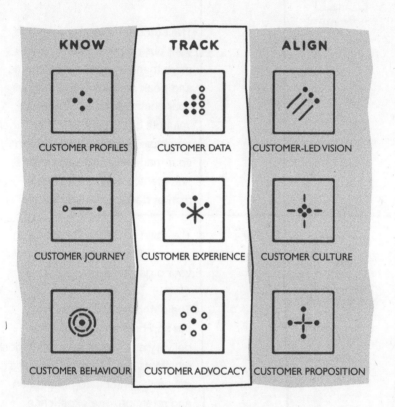

Figure 21: TRACK and the three capabilities

TRACK Customer Capability	Context	Overview
CUSTOMER DATA	Facts + intelligence	The main question: Do you use your customer and sales (transaction) data to drive business decisions? The outcome: Digging deep into your business data can provide more than just seasonality curves and peak periods. Understanding your customer base, your most valuable customers (MVC) and their purchase behaviours can inform your marketing and sales efforts, and identify new product and market development opportunities.
CUSTOMER EXPERIENCE	Reality + improvement	The main question: Do you gauge what it's like to be a customer of your organisation? The outcome: Understanding the gap between your service delivery and customer expectations highlights the issues and specific drivers behind customer attrition and retention. The experience view brings focus to the areas for improvement that will make the most impact on your customer and on your performance.

TRACK Customer Capability	Context	Overview
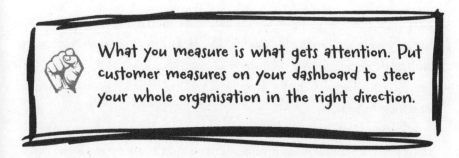CUSTOMER ADVOCACY	Future + foresight	The main question: Do you know how your customers feel about you: are they advocates, apathetic or assassins? The outcome: Different to satisfaction, keeping track of customer intent and their propensity to refer gives an insight into your future performance. It tells you how your customers feel about you and highlights how active or inactive they are at being an extension of your sales force.

These three capabilities enable your organisation to build the awareness you need to be a successful customer-led organisation. How customers interact with your business, what their experience is and how they truly feel about you.

We'll cover these in more detail in the coming chapters with lots of stories and examples.

Now we understand the importance of tracking our performance from our customers' perspective, let's get into the nitty gritty of the three capabilities that sit under this transformative discipline.

> What you measure is what gets attention. Put customer measures on your dashboard to steer your whole organisation in the right direction.

Chapter 21

CUSTOMER DATA: UNLOCKING THE INTELLIGENCE ALREADY IN YOUR BUSINESS

The strategic question we're setting out to answer is:

Do you use your customer and transaction data to drive business decisions?

When we ask business leaders about assets, they usually respond with the traditional ones. You know, cash in the bank, their people, their brand, their proprietary technology. But in the Customer-led Revolution your Customer Data will be one of your greatest assets.

WHAT IS CUSTOMER DATA?

Keeping the complex simple, we see data as **a collection of facts**. Depending on your organisation, this can include sales figures, customer feedback, addresses, demographics, frequency of purchase, sale price, number of products purchased... the list is endless. And like facts, some can be useful or useless to you.

Customer Data can appear in many forms and places right across everything you do. Because many organisations view data as scary and aren't sure what to do with it, they have let it grow organically, unintentionally. You see this in systems everywhere. In fact, as customers of other organisations yourselves, we're sure you've had that frustration of seeing disconnected internal data systems from the outside in. It has been seen as an admin item in a transaction, not as a valued currency.

WHY IS CUSTOMER DATA SO CRUCIAL TO YOUR FUTURE?

In the past, Customer Data required special skills and capabilities, usually reserved for large scale organisations who could afford to employ a propellorhead to do some 'smart maths stuff'. But, due to advances in technology, the machines can now do the work for us lay folk!

Customer Data is the foundation for moving your organisation from having a transactional relationship (product view) with your customer to having an experiential relationship (customer view). It gives you the collection of facts to enable personalisation of the experience, and give you a robust platform to give actionable insights that improve your tactical and strategic decision-making.

LINKING IT UP FOR INSIGHT

In its various forms, your Customer Data is rich in what it can tell you. It can tell you more than just seasonality curves and peak periods. It can help you find hidden inefficiencies, identify your most valuable customers and reveal hidden growth opportunities.

> CUSTOMER DATA IS THE FOUNDATION FOR MOVING YOUR ORGANISATION FROM HAVING A TRANSACTIONAL RELATIONSHIP (PRODUCT VIEW) WITH YOUR CUSTOMER TO HAVING AN EXPERIENTIAL RELATIONSHIP (CUSTOMER VIEW).

There's a strong need to go beyond the basic sales figures, or transaction data by linking your various data sources together. In Chapter 17 we spoke (p138) about breaking your customer base down into Customer Profiles. Imagine if you could tag your existing data to your five to eight different profiles. In a Tourism sense, what if your data told you that one particular customer profile travelled weekdays, when everyone else travels weekends? Imagine what that data could do to help you build new products, services and messages that filled a traditional 'trough' in your business performance?

Ultimately, data helps you make better decisions based on fact, not opinions.

We've shown you the power of the external view through understanding Customer Behaviour. Customer Data is the internal view, the knowledge, insight and experience you've gathered within your organisation. It's about how your customers interact with YOUR business within THEIR lives. Putting them together can help identify gaps and opportunities for growth.

THE PROBLEM WITH DATA THAT THE CUSTOMER CAN SOLVE

In Peter's early career, he worked for Australia's leading battery manufacturer. And you thought you had sexy products! Being a manufacturer was a very data driven business. They had some great data accumulated over many years, maybe even too much. Without boring you with the details of battery production, it's important to forecast WAAAY in advance due to the manufacturing lead time. At an aggregate level, things looked okay. It wasn't until Peter started speaking with Marvin, their Marine Customer Profile, that he struck gold. Marvin told him that EVERY September, the company would run out of Marine batteries, and he couldn't get enough.

While the sales data showed sales were good, the business was clearly missing a trick. Each year, the forecast was adjusted incrementally, but clearly never enough. And when they ran out, they couldn't just open the flood gates to quickly fix the problem.

The reality was that demand spiked in September as owners who'd docked their boats for the winter were ready to take to the water again, only to find their marine batteries flat as tacks. As a manufacturer, they couldn't have known this but by listening to the customer, the team chose to increase production to meet market needs and owned the marine battery market for decades to come.

IT'S ABOUT THE RIGHT MEASURES FOR YOUR ORGANISATION

Remember all the dials and levers in the Concorde? The pilot can't look at everything all the time. And, as leaders in your organisations, neither can you. Much like the pilot, you need a dashboard of key measures to help you keep on track, stay in the air and away from the mountains.

Customers are the ultimate reason you're in business. So, if you think about your dashboards today, are you flying blind? Do you have too much useless data? Do you have all business measures? Or do you have those three to four customer measures that make sure everything is tickety-boo?

CUSTOMER DATA: GET THE FACTS TO BUILD YOUR INTELLIGENCE

Now we understand the importance of Customer Data for better decision-making, let's take a deeper look at our Customer Strategy Framework™ and the guiding capability of Customer Data.

We see Customer Data as one of the forgotten assets of an organisation. It helps you gather the facts to help you build your organisation's collective intelligence and make better, more informed decisions. It forms the backbone of personalising your customer experience, reducing burden and frustration and making your whole organisation much more efficient.

p187

IS THERE A HOLE IN YOUR BUCKET?

In our work, we've found that there is one primary customer measure that very few keep track of. But those that do are usually the ones at the forefront of customer-led practices.

We call it Customer Flow Rate (CFR). Put simply, it's the difference between the number of new customers you have flowing in, versus the number of customers flowing out. The 'bucket' is your hidden asset – your active customer database. At a simple level, think of it like water flow. If you have a small amount coming in, but a large amount going out, your bucket will empty. Similarly, if you have a large flow in with a small flow out, your bucket will fill up – possibly overfill (which can be a problem in itself too).

We did some work with a well-known financial services company who were winning marketing awards for customer acquisition. However, at the same time, they were losing almost 40% of their customers within the first year. It wasn't until we looked at the flow rate that we realised – this was a BIG problem. Is this a good business? When unhappy customers leave, they also tell more potential customers just like them about their (poor) experience.

Why is this important to you? These inflows and outflows cost money. What if your customers stayed engaged with you beyond the one and done transaction, returned again, bought more stuff, brought other people with them or just amplified their advocacy

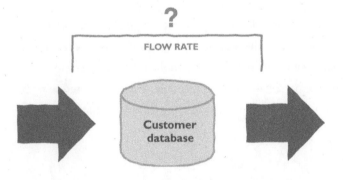

Figure 22: Customer Flow Rate – your inflows, outflows and 'bucket'

for you? How much better would your organisation perform? By focusing on this simple measure on your dashboard, you can gain deep insights into what to do next.

Don't assume just because one measure is going well, that there's not a leak somewhere else.

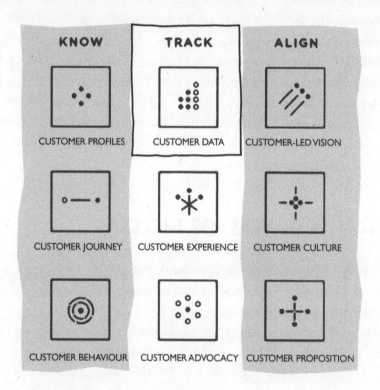

Figure 23: Customer Data capability within the Framework

The core question

Do you use your customer and transaction data to drive business decisions?

Does your organisation *really* do this well, or is there some scope to be a bit smarter? Sales trends aren't it. Neither is the inconsequential battery voltage for the Concorde pilot.

Why does it matter?

Understanding your customer base, your Most Valuable Customers (MVC) and their purchase behaviours can inform your marketing and sales efforts, identify new product development opportunities, enhance personalisation and open up new markets.

Similarly, understanding customer complaints and the points in the customer journey when they most occur is also valuable. But, how far away or close to the point where you ask for their Net Promoter Score (NPS) are those complaints? One of our clients was tracking exceptionally well on their NPS, which they measured at the point of sale of their product. But most of their customer complaints came at the point of delivery of that product – AFTER they'd given the score and when they started to really feel the pain of delayed delivery, broken or incorrect products. By then, they'd already scored the business and rated it far higher than they would have at this later point in the journey.

THE FIVE DRIVERS FOR SUCCESS

There are five key drivers or ingredients you need in this discipline for success. Let's take a look. As you read the statement, ponder your answer – what's your gut feel? Read over the best practice and explanation to see what good really looks like. Then, go back and consider again how strong you are in this area. What gaps and opportunities emerge?

Accurate records are only the start, but the leading organisations focus in on these five drivers to step up their operations.

#1 You actively monitor your customer flow rate* across acquisition, retention and attrition

Best practice: Customer flow rate is a core KPI on the management dashboard that directs the marketing, sales and customer care functions and informs the strategic choices made across the organisation.

---

* The ratio of the number of customers you have coming in versus going out.

The rate of inflows and outflows of your customers give you immense insight into your total operations. If you're winning lots of customers, but losing them just as fast, your organisation won't just be standing still – it will be going backwards. There is an inherent cost in attracting, converting and serving your customer. Think about when you last bought a mobile phone. It takes a while to get your head around the new features, but once you do, you're pretty self-sufficient. Same goes for your customers. Once you invest in educating them, there is more of an incremental cost to keep serving them. The hard work is done early in the relationship. By measuring customer flow rate, you can see what is happening and whether you're heading to empty or not!

#2 You regularly review your revenue and profitability by customer, tracking their lifetime value*

Best practice: Management dashboards showcase the performance of primary and secondary customer segments, and highlight growth opportunities and competitive risks over the lifetime of the customer.

Topline revenue only tells you one story. Imagine if you could see your profitability and revenue by Customer Profile. In many organisations, we see regular instances of customers costing considerable money to serve. By identifying the trends that are driving inefficiency or ineffectiveness or simply identifying plain old unprofitable customers, you can use the customer-led agenda to drive direct impacts to the bottom line of your organisation. 'But – we have to serve them,' we might hear you say. Challenge yourself and your team here – do you really?

The concept of customer value is raised here. Who are our most valuable customers? If you want to fill a timeslot on any board meeting agenda, ask that one simple question. The reality is value means very different things to different people. That's when you know you're off track and need to find your true north, getting everyone on the journey, with complementary viewpoints and focal points.

Think of the MVP in a sports game – who do you want on your team and on your bench?

---

* The total worth of a customer over the period of your relationship with them.

#3 Your customer records are complete, accurate and up-to-date

Best practice: The single customer view is actively monitored and used to refine offerings, enhance cross-sell opportunities and build longer-term relationships with customers beyond a single transaction view.

Good quality Customer Data is the fuel for the customer-led high-performance engine. If you owned a Porsche, you wouldn't put cheap nasty fuel in – so don't do it to your customer engine! We find that many organisations try to do it themselves and often fail. But, you don't need to do it alone. You can enlist your customer to help. Simply by presenting the customer with the upside benefits to them of better, clean and accurate data, they can help you whip it into shape. However, if you present it that they're helping you to fix something that you should already know, it won't land so well.

We've seen government agencies bring their customers into the issue, sharing the need for quality data on both sides. For the customer, it means timely, accurate payments. For the organisation, it means greater efficiency, which in turn often means greater payment amounts or enhanced services for customers. It's a win-win.

#4 You keep track of the sources that drive customers to you

Best practice: Tracking systems highlight channel performance and referral conversion to balance the best ROI on marketing and sales efforts, with regular reviews of what's working and what's not working.

We all know that word-of-mouth referral is still one of the strongest and most trusted forms of growth for any organisation. But, are you tracking it? Do you know which sources are the best drivers and highest quality converters for you?

By hanging out with the right people in the right customer 'watering (p139) holes' and tracking what works and what doesn't, you can begin to refine your marketing and sales efforts. Like the old saying, 'I know that half of my advertising spend is wasted, I just don't know which half.' Maybe you can make it more sixty-forty!

Once you are actively tracking what works, you can then invest in and amplify those channels to get even greater ROI to fuel your growth.

#5 You monitor your share of customer spend for your type of offering against competitors

Best practice: Beyond market share, total customer spend potential is calculated to reveal product development and extension opportunities that deliver enhanced customer loyalty, improved revenues and more profit.

Now, this is one of the tougher concepts to make real. How the heck can you measure it? For larger organisations who invest in it, they can see market share against their competitors. Why is this a useful metric? If your business is growing at 30% year on year, is that a good thing? On the surface, it sounds okay. But what if the rest of your industry is growing at 50% per year? In reality, you're going backwards relatively, getting less and less of the customer wallet over time.

This works well in professional services firms that offer a range of services. One client in particular has built out their offering from accounting services to offer legal, HR, marketing and financial advisory. This is where the share of wallet and 'customer for life' kicks in. Similarly, for tourism associations, imagine if you could build civic pride in a way that encourages people to stay longer, spend more and visit more often to your region. You're increasing the share of wallet over time.

SELF-ASSESSMENT: HOW DO YOU STACK UP?

Now that you're familiar with the five key ingredients for success and what best practice looks like, it's time to do a bit of self-assessment and ask yourself, how do we stack up?

To get an initial benchmark, check out the statements below and circle the one that best matches your current situation. Mark yourself on the harder side, there's no gold stars here, just learnings and opportunities.

 Customer data is at the heart of our organisation + drives everything we do

Data? We gather no customer or transaction data at all	We have an outdated system where we capture the basics, but we don't really understand the value of it	We gather some customer + transaction data, but we don't do much with it right now	Data is an important element in our decision making. We use it actively + regularly to create useful insights	Yes, we eat customer insight for breakfast. It's at the heart of every decision we make

This quick assessment is a simplified version of our full-blown Customer-led Accelerator Program. But, straight away, this gives you an initial idea of how you stack up.

Share it with colleagues and see what they think. It's a great way to open up the conversation on customer. What answers do you think you'd get if you asked your senior leadership team? Are you aligned or are you on completely different planets?

 Refer to the section 'How to use this book' for tips on who to ask in your organisation, how and why.

RED FLAGS AND ROADBLOCKS

Let's look at some of the red flags and potential roadblocks for Customer Data.

Red flags	Potential roadblocks
■ You're looking at your traditional internal measures only, perhaps on dashboards that have very few, if any, customer measures. ■ You feel like you're spending time looking at data that's out of date by the time you see it and it's not helping you make decisions. ■ You have plenty of Customer Data but none of it is complete enough to give you valuable insights on which to build robust decisions.	■ Fragmented or limited IT systems and policies that stop you seeing the full picture of your customer, including their flow rate, lifetime value and interactions across your business functions. ■ Continuing to use the easiest measures and tools to build a picture of your performance, ignoring those that may require effort but will also uncover the greatest opportunities in the future. ■ Investing in obtaining quality Customer Data is perceived as a waste of resources, or put into the 'too hard' basket, and gets deprioritised among the day-to-day operations.

WHEN YOUR ORGANISATION BUILDS THIS CAPABILITY

Imagine your organisation with a robust Customer Data capability in place. You'd be enjoying the benefits of a connected, single customer view where your data systems, operations and interactions all revolve around the ultimate reason you exist.

You're able to heighten your customer experience and reach new levels of personalisation that leads to stronger connection and advocacy. Your team continually analyse your existing data to find trends that unlock new growth opportunities and cost-saving efficiencies that hit directly to your bottom line.

Your Customer Data is seen as a valuable asset by the entire business that is used by all functions to make collective decisions for the good of the customer and the organisation. Instead of being a pain in the @ss, Customer Data becomes one of your competitive advantages. How much more efficient and effective would you be?

With the capability of Customer Data in place, let's now take this TRACK discipline even further as we help you get a gauge on your customer's experience to find out how you're performing from their perspective at the key moments that matter.

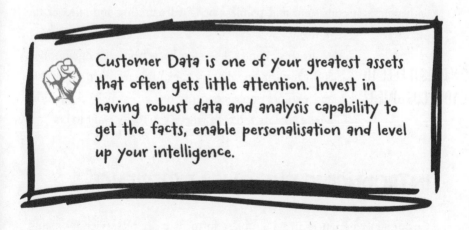

Customer Data is one of your greatest assets that often gets little attention. Invest in having robust data and analysis capability to get the facts, enable personalisation and level up your intelligence.

Chapter 22

CUSTOMER EXPERIENCE: STEP INTO YOUR CUSTOMER'S SHOES AND GET THE FULL PICTURE

The strategic question we're setting out to answer is:

Do you gauge what it's like to be a customer of your organisation?

So, what IS it like to be a customer of your business or organisation? Truly. We don't want the marketing or sales answer, we want the reality, the truth. How does it feel to be your customer? Throughout my interactions with you, is it consistent and painless or is it frustrating and all over the place?

HOW DOES IT FEEL TO BE YOUR CUSTOMER?

In this chapter, let's step back from our organisation and get clear on what we mean by customer experience and explore some concepts to help you level up from where you are today to where you really want to be.

INTRODUCING CUSTOMER EXPERIENCE

Customer Experience, in its simplest form, is a set of service moments, intentionally (or unintentionally) designed. These service moments (the S in the diagram below) support the delivery of your offering and occur right across the Customer Journey.

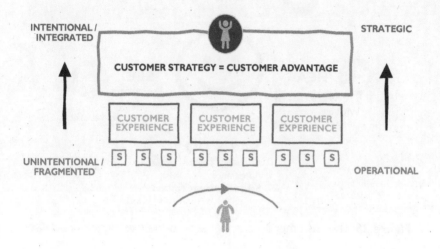

Figure 24: Customer Experience and the relationship to Customer Service

Our approach, you may find, is similar to others you've seen. Or maybe it's not. The power, however, is in the interaction of the Customer Experience capability with the other elements of the Customer Strategy Framework™. The power is in the wider perspective and the deeper understanding.

Typically sitting alone as an individual focus, it's true meaning and power comes to life when you KNOW your customer, TRACK your performance from their perspective and ALIGN your business to your customer.

There are a number of frames through which to see the Customer Experience, using the five human senses and beyond:

- what do they hear or smell?
- what do they see?
- what do they do?
- what do they think?
- what do they feel?

What really counts?
Major preoccupations
Worries and aspirations
THINK & FEEL

HEAR
What friends say
What influencers say
Ambient sounds

SEE
Environment
Friends
What the market offers

SAY & DO
Attitude in public
Appearance
Behaviour towards others

Figure 25: The customer frames that absorb the experience you deliver

YOU OWN THE CUSTOMER EXPERIENCE

A great way to view Customer Experience and Customer Journey is: the customer owns the Customer Journey, you own the Customer Experience.

THE CUSTOMER OWNS THE CUSTOMER JOURNEY, YOU OWN THE CUSTOMER EXPERIENCE.

The customer has certain expectations of life and providers in general, and of you and your business, when they choose to interact with you. And in everything you do, every day in your business – all your choices, your strategies, priorities and actions, come together to either meet, exceed or fall short of your customer's expectations. Many businesses struggle with this. How do they ensure their customers' expectations are met, let alone exceeded?

To gain clarity and drive for your improvements, answer this question. How do you want your customer to feel? We call it intentional emotion.

Many businesses will say 'satisfied' or 'happy' – but how passive and unenergetic are those words? Talk about middle of the road or mediocre. Yawn!

How about excited or inspired or connected or amazed or in love with us or grounded or deeply touched – there are so many different ways to say happy and the more specific and descriptive you can be about your intentional emotion, the more clarity you'll have around what you and your team have to do to achieve that emotion in your customer. Most businesses want their customers to be 'happy' but take it up a notch or three and you'll have yourself a real competitor advantage.

TO GAIN CLARITY AND DRIVE FOR YOUR IMPROVEMENTS, ANSWER THIS QUESTION. HOW DO YOU WANT YOUR CUSTOMER TO FEEL? WE CALL IT INTENTIONAL EMOTION.

209 | Customer Experience: step into your customer's shoes and get the full picture

IDENTIFYING THE CRITICAL MOMENTS FOR YOUR CUSTOMER

Often times, we can be so busy focusing on delivering our product or service – the processes, the operations, the people, the costs and the like – we forget to think about what's going on for the customer.

As shared earlier, identifying the critical moments for your customer can be the key to success for your business. By finding and focusing on (p161) those moments that matter most to them, you'll find ways to connect with them and solve their problems, that others will have missed.

POOL OF LOVE AND FORGIVENESS

We love this concept which we mentioned briefly earlier. The pool of love (p170) and forgiveness is something you have in any relationship – personal or professional.

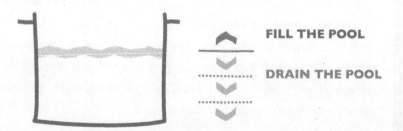

FILL THE POOL

DRAIN THE POOL

Figure 26: The pool of love and forgiveness

CUSTOMER SATISFACTION: MEASURES A MOMENT IN TIME – CHANGES IN AN INSTANT

Figure 27: The satisfaction equation

One of the most common measures we see in organisations today is 'customer satisfaction'. While it has its place, it can miss the mark. As a lagging indicator, it tells you what has happened in the past, not what might happen in the future. It also only measures a moment in time, meaning it can change in an instant.

Imagine this situation. We're your boss and we've decided that you've done a great job this year and deserve a bonus. How would a 50% cash bonus of your total salary package be? On a scale of 1-10, where 10 is very satisfied, how satisfied are you with your bonus? You're pretty happy, huh? Likely a 9 or a 10?

Now, recall a colleague you've worked with at some point in your career that you don't particularly like. You've just heard that they got a 75% cash bonus. **Now** how satisfied are you with your bonus?

What changed? Nothing really. Except the moment in time. With new information or influences, satisfaction can change. We're not saying to stop using it as a measure as it is useful, but think about what you are measuring and where you are measuring it in your experience delivery to get the most out of it.

Let's use your customer as an example. Each interaction they have with your business either fills the pool or drains the pool. Good stuff – fill. Bad stuff – drain.

Some ways this might apply for customers:

- go onto your website and can't find your phone number – drain
- call your business and are greeted with a warm, welcoming voice – fill
- say you'll call back but don't – drain (often BIG, fatal drain!)
- deliver your offering ahead of expected delivery date – fill.

You get our drift. Do good things, fill the pool. Do not-so-good things – drain it.

ENGINEERING DELIGHT: THE EXPECTATION MATRIX

Customer service experts have been telling us for years that we should surprise and delight our customers. But very few of us know what that means or how to do it.

By using the concepts in this chapter, you'll not only surprise and delight your customers, your reviews will improve, your staff will be happier, you'll be more profitable and you'll have a deeper connection with your customers.

Here's a great way to look at surprise and delight and a great way to present it to your team.

Think about energy within a relationship – the ups and downs.

When you do something that I expect, I have a neutral emotion – I expected it, so you should deliver it.

When you don't do something I expect, I have a negative emotion – you've let me down.

When you do something I don't expect – I have a positive emotion or reaction. You've possibly wowed me or at least surprised me by going above and beyond.

When you don't do something I don't expect – I have a neutral emotion because I didn't expect you to do it so it doesn't really matter to me.

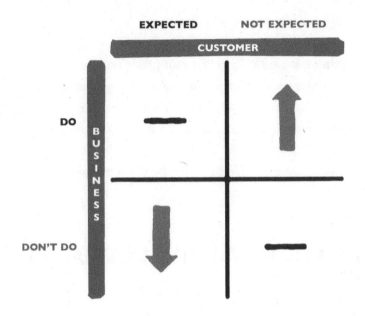

Figure 28: The expectation matrix

Get your leaders and your team members to ask themselves, in which quadrant do I normally operate in? Where is my mindset, how do I think about serving the customer? If they're operating in the 'do what I expect' quadrant, you'll find that's why you're not achieving those 'wow' moments, that surprise and delight your customers.

If you're operating in the 'don't do something I expect', this means you'll be falling short of your customer expectations. Time to move out of there, find out what's important to your customer and start doing that. Then work on moving into the 'do something I don't expect' quadrant by understanding your customers better and surprising them with things that are important to them, but they don't necessarily expect that you'll do. It's a powerful tool and one you can get your team to use to help inform their priority actions.

WHAT'S YOUR 'WHOOOSH'?

If you've ever bought an iPhone, you might notice that everything is intentional, even down to the 'whooosh' sound the box makes when you 'unveil' your new toy. It is something special, something unique, something mystical – that adds to the overall perceived value of the offering.

The product itself is just electronic components and clever design, probably only worth a fraction of what you pay. It is the integration of the product and the service elements of the overall experience – that's what you are buying. When it comes to the service elements, think about the in-store experience – the process, the number of staff available to help, the learning modules to show you how to use the product to its full potential. It's more than just the product. And that is a big part of why organisations like Apple 'get it' – not for the sake of it, but because it makes them more money in the long run.

Which begs the question – what is the whooosh for your organisation?

WE FORGET TO LOOK AROUND

There's a concept in Japanese culture called oyakudachi, which translates to 'walking in the other's shoes' or 'putting yourself in the other's shoes'. This concept was our inspiration in the development of this capability of Customer Experience.

In business, it's common to get so busy looking inwards, caught up in operations and sales figures and internal culture and dramas and meetings and internal politics and egos (need we go on?), that we can lose sight of what it's like to be a customer of our business.

We forget. It's completely normal. The thing is, when we forget as the leaders, our staff forget as the followers. It's a little like when you're riding a motorcycle or a pushbike – look where you're headed and the bike will follow. Look down at the potholes and the cracks in the road (in business, the sales figures or the issues), and that's where your team will look. It's also the most dangerous approach, as not only do you lose sight of where you're going, you tend to ride smack bang into that pothole when you focus on it.

Some of your senior team will be great at looking around – seeing the whole picture and working with other functions to achieve the organisation's overall goals. Others will be inwardly focused, working as a silo on their own priorities and goals.

In our experience, even the latter can be turned around, once they realise the value of taking a wider view and the opportunities it can afford them.

But when you stop and look around, at your surroundings, your team, your internal culture, your deliverables, your reputation, your customer experience – boy oh boy, does the world open up. Once you see it, you can't unsee it.

It is a liberating – albeit somewhat confronting – experience to step into your customer's shoes and see your business as they do. But the beauty of doing it is this – once you see it, you can't unsee it.

You may think it's not worth your time to make an online purchase on your website, or walk through the gardens of your resort, or call your call centre with an issue or use one of your products. But it can be one of the most fruitful, rewarding, game-changing experiences you'll ever have.

ONCE YOU SEE IT, YOU CAN'T UNSEE IT. One of our favourite stories is from our client who ran an establishment on the famous Sunshine Coast of Queensland. Among countless findings in her Experience Review, we noted the unsightly industrial bins that lined the entrance to her venue. They were ugly, dirty and yes, unsightly. When she read the report, she exclaimed, 'I have driven past those bloody bins for years, every single day and I NEVER NOTICED THEM!' She couldn't believe it. Needless to say, the very next day those bins that once 'greeted' her customers, were gone! They had to come back of course, but when they did, they'd been skinned with beautiful imagery of the beach that lay behind the building (a clever way to show the view they get from the venue). No longer an eyesore AND a clever marketing tactic!

You may not be able to change it, but you can change the experience of it.

You may already have a practice of secret shopping in your business. This is one form of seeing your business through your customer's eyes and doesn't have to be overly formal, tedious or time consuming. Some businesses put team members in different departments temporarily to widen their experience. There are many great ways to help your team understand the workings of the business and how they impact the delivery to the customer, as well as seeing the experience from the customer's perspective.

IF YOUR EXPERIENCE IS LACKING, CUSTOMERS WILL WALK - OR TALK - OR BOTH

What amazes us in our work is this: businesses and organisations work SO hard to get new customers. Marketing, social media, advertising, PR, incentives, promotions, price cuts, referral campaigns, returning customer campaigns, e-newsletters, billboards, television, radio… The list goes on…

But what about keeping them?

We feed them into the sausage machine of acquisition, then move on to the next mark, all the while checking our profit and loss, sales figures and revenue targets.

If your experience is lacking, it doesn't matter how good your marketing is – your customers will walk. Not fulfilling a marketing promise is one of the biggest no-no's in our eyes. If you make promises to customers to get them to buy you, then please, fulfil those promises. And not just once, but over and over.

> **YOU MAY NOT BE ABLE TO CHANGE IT, BUT YOU CAN CHANGE THE EXPERIENCE OF IT.**

It's the old Homer Simpson adage – 'they get you hooked, then they jack up the price!'

When you don't fulfil promises and your customer experience falls short of the customer's expectations, not only will they walk, but they'll talk too. They'll tell everyone they know, and a few thousand of their closest friends on social media and even more on review sites.

No matter how much great marketing or how many fancy promises you make, your customers will be at the other end, diminishing your brand, putting your reputation into question and dissuading those customers you're trying so hard to win.

p198 Remember the example we shared earlier about the organisation who at one level was winning marketing awards for their amazing campaigns, attracting customers in droves, driving brand awareness and generally being awesome. Great! Except at the same time, that same organisation was experiencing an attrition rate after the first year of – 40%.

How do you think THEIR customer experience measured up to the promise? Not so well.

WHEN THEY TALK: DRIVING AVOIDABLE CONTACT IS A HIDDEN COST

Many of us worry about the impact of a customer 'talking' in online reviews and social media. A very real fear, of course. Reviews on social media are like word of mouth on crack, and good or bad, many thousands – even millions – of people can be exposed to it.

Customer complaints, particularly in a public domain, can be damaging to your reputation and worse still, they tend to be around forever.

According to Qualtrics, negative online reviews can have a devastating effect on your brand (not the odd one here and there, mind, don't panic – everyone can spot a hater from a mile away). Apparently, 3.3 is the minimum star rating of a business consumers would engage with, 94% say an online review has convinced them to avoid a business, and four out of five consumers have changed their minds about a recommended purchase after reading negative online reviews. In fact, businesses risk losing as many as 22% of customers when just one negative article is found by users considering buying their product, with three negative articles increasing that risk to 59.2%.*

---

* www.qualtrics.com/blog/online-review-stats/

What we often forget is the hidden cost of customer complaints. Far from the outside world, we're talking about the internal impact. The cost of customer complaints to our business's bottom line. The blow to efficiencies. Even the impact on our team members, culture, employee experience and the vibe of our organisation.

Often termed 'avoidable contact', it's the draw down that customer complaints have on the organisation. It's the phone calls made to our customer contact centre by unhappy customers. The admin involved in processing written complaints and capturing call content, not to mention the refunds and the replacements. The phone call tennis between team members and customers. The emotional toll on staff.

Avoidable contact is just that – avoidable. Many businesses think customer complaints are just a part of life, the reason there's a Customer Service team.

What they forget is that by improving the Customer Experience in the areas that matter most to the customer, these complaints and contacts will reduce, directly impacting their efficiencies, cost-base and the effectiveness of their efforts.

Don't get us wrong, there's a place for Customer Services and a customer complaints process. But when it becomes the catch-all for mistakes and issues, when it becomes the 'oh well, we'll know it's a problem if they call Customer Service' – that's when you know that you're off track. You're being reactive rather than proactive. And there's no doubt there'll be some great savings to be made on your bottom line by improving the Customer Experience and getting ahead of the issues.

 ## CUSTOMER EXPERIENCE: SEE THEIR REALITY TO DRIVE YOUR IMPROVEMENT

Now we understand the importance of Customer Experience and how it drives – or diminishes – our connection with our customers, let's take a deeper look at our Customer Strategy Framework™ discipline.

The core question

Do you gauge what it's like to be a customer of your organisation?

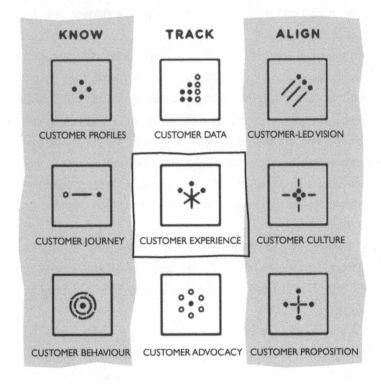

Figure 29: Customer Experience capability within the Framework

Why does it matter?

Understanding the gap between your service delivery and customer expectation highlights the issues and specific drivers behind customer attrition and retention. The experience view brings focus to the areas for improvement that will make the most impact on your customer and on your performance.

There are five key drivers or ingredients you need in this discipline for success. As you read the statement, ponder your answer – what's your gut feel? Read over the best practice and explanation to see what good really looks like. Then, go back and consider again how strong you are in this area. What gaps and opportunities emerge?

#1 You intentionally design the experience you give your customers throughout their journey

Best practice: The functional, rational and emotional aspects of the Customer Journey are used to design intentional Customer Experiences by Customer Profile, clearly articulating how they should feel at every moment.

Ask yourself: do you design your Customer Experience – the way you deliver your product, service or offering – based on a deep understanding of your customer's needs, wants and expectations?

Do you put your customer first or do you base all your operational decisions on what you need as a business, what's easier, cheaper or less painful for you? Do you sacrifice your own comfort for that of your customer or the other way around?

Think of a time when you started a relationship with a business, be it for work or play. You've been through the sales process, usually with a salesperson, but then what? Have you been efficiently handed over to the person in charge of the next stage of your journey, or have you been left to figure it out by yourself? So many businesses make the mistake of nailing the sale, then leaving it to the customer to figure out the rest. The best customer experience examples involve the business taking care of the customer, guiding them through the steps and stages of their experience and fulfilling their needs along the way.

In your organisation, it might feel that this is just too big a task. So start small. It could be the smallest, most seemingly insignificant element that you think won't make a difference, that might. By understanding your customer better and what's important to them, these decisions and minor tweaks will be a walk in the park.

A Tourism industry client was struggling with attracting new customers, even though the ones they had loved their property. By delving into who their customers were and identifying their needs, we helped them identify an opportunity in one of the smallest elements of their Customer Experience – their phone number.

Their customer was an older demographic who wasn't super confident online. They liked to speak to someone, to ask questions and confirm details. By looking deeper at our client's Customer Experience, we found that locating their phone number on their website was difficult. In fact, it was practically hidden.

Considering their customers aren't great online, hiding a crucial detail like their phone number was business suicide. The answer – easy. We put their phone number on the top righthand corner of their home page. And the calls came in.

Mapping out even a simple outline of your Customer Experience can help you identify the big and small things you can do to improve it. Intentionally designing the elements at each step – even better.

#2 You regularly 'stand in your customer's shoes' to review yours and your competitor's offerings

Best practice: Staff are encouraged to observe, experience and process the customer perspective with regular feedback to decision-makers. Secret shopper exercises are undertaken with competitor businesses to benchmark performance and identify improvement opportunities.

Secret shopping is not a new concept. But stepping into your customer's shoes every single day, in everything you do, is a powerful and underestimated business tool.

Forget paying secret shopper companies the big bucks to sneak around your business – get your team to do it for you. You'll soon find the team members that have bought into being customer-led, and those that haven't.

Your staff are often the closest to your customers, most definitely closer than you and your senior leaders are on a daily basis. By getting them to own the customer view and giving them the permission to tell you the good, the bad and the ugly about the experience, you'll uncover countless improvements.

#3 You monitor customer satisfaction at key moments in your experience delivery

Best practice: Regular customer satisfaction surveys are deployed at key service moments with results shared at all levels to inform ongoing continuous improvement.

Ah, customer satisfaction surveys. In the next chapter, we'll talk more (p229) about customer satisfaction versus customer advocacy but for now, let's talk about the former.

Checking in on your customers and their experience of your organisation offering is crucial to improvement. Issues can't sneak up on you if you consistently check in with your customer to identify the things you're doing well, and the things you're not.

You may already be doing some form of satisfaction or customer surveys in your business, which is great. But are you sharing them? Are you figuring out the issues and making tracks to address those issues? Many businesses get the data, but not many take action on it.

Customer champions, action groups, customer leads – having people in charge of taking the insight and actioning it is next level, and sees those businesses who adopt these practices charge ahead of their competitors.

#4 You identify and track the key drivers of positive experience for your customers

Best practice: Customer research reveals the key drivers that impact positively and negatively on the overall Customer Experience, directing whole-of-organisation focus on the most valuable improvement efforts.

This is a goodie, mostly because as business leaders, we don't often do it. In fact, we're often so busy looking at the negative, we forget to look at the positive.

Over recent years, the focus on customer reviews has skyrocketed. And rightfully so. No longer do unhappy customers tell 12 people (remember the old rule, a happy customer tells 4 people, an unhappy one tells 12). They tell, hundreds or thousands or even millions, depending on their audience following and where they post.

It's important to drive improvements that address these negative issues, fix the problems and produce a better and more positive Customer Experience. Reviews and feedback are useless if you don't use them.

But in the obsessive focus on negative reviews and feedback of recent years, we've lost the magic of the positive. There's much to be learnt from positive reviews and feedback.

By identifying the key drivers of positive experience for our customers, we can learn what we need to **do more of**. Because let's face it, we're all doing some good stuff. Our staff can be trying their best, yet if we keep focusing on the bad stuff, it can feel pretty demoralising and demotivating. Tip: the use of testimonials is a powerful tool. 'Our customers love…' is a powerful, engaging statement that not only tells potential customers that you HAVE customers, but also showcases the best parts of your offering.

Focus on the positive as well as the negative, and learn what you need to do more of, not just what you need to stop.

#5 You have a clear and effective process for handling customer complaints and service recovery

Best practice: A simple, effective complaint handling process is clearly communicated to the customer and delivered as promised by the organisation. Staff are empowered to take action within agreed parameters.

We're not talking long-winded, difficult, hard for the customer, convoluted, jump-through-hoops, lose-the-will-to-complain type processes. We mean simple. Effective.

If your customer wants to complain, they will. They'll find a way. Whether it's through your simple and effective complaints process or via Google reviews, Tripadvisor or social media, they'll find a way.

Setting up a simple process, then letting your customers know that if they have a problem you WANT them to complain directly to you, is groundbreaking for customer relationships.

No one likes bad feedback. Give us bad feedback and we feel like we've been kicked in the guts. Or somewhere slightly lower than the guts, in the nether region. We take negative feedback (which we can get once in a while, we won't lie, usually from people who aren't our ideal customers) badly.

But once we've come through the hurt, rocked back and forth and perhaps had a glass of wine or two, we see it for what it is – gold dust. Opportunity. Permission. Permission from our customer to do better. To serve them better. To make amends.

By giving them permission to tell you what they really think – in the moment preferably, not afterwards – you give yourself the opportunity to recover the situation and save the relationship. In fact, some of the best customer relationships have come from a bad situation or experience. Or in some cases, simply accept you can't please everyone and let those customers go.

We recently met a tour operator who received a two-star review from a customer. Instead of getting all hot under the collar about it, he checked the tour the customer had booked, realised that it was completely the wrong tour for them, contacted them, gave them a discount on a better-suited tour and bam – two-star review gone, replaced by a five-star review. Not only that, he then went and revised the way he presented his tours online and changed the descriptions, images and the 'perfect for...' message, to ensure customers could find the right tour for them, avoiding the same issue happening again for another customer. Magic!

RECOVERING THE EXPERIENCE WHEN IT GOES BAD

We once stayed at a resort on the Gold Coast, famous for its waterpark and family facilities. Sold by the prospect of an affordable family break close to home, we booked. Thanks to the images on the website, we were aware this was not a five-star stay, but the rooms looked comfortable enough and considering we'd be by the pool most of the day, it didn't bother us.

What did bother us was that from around 9pm, after we'd settled the kids in bed and were sitting on our balcony enjoying a glass of red (with a 'gorgeous' view of the carpark), the wafting smell of cigarette smoke blew over us from above. Thinking it would only be for a short time, we stayed on the balcony until it got too much and we decided to turn in for the night. That's when the real fun began. Cue loud voices from the same balcony above. Then the slamming of the sliding door every five minutes, accompanied by loud voices, until well past midnight. Wasn't this a family resort? Apparently not, according to our neighbours who partied well into the night.

Things got worse the next morning, when we found that someone had tried to wrench our personalised plates off our car, bending the plates and damaging the bumper bar. Parked in the nearby open carpark, we had been assured by a hotel staff member that it was safe.

Far from the safe, relaxing family holiday we'd envisaged, we complained. Tired, frustrated and let down, this was not what we pictured our family trip to be. Expecting to be moved to another room, we were shocked that the manager upgraded us to their sister property next door, a five-star apartment building that shared access to the kids' facilities of the resort, but also had an adult-only pool and facilities. We were also given free access to the underground carpark to protect our car for the remaining nights of our stay.

How's that for service recovery? Not only did the manager take our complaints very seriously (they spoke with the neighbouring guests who were told to leave if they had another night like the previous one), he took the opportunity to completely redefine the way we saw the hotel. He probably realised that although our spend was at the three-star resort at the time, in reality our expectations were probably more of the five-star apartment building next door. So where would we stay next time? Clever, right.

The key here is to give your staff permission to recover the relationship in the moment. If you're in hotels, it might be a room upgrade or a free drink at the bar, in a restaurant it might be a free dessert – better still, give them a suite of options and let them choose. Giving customers sorry gifts that don't matter to them might even make the situation worse. But empower your staff to own, care for and recover the customer relationship and watch them shine.

SELF-ASSESSMENT: HOW DO YOU STACK UP?

Now that you're familiar with the five key ingredients for success and what best practice looks like, it's time to do a bit of self-assessment and ask yourself, how do we stack up?

To get an initial benchmark, check out the statements below and circle the one that best matches your current situation. Mark yourself on the harder side, there's no gold stars here, just learnings and opportunities.

 We put ourselves in our customer's shoes to see our organisation through their eyes

CUSTOMER EXPERIENCE

| Our customers fit around the way we operate, not the other way around | We are mainly process-based, with little consideration for the customer | We try to balance our process + efficiencies with what's important to the customer | We allocate time to observe our customers + our people to see how they interact on a regular basis | We regularly + actively engage with customers to empathise with + identify their needs, wants + challenges |

This quick assessment is a simplified version of our full-blown Customer-led Accelerator Program. But, straight away, this gives you an initial idea of how you stack up.

Share it with colleagues and see what they think. It's a great way to open up the conversation on customer. What answers do you think you'd get if you asked your senior leadership team? Are you aligned or are you on completely different planets?

 Refer to the section 'How to use this book' for tips on who to ask in your organisation, how and why.

RED FLAGS AND ROADBLOCKS

Let's look at some of the red flags and potential roadblocks for Customer Experience.

Red flags	Potential roadblocks
■ People within your organisation think that customer service and Customer Experience are the same thing. ■ Customer Experience is seen as the same thing as customer journey and you own both of them; and all customers should have the same Customer Experience. ■ Your Customer Experience is owned by the Customer Services team and the rest of the organisation plays no part in it.	■ Not being intentional with how you design and deliver your Customer Experience at every level of your business and across the Customer Journey. ■ Not being clear on the intentional emotion you want your customers to feel at each stage of their Customer Journey; and not having it shared and understood across the organisation. ■ Measuring the wrong moments to save face instead of using customer feedback and satisfaction to direct focus and drive improvements.

WHEN YOUR ORGANISATION BUILDS THIS CAPABILITY

Imagine if you could remove all the friction for your customer throughout your customer experience. You'd get less customer complaints and have happier customers who are more satisfied. Your staff would enjoy more rewarding interactions with customers, have higher job satisfaction and be more connected to your organisation's goals and objectives. You'd stretch far beyond a focus on tactical customer service to become remarkable, a leader in your industry who's revered for delivering a consistent experience every time. Instead of having to compete on product features or the death spiral of price, your customers would value you for your experience and it would be a competitive advantage in and of itself. As price becomes less important, you'd get direct impact on your profit line enabling you to fuel growth and drive sustainability. How different would your organisation be once you've built up this capability?

With the capability of Customer Experience in place, let's now take this TRACK discipline even further as we go beyond the traditional business concept of customer satisfaction to how your customers truly feel about you and how they can become an extension of your sales force.

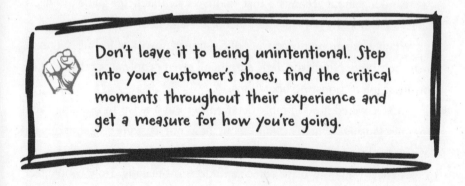

Don't leave it to being unintentional. Step into your customer's shoes, find the critical moments throughout their experience and get a measure for how you're going.

Chapter 23

CUSTOMER ADVOCACY: THE CRYSTAL BALL FOR YOUR BUSINESS

The strategic question we're setting out to answer is:

Do you know how your customers feel about you: are they advocates, apathetic or assassins?

Let's talk about the 'F Word'. It's always great to open a workshop or keynote event saying that you're going to talk about the F word. Of course, we're talking about 'feelings' – that emotive state that helps guide our decisions alongside the rational and functional elements.

When we open up the concept of Customer Advocacy, feelings begin to rear their head. Not particularly surprising given people are at the heart of business interactions and operations.

p184 We've covered it off in more detail earlier but it is worth bringing back to consciousness when we talk about how our customers feel about <u>us</u> as the business, not just how they feel along their customer journey or experience. Emotions drive choice and decision-making. How people feel informs what they say and do. Whether they'll come back. Whether they'll bring others too or actively kneecap you in your daily efforts.

In short, how do your customers feel about your organisation today? We don't mean whether they're satisfied – because satisfied is a state, not an emotion. What emotions are aroused when they think about your organisation? The answer massively impacts on their actions over the short, medium and longer term.

Customers with positive sentiment towards you become an extension of your sales force. Word of mouth has, and always will be, the most powerful marketing and sales tool of all.

WHAT IS CUSTOMER ADVOCACY?

Advocacy is simply a measure of the sentiment that your customer holds towards your organisation. It is how much they are willing to put their own reputation on the line for you. It's a big deal – no one wants to look bad in front of their peers or friends. Advocacy is the sentiment they hold towards your organisation and depending on the level of the sentiment, they'll either advocate, sit on the fence or actively dissuade others from using you.

Customer advocacy is not about satisfaction, though it is often confused with it. Where satisfaction addresses operational or tactical issues at certain moments, advocacy is a strategy tool with a longer term horizon around customer connection and competitive advantage. It gives you an insight into your future performance – we call it the crystal ball for your business.

> **CUSTOMERS WITH POSITIVE SENTIMENT TOWARDS YOU BECOME AN EXTENSION OF YOUR SALES FORCE.**

While they're different, satisfaction is related to advocacy and is more a precursor. I can be satisfied, but I might not necessarily advocate for your organisation. Similarly, if I'm not satisfied, chances are I won't be advocating for your organisation. Where satisfaction only measures a moment in time, (p210) advocacy is about how your customer feels about you. Yep – feels – the emotional connection that they have (or don't have) with your organisation.

It can also apply to how your employees feel about your organisation. This is employee advocacy. In our experience, cracks in performance appear when these two are out of sync. By comparing the two advocacies (customer and employee) you can get a better understanding of what needs to be improved to make your organisation a force to be reckoned with.

THE RISK OF IT TURNING TO CUSTARD

We love being advocates for quality products, services and offerings. But sometimes it can go wrong.

We recently referred a friend who runs a swimwear retailing group to a professional services firm whom we're strong advocates for. In doing so, we put our own reputations on the line. The swimwear group was going through a management buy-out process and needed fresh advice and robust numbers to make it all happen. It seemed like the perfect marriage. Except, that it wasn't. We expected our swimwear friend to have a straightforward, quick, enjoyable experience with this firm. What they got was a long, frustrating, drawn-out process that took way longer and was more painful than it needed to be, or that we'd expected.

The result? Embarrassment on our part. Incredulousness, frustration and disappointment on our friends' part. Will we still be advocates for this company moving forward? The chances are low.

THE THREE TYPES OF CUSTOMERS IN EVERY ORGANISATION

Tracking advocacy starts by understanding that the customers of EVERY organisation – regardless of sector, size, industry – fall into one of only three buckets. Knowing how many customers you have in each bucket helps you to understand where you are today, and most importantly, gives you an insight into your possible future. It's why we call it the crystal ball. Identifying the three customer types – Apathetics, Advocates or Assassins – helps you and your team to focus in on what matters most.

Apathetics – an apathetic probably likes your product or service, but it wasn't a slam dunk. They may mention their experience in the right context, but they are unlikely to personally vouch for you or your organisation. We call these the fence sitters as they have a high propensity to switch to another supplier.

Advocates – an advocate will go out of their way to recommend your product or service to everyone they know, often unprompted (basically you don't have to ask them to!). They are willing to put their personal reputation on the line to recommend you.

Assassins – an assassin will proactively take any opportunity to dissuade people from using your product or service. We call it actively kneecapping you. They will often speak louder than even your biggest fans.

One of the methods to gather this insight was created and popularised in the early 2000s by Fred Reicheld of Bain & Company,* a leading global strategy consultancy. Over the last two decades, his Net Promoter Score (NPS) methodology has been widely adopted across the globe in an attempt to get a handle on quantifying the number of customers in each bucket (they call them, promoters, passives and detractors) and gaining an understanding of why customers are in each bucket.

WHY DOES IT MATTER WHAT SHAPE YOU ARE IN?

Your performance and future can look very different depending on how many of each of these types of customers you have at any given time. Depending on where you're at, it drastically changes what you need to do as an organisation.

For example, if you have a lot of assassins, how strong do you think your business is? How does your future look? Not pretty, is it? Conversely, if you have lots of customers in the advocate bucket, your future's looking pretty bright, right? Correct. In fact, you have yourselves an unpaid sales force who effectively do your marketing and sales for you – winning!

But what about if you have a whole bunch of apathetics? How does your future look? You're probably sitting there saying, well, that's still pretty

---

* www.netpromotersystem.com/about/

good, right? They're fairly happy with us, they're still buying stuff from us, we're fine. Our future looks bright!

So, which is the most dangerous mix of customers, do you think? You're likely thinking, 'Well, assassins of course, duh!' But, that's not correct.

We see apathetics as the most dangerous customer of all. At least with assassins, you know why they dislike you and you can use that information to improve your business and customer experience. With advocates, they're loving you all over the place, openly telling you and everyone else what they love about you – so you can just keep doing more of that stuff.

But apathetics – we call them the silent assassins. These fence sitters will ditch you at a moment's notice if a supplier up the road is selling the same product for five bucks less or if a hotel in town offers a similar room for $10 cheaper a night (even though it's not quite as nice).

But they're so indifferent to you that they don't really tell you why – so you're not learning from them what you could fix or what you could do to create a greater customer connection… they can't even be bothered telling you.

So instead of having a nice heavy bucket of apathetic customers that are still buying from you, you have a house of cards – an unstable business that is affected by the decisions made by indifferent customers – customers who don't really care for you, have no real connection with you and will ditch you at the drop of a hat.

MORE THAN A 'SCORE'

For those of you who are already using the NPS method in your organisation, one of the pitfalls we see is getting stuck on the 'score'. The Net Promoter Score is the percentage of promoters, minus the percentage of detractors (hence, the net promoter). We see in some organisations that chase the score, they can become fixated on it, or become complacent and miss the point of it.

One of the biggest drawbacks of only looking at the score is that you miss the whole impact of where your customers sit. There's a need to go beyond the NPS score and look at the shape you're in. In our work in this area over the last two decades, we have identified a range of eight different advocacy shapes with eight remedial strategies to move forward, as outlined in the following diagrams.

Take a look at the diagrams – which one is your advocacy shape? What's fascinating is that you may have the same overall score as another business, but your advocacy shape will be completely different depending on where your advocates, apathetics and assassins sit. Your advocacy shape informs the strategies you should employ to improve your scores. So, what shape are you in?

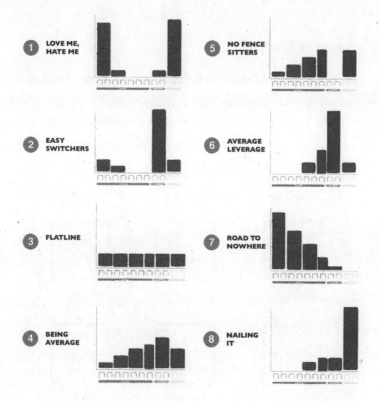

Figure 30: The eight advocacy shapes – each requires a different strategy

CUSTOMER ADVOCACY: SEE INTO YOUR FUTURE WITH GREATER FORESIGHT

Now that we've shared our perspective on Customer Advocacy and where it fits within the overall navigation towards being a customer-led organisation, let's specifically look at the elements you need to have in place to start making this capability pay dividends.

The core question

Do you know how your customers feel about you: are they advocates, apathetic or assassins? Not just gut feel or anecdotally. Do you actually measure it, understand it and embrace it?

Why does it matter?

As we've established, advocacy is different to satisfaction. Keeping track of customer intent and their propensity to refer gives an insight into your future performance. It tells you how your customers feel about you and highlights how active or inactive they are at being an extension of your sales force.

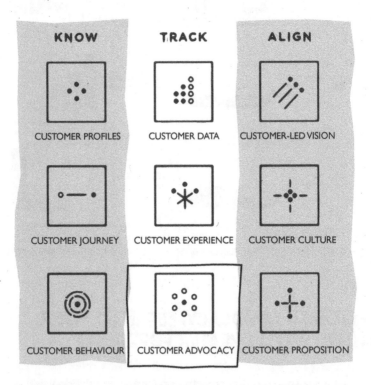

Figure 31: Customer Advocacy capability within the Framework

THE FIVE KEY DRIVERS/INGREDIENTS FOR SUCCESS

There are five key drivers or ingredients you need in this capability for success. Let's take a look. As you read the statement, ponder your answer – what's your gut feel? Read over the best practice and explanation to see what good really looks like. Then, go back and consider again how strong you are in this area. What gaps and opportunities emerge?

#1 You measure what proportion of customers are advocates, apathetic and assassins

Best practice: Regular advocacy campaigns track business performance and overall customer health, to inform both the strategic direction and the operational improvements required for maximum impact.

This can be a revelation for many courageous leaders. We often don't think of our customers in this way. In fact, it's a great way to engage others in your customer-led transformation. Simplifying the overall complexity of your operating landscape back to the three customer buckets brings a new level of clarity and focus.

There's two important parts to this – 'measure' and 'regularly'. You need to have a robust measurement approach in place <u>and</u>, this needs to be done regularly. Not a once-off.

Also, once you have the data, you need to do something with it. We've seen a lot of instances where organisations are tracking NPS or other measures, only to do nothing with them. Use them to drive change, bringing the customer voice to the decision-making table and you'll be ahead of the game.

MEASURING AT THE WRONG TIME DOESN'T HELP

We met with a potential property management client who took great pride in their NPS scores. When we challenged them on the point in time they were measuring the NPS and the significant skew it was creating in their results, the client was adamant that they didn't want to change. Why? Because they knew that it would fundamentally change their score, which they took great pride in celebrating and promoting at every chance. In fact, measuring their NPS at the 'correct time' would have dropped their score considerably, given the poor experience afforded to their customers at key points in their customer journey. Good for PR – yes. Good for improvement planning and future growth – not so much!

#2 You have a clear strategy in place to improve customer advocacy for your organisation

Best practice: A customer strategy or customer improvement program engages the organisation cross-functionally with a common goal of driving positive customer sentiment, loyalty and connection.

Advocacy is a HUGE asset for any organisation. And, like any asset in business, you need it to work for you – not just sit there dormant. You wouldn't buy some fancy physical machine or resource and just let it sit there. You need to leverage it to help you grow.

This is where intentionally designing a Customer Advocacy Strategy is paramount. Not just taking the advocacy for granted or a 'yay – aren't we loved' and moving on. How can you leverage this asset that you've built to help you achieve your objectives?

In our experience, this is one of the quickest wins. The asset is there, often untapped. Imagine that if 30% of your customers went and raved to three other people about your organisation – what would that do to your overall results?

#3 You proactively analyse customer feedback and use it to drive improvement

Best practice: Customer issues identified through feedback are actively and systematically addressed, favouring sustainable, impactful improvements over quick-fix solutions.

No one likes a bad report card. It is the brave leader that asks the question that they might not want to hear the answer to. You've got the data and insights, this is now taking it further and getting a cross-functional team to gather improvement ideas and put them into action. Your customers love it too. Not only because things improve, they can see that you heard them, are taking action on their behalf and that they matter.

In the late 2000s we were engaged in helping a UK government agency to become customer-led. One of the first things we noticed was that, while there were lots of people available, they never came together to really analyse customer insight in a systematic way.

Simply by formalising a quarterly review that included key people from inside and outside the organisation, sharing the insights and then creating and monitoring actions, a new level of momentum was achieved. Later on, both customer and stakeholder insight were brought together into the same process, which became the 'Insight to Action' Framework that helped transform the organisation.

#4 You scan public opinion to gauge customer sentiment towards your organisation

Best practice: Customer 'watering holes' (including forums, review sites and social media) are systematically reviewed and analysed to identify the roadblocks to advocacy and prioritise what matters most to customers.

Formal customer research is great, but checking out what customers are saying about you on more informal channels can be just as valuable. Again, this doesn't have to be some highly detailed 'Media Monitor' style campaign (though these are good too!). It means dropping into the main places where customers gather together. This will change massively depending on what your organisation does and also for specific customer profiles. But, it is worthwhile thinking it through to see what the corridor talk is, be it on review sites, social media groups or even in the media.

A word of warning. Remember this is unstructured and uncontrolled opinion. It's not fact and gives you more of an anecdotal perspective. And, like toilet doors and walls, sometimes it's not pretty – the sentiment or the colourful language! But, it can also give you a handle on the positive and negative emotions that are bubbling beneath the surface.

#5 You actively encourage customers to share their experiences of your organisation with others

Best practice: Through an intentional advocacy strategy, customer advocates are identified and engaged to talk about their experiences and amplify their positive sentiment to their peers to help win new customers.

This one sounds obvious, yet many organisations are afraid to do it. In management literature they refer to the 'Knowing-Doing Gap', where firms gather experience and insights but fail to implement them. It's a bit like weight loss and the multi-billion-dollar fitness industry that feeds on it. We know we need to eat healthily, exercise, drink less alcohol… but it's the doing that lets us down!

Similarly, we know that word of mouth is great and that having customer advocates will grow our business or achieve our goals, but it just sits there. When you turn the dial on authentic Customer Advocacy, great things follow.*

You may find your customers are more than happy to shout your praise. In Tourism, where there are lots of small businesses, we encourage them to get over the fear and ASK their customers to come back, to tell others, to write reviews. By telling them, 'Your kind words help our business grow,' you're giving your customers the chance to have a role in your success. How good is that for your customer connection (AND your business growth!)?

---

* Authentic is not some influencer saying you're great. It's your customers putting themselves on the line for you.

We saw this recently in the car tyre sector. One of the disruptors of the supply and fit tyre industry proactively asked customers to provide video reviews, which is great. Except it was in return for a discount or cash back on their purchase, which authenticity wise, was not so great. This is not true advocacy. It's cash for comment. And customers see straight through it. Even if they don't see it straight away, they work it out when they go through the purchase process and get asked to do it. It can leave them feeling duped, cynical and less trusting. Ever had someone ask you to give them a five-star Google review, regardless of how good their service was? Same thing!

The question for you, the brave leader, is this – are you really maximising your asset? Is it laying dormant? Or worse, are you doing a dodgy that potential customers see straight through?

Truly engaged customer advocates will be willing to stand tall for you. In fact, they're probably waiting for you to ask them.

SELF-ASSESSMENT: HOW DO YOU STACK UP?

Now that you're familiar with the five key ingredients for success and what best practice looks like, it's time to do a bit of self-assessment and ask yourself, how do we stack up?

To get an initial benchmark, check out the statements below and circle the one that best matches your current situation. Mark yourself on the harder side, there's no gold stars here, just learnings and opportunities.

What is customer advocacy? Isn't that just customer satisfaction?	We've heard of customer advocacy but wouldn't have a clue where to start with it	We don't formally track customer advocacy though we have some customer feedback	We regularly track customer advocacy + use the results to help guide the organisation	Yes, customer advocacy is one of our KPIs + core to our planning. It drives our organisation

This quick assessment is a simplified version of our full-blown Customer-led Accelerator Program. But, straight away, this gives you an initial idea of how you stack up.

Share it with colleagues and see what they think. It's a great way to open up the conversation on customer. What answers do you think you'd get if you asked your senior leadership team? Are you aligned or are you on completely different planets?

 Refer to the section 'How to use this book' for tips on who to ask in your organisation, how and why.

RED FLAGS AND ROADBLOCKS

Let's look at some of the red flags and potential roadblocks for Customer Advocacy.

Red flags	Potential roadblocks
■ You don't have a handle on how much referral business your organisation gets and where it comes from. ■ Your organisation makes kneejerk reactions to customer feedback and reviews without taking a broader, more considered approach. ■ Your existing customer metrics are all looking positive but you're still experiencing efficiency and effectiveness issues.	■ When gathering customer sentiment, you make sure it's at the right moment to give you a good score, rather than checking that its driving improvement which feeds into a coherent advocacy strategy. ■ Team members who are used to gaming the system by asking customers to give them high scores that skew results and make your insights less valuable. ■ Traditional thinking that you need to survey customers with expensive, complex research methods instead of being able to quantify the core of your referral engine – your customer sentiment.

WHEN YOUR ORGANISATION BUILDS THIS CAPABILITY

Fast forward to see your organisation with a strong Customer Advocacy capability. Your three customer buckets are central to your organisation's dashboard. You have a clear strategy in place to leverage the advocacy asset that you've built up to drive more sales or positive interactions with your organisation. These advocates have become an extension of your sales force, reducing your need for push or tell marketing where you now invest in supporting and building your advocacy community. The connection with customer is deeper than ever before with your organisation owning a healthy share of wallet – they're coming back more often, spending more and telling everyone they know about you. How different would your business be today?

This rounds out the three capabilities that help you truly TRACK your organisation's performance from the customer's view – leveraging your data, intentionally designing your experience and building strong advocates for your future. We've shared a view of what your future organisation could look like with these three things in place.

So at this point, we've now shared two of the three disciplines and the three capabilities required for each. By now, you should be seeing ideas emerging, quick wins and also having some a-ha or (oh-sh!t) moments.

But these two disciplines can't stand alone. Let's get into the final area – ALIGN. It's great to KNOW your customers and TRACK your performance from their perspective, but your organisation needs to be aligned from boardroom to back office and everywhere in between to truly succeed.

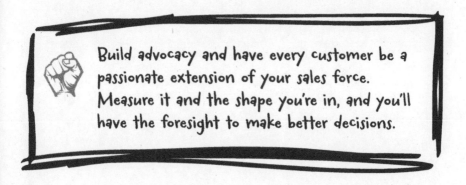

Build advocacy and have every customer be a passionate extension of your sales force. Measure it and the shape you're in, and you'll have the foresight to make better decisions.

Section 6

ALIGN

Welcome to the third discipline of the Customer Strategy Framework™: ALIGN.

What sets the world leaders in the Customer-led Revolution apart, beyond knowing their customer and tracking their performance from the customer view, is ensuring that their organisation is aligned around the customer – at all levels. They have a solid vision of where they're going that includes the customer, they've built a strong customer ethic and culture with a clear focus on who they are, what they offer to customers and where they sit in the wider landscape.

So, here's the big strategic question to ponder through this section: Do you align your organisation to the customer?

Chapter 24

SO, YOU THINK YOU'RE ALIGNED AROUND YOUR CUSTOMER, BUT WHERE'S THE PROOF?

Aligning your organisation around your customer is where it all comes together. You can have the best knowledge of who your customers are and what their needs are, and what makes them tick. You can have the best understanding of how they perceive your organisation and how you're performing in their eyes. But, unless you rally the team around the customer and put all of this into action, you'll fail to get traction.

WHAT DOES BEING ALIGNED REALLY MEAN?

Being aligned is a pretty simple concept and we find that it's not the under-standing of the concept that trips people up. It's in the actual doing. How many times have you thought you were on the same page with someone in your life – either professionally or personally – only to find that when push comes to shove, you're actually not?

Many business leaders we meet think they and their team are pretty aligned which is great! It's when we dig into the Customer Strategy Frame-work™ and ask them some pretty telling questions that they realise they might not be as aligned as they thought – not only internally with their team, but externally with their customer.

But awareness is a good thing. Because by identifying the gaps and realising where there is misalignment, you can fix the issues that are ultimately holding you back.

Awareness means ensuring everyone is rowing in the same direction, to the same place.

We used this analogy, along with the concept of true north, to help leaders visualise the problem and the need for alignment.

Alignment is everyone – from boardroom to back office – knowing where they're heading as an organisation, what role they play in getting the organisation there and how important the customer is in the process.

In our analogy, we talk about everyone rowing in the same direction, to the same place.

Let's imagine there's an island – it's our strategic vision and goals. Let's call it Vision Island. The organisation as a whole is rowing towards that future state – that blissful place where we achieve our goals and objectives, smash the competition and become all we've ever dreamed of being as an organisation.

> **AWARENESS MEANS ENSURING EVERYONE IS ROWING IN THE SAME DIRECTION, TO THE SAME PLACE.**

Now, not everyone can fit in the one boat, unless you're a small business. And it wouldn't make sense to try to fit everyone in the same boat because, well, some departments need slightly different tools to propel their boat. Some need more or less people. Some travel a little faster than others. It's natural in business and something that makes business interesting – and challenging.

So, depending on the size of our business, we might have lots of boats. Or just a few. There might be the C-suite boat. The senior management boat. The Marketing boat, the Sales, Finance, IT and HR boats. Each boat houses the department or function lead and their team, each rowing and functioning their part of the business on their way to Vision Island.

Now the function leaders have to get out of their boats regularly to join the senior management or the C-suite boats, trusting their team to keep their function's boat moving at the right pace, in the right direction while they're away.

Some function leaders are amazing at keeping their boat on track and their team rowing at a pace that benefits the business and matches the overall objectives. Some aren't so much, encouraging their team to stray a little off course for the purpose of their own achievement or motivation. Some are great at leading their boat until they have to get out, then their team are off merrily 'sailing' (yes, sailing, not rowing!) in their own direction (often to the closest tropical island complete with pool bar and spa). The function lead has to get them back on track each time, spending valuable time and effort recorrecting their course.

Some teams row side by side, encouraging and motivating each other to keep going. They share sustenance and input to help drive each other forward. Some prefer to work alone, a short (or long) distance from the rest of the boats.

So where are they going?

Now, if the senior leaders have looked to the horizon, raised an arm, pointed a finger and said, 'We go that way!', without so much as a navigational guide or coordinates to pinpoint the destination – that's when things can start to go wrong.

Teams might voraciously and passionately row their boats in the direction given. Even with the right team in place, who are connected with the purpose and vision of the business – what they believe is their true north – they will still go off course without the specifics.

We find this all the time in the organisations we work with – the senior leaders have given a rough direction of where they want to go, then spend their time yelling at (sometimes motivating, sometimes berating) their teams to forge forward. The team passionately and energetically obey, driven to help the business achieve. But they soon tire. They might even lose hope, feeling like they're never going to make it. The goalposts keep changing. The horizon seems so far away. Some stop rowing (some never rowed in the first place). Some try but tire quickly. Most become disillusioned. Some jump out of the boat altogether. Others just lay back and enjoy the ride.

Why? Because they don't know where they're really going. They have a sense, sure. But they don't have a clear and manageable and achievable goal that says, 'we're going this way' and 'we'll know when we get there because this, this and this will happen' and 'success looks like this'. For some, it can seem relentless, especially if the senior leaders keep changing their minds, the direction and the pace.

When the senior leaders and the team are aligned on where they're going, what they're aiming for and how they're going to do it (their values), it's a smoother sail towards their shared destination.

EVERYTHING SHOULD STACK ON TOP OF EACH OTHER

Let's look at it another way. Think about your business as a set of building blocks. Each building block is a department or team within your organisation. And you have your foundation blocks, which depending on how you approach your business, could be any of the following:

- your vision and values – the cultural part of your business on which everything is built
- your strategy and plans – the business part of your business on which your actions are based and your priorities set
- your core department of HR (People and Culture) or the other departments that are identified as core to your business (Operations, IT, etc.) – the operational part of your business on which your business functions.

Once you've got your foundation blocks in place, you stack the other departments or blocks on top based on your priorities and strategy.

If you hurriedly stack your blocks on top of each other, more focused on the race against competitors or the inner demands of the business leaders than with the quality of your infrastructure, there's a good chance you'll run into trouble. Blocks haphazardly stacked and ordered, either with total disregard to the integrity of the structure, or otherwise manipulated and influenced by only one part of the business. This is when things go wrong.

At some stage, the blocks will tumble, possibly like this:

- one part of the business (who screams the loudest) demands everything be built on their strategy, plans and priorities
- one leader in the business (again, who probably screams the loudest) refuses to see the views or priorities of the other functions, insisting that theirs is the most important (so demands resources of time, people, attention, budget)
- the wider team are not consulted as to how the blocks should be stacked, in which order and at what pace, leaving them disengaged and disconnected from the business
- senior leaders compete internally about whose blocks are most important, demanding crucial resources for individual agendas and priorities, while not supporting each other in the achievement of the wider business goals and objectives.

You get our drift. Having misaligned building blocks within your business will only create trouble, be it in the long-term or the short.

We're not saying you can't realign your business blocks if you notice that some of the things listed above are happening in your business. But realignment must be done with intent. And to make it truly sustainable for the long-term, we believe it should be done with the customer at the heart.

Being aligned internally is a wonderful thing.

You'll be able to feel almost intuitively whether you're aligned in your business. You'll just know. If you're aligned internally, things will feel right. They'll feel like they're in flow, even if things aren't perfect. Here's some examples – departments will work well together, business leaders will be open and connected with each other, staff will be engaged and excited about their roles, work will be done, deadlines will be met, targets will be achieved or exceeded, customers will be happy.

BEING ALIGNED IS ONE THING – BEING ALIGNED AROUND YOUR CUSTOMER IS ANOTHER.

You'll also know when you're not aligned. The opposite things will be happening – staff will be disengaged (high turnover, lots of sick leave, not achieving their goals), targets will be missed month after month, senior leaders will be disconnected from each other and their staff.

And you, as a senior leader, will feel it all. You'll know because you know what you're looking for. You'll know what good looks and feels like. You'll know what works and doesn't work. And you'll likely be hearing it from your team members and leaders, not to mention your customers. You'll see it in your results.

Being aligned around your customer is a whole new kettle of fish.

It helps if you're already well aligned internally – if you are, then it's just a matter of figuring out what's important to the customer and doing more of that (completely oversimplified, we realise this!).

> **CUSTOMERS CAN BE THE GLUE THAT HOLDS YOUR TEAM TOGETHER AND STICK, IF CLOSELY ALIGNED TO YOUR STRATEGY AND VISION.**

If you're not aligned internally and you're suffering from some or all of the things we listed above, don't despair. Using the customer to help you align your organisation and departments can be the thing you need to get everyone on the same page. Customers can be the glue that holds your team together and stick, if closely aligned to your strategy and vision.

Staff and team members, senior leaders, C-suites – when you put customer and what they need from you in front of them, they're hard pressed to say, 'No, thanks.' We've seen once fragmented teams with disengaged and disillusioned staff come together to create incredible plans and priorities, based around the customer.

WHAT DOES BEING OUT OF ALIGNMENT LOOK LIKE?

Getting out of alignment can happen slowly, over time, decision by decision, or it can happen in one area of the business and spread to the others. It usually comes from the top – a misaligned leadership team spells disaster for a business and inherently breeds cross-organisational misalignment.

The following problems can happen, either in isolation or en masse:

- teams pull against each other, creating inefficiencies and internal rivalry
- teams compete with each other for resources, creating friction
- individual agendas and egos become prevalent
- low staff morale and toxic culture
- people start to do the wrong things at the wrong times, either inadvertently or intentionally
- you start hiring the wrong people and creating an even bigger problem
- high staff turnover, usually with the good people leaving
- high customer turnover due to the inconsistency in customer experience and service delivery.

If any or all of the above are happening in your organisation, chances are, you're misaligned. Not only from your customer but from your purpose (your why), your strategic objectives, your vision and your values. Time to change.

THE NEED TO BUILD YOUR ORGANISATION'S CAPABILITIES (ALIGN)

A common mistake we see business leaders make is thinking that they are aligned in their organisations, or worse still, have no idea whether they are or not. In fact, it's often this lack of awareness that sits at the heart of the issue.

They may know something's not right, but they don't know why. Instead of looking at the way their organisation works together, at the functions, business units, personalities and culture, they blame sales or the market or the customer for their lack of success.

The three capabilities of ALIGN: Customer-led Vision, Customer Culture, Customer Proposition

By building your business capability in these three areas, you'll find yourself making more efficient, effective, powerful, impactful decisions that are more aligned with your customer and what matters to them.

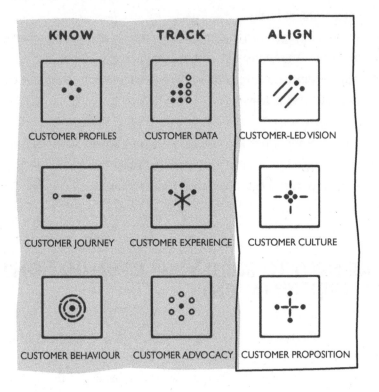

Figure 32: ALIGN and three capabilities

Let's touch on the three ALIGN capabilities before we delve into them in more depth in the coming chapters.

ALIGN Customer Capability	Context	Overview
CUSTOMER-LED VISION	Common purpose + connection	The main question: What are the goals and objectives for your organisation and where does the customer sit in your overall vision? The outcome: Putting the customer at the heart of your organisation requires a business-wide commitment from the top down. Your values, incentives, internal communications and measurements combine to position you as a truly customer-led entity.
CUSTOMER CULTURE	Alignment + consistency	The main question: How well is your organisation aligned with your customers, from boardroom to back office? The outcome: Being truly customer-led is an all of organisation effort. It requires an understanding of how well all functions stack together to create a unified and intentional customer experience through your structures, processes, people and incentives.

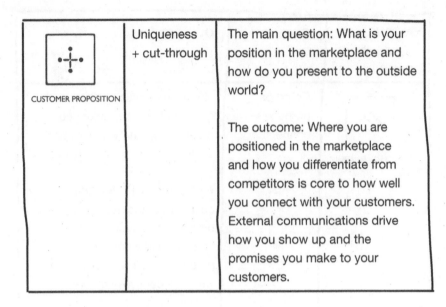

CUSTOMER PROPOSITION	Uniqueness + cut-through	**The main question:** What is your position in the marketplace and how do you present to the outside world? **The outcome:** Where you are positioned in the marketplace and how you differentiate from competitors is core to how well you connect with your customers. External communications drive how you show up and the promises you make to your customers.

These three capabilities provide the alignment foundation to give your people the direction, guidance and the clarity to deliver on your strategy to become a customer-led organisation. Where you want to be, the behaviours you expect from your people and the promises you make to the customer.

We'll cover these in more detail in the coming chapters with lots of stories and examples.

Now we understand the importance of aligning our business to the customer, let's get into the detail of the three capabilities that sit under this discipline.

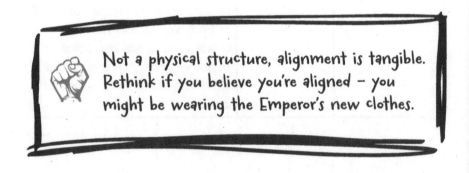

Not a physical structure, alignment is tangible. Rethink if you believe you're aligned — you might be wearing the Emperor's new clothes.

Chapter 25

CUSTOMER-LED VISION: WHAT GETS YOUR TEAM OUT OF BED IN THE MORNING?

The strategic question we're setting out to answer is:

What are the goals and objectives for your organisation and where does the customer fit in your overall vision?

DO YOU HAVE A VISION? AND WHERE'S THE CUSTOMER?

If customer is so important to your organisation or business, then where are they in your vision?

Organisational visions are normally all about you – the organisation – where you want to be in the future (usually 5 or 10 years) in relation to the market or your competitors or even your current position. A good vision will also be purpose-driven, unique to your organisation, inspiring, challenging, motivating and memorable.

But they rarely include the customer.

To truly put the customer at the heart of everything you do, you must put customer in your vision and make it a priority of your senior leadership team. Without formality around the customer and where they sit in your organisation, you are leaving things to chance. Even the best visions can soon be forgotten, even after motivating and exciting teams at their inception and launch.

Visions also have to be compelling enough to get you, your senior leaders and the entire team out of bed in the morning. Not dragging, not moaning, not just-one-more-snooze-ing – jumping, leaping, bouncing, even rising is better than your stock standard wake-up. We love rising – rising to the occasion, to the challenge, to the top...

(p56) Remember the story of the NASA employee, mopping the floor of the NASA building, who told President Kennedy, 'I'm helping to put a man on the moon, sir.' We bet this guy bounces out of bed every day to go to work, with a vision like that!

Now THAT is vision, that is purpose. When your cleaners are engaged with your vision, then you know you're on a winner. Being connected to that vision through the right values, practices and reward system is also (p281) crucial – we'll cover that shortly.

WHAT IS A CUSTOMER-LED VISION?
YOUR PURPOSE, YOUR VALUES/PRINCIPLES

A Customer-led Vision is part of a bigger picture, with vision at the top.

The old school view is to use the customer to achieve an outcome for the organisation. Therefore the customer is a means to an end. We challenge that there is a new and better way of thinking – that the customer IS the outcome. It's seemingly small but it's a radical change in philosophy. In a Customer-led Vision, the customer is the vision, and helping the customer achieve their goals becomes the modus operandi of the entire organisation. As a result, the organisation is by default, successful.

A Customer-led Vision needs the following three components to be truly impactful, long-term and adopted within an organisation. Traditionally, these elements have been treated separately, but the power is in the combination, especially when it comes to customer.

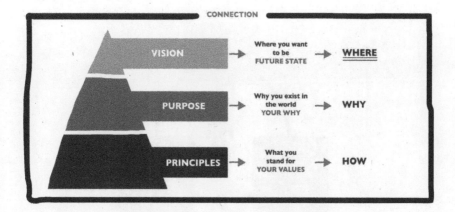

Figure 33: Vision, Purpose and Principles

Let's look at the elements in the above diagram:

Vision is all about *where* you want to be. The future state of your organisation. The island you're rowing towards. What does that island look like, what's happening there? The sharper and clearer you can be about this, the better and the more likely your team will connect with it.

Purpose is your *why*. Why you exist in the world. Why you do what you do. It's why you get out of bed in the morning. More heart-centred, it can be linked to your own personal purpose as well as your customer. The more emotional and clear your purpose can be, the better. In fact, one of the biggest hurdles for a lot of businesses we meet is their purpose – they've fallen out of love with their business or role, they've lost connection with their why – why they joined the organisation, why they started the business. We help them fall back in love with it by connecting with the ultimate reason they're in business – their customer.

Principles are your *how*. They're what you stand for, what your values are. They are crucial to how you and your team deliver your offering to the world. Having a team connected with your why and your principles or values, will give you a much greater chance of success. And the how is where much of the gold (or when misaligned, sh!t) lies.

A Customer-led Vision is simply these three elements combined, with customer at the heart.

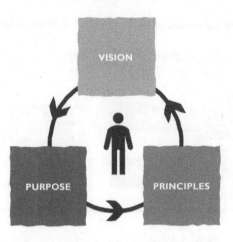

Figure 34: Vision, Purpose and Principles – with the customer at the heart

Let's look at another way to help us solidify our thinking. On the left is the present – where you are today. On the right, your vision – where you want to be in the future. So, how do you get from where you are to where you want to be?

The arrow is your journey. No matter what, whether it's a good fruitful journey or a rocky hellish one, you're still on a journey as an organisation, as a senior leadership team, as a professional and an individual.

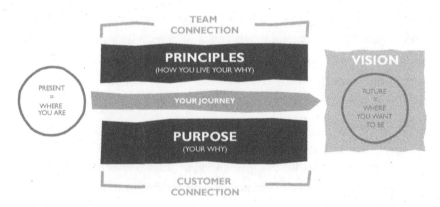

Figure 35: Vision, Purpose and Principles – your team and your customer

Your purpose, below the journey arrow, is your why. It's why you do what you do every day, why you get up in the morning, why you make the decisions you make. If you're on purpose, you'll be making decisions that are focused on your vision, your future. If you're not, then chances are your journey will be much longer and unlikely to see you reach your vision state. (This will likely look like zigging and zagging, being pushed and pulled in all different directions by internal unrest (rivalry, resource competition, misaligned leaders, personal agendas, etc.).

Your purpose, your why – is what creates customer connection. Even more these days, customers want to connect with an organisation and why they do what they do.

Your principles (or values), above the journey arrow in our diagram, is your how. It's how you live your why every day. Your behaviours, your KPIs, your delivery of your offering. If you're on principle, your staff are connected with your why and know how to deliver to the world. You employ people based on your principles, not just on the skills they have or the length of time they've worked in your industry. It's way beyond that. It's about heart.

Your principles and values, your how – is what creates team connection. Team members understand your vision and know how to behave in order to get you there. They have values to connect with that reflect their own personal values, and what it means to live them.

YOUR VALUES CAN MAKE OR BREAK YOUR CUSTOMER CONNECTION

Be clear on your values as a business. What do you stand for? Who are you? What makes you, you? By being clear on these elements (think of it like your identity, Customer-led Vision, your values, even a customer charter), making sure your staff are clear and living them, then communicating them with your customers, you give them something to connect to, something to differentiate you from the rest. It's really very powerful. Tip: don't pretend to be something you're not, don't try to be the same as your competitor and please, don't make promises you can't keep!

WHY IS IT SO IMPORTANT TO HAVE A CUSTOMER-LED VISION?

Having a Customer-led Vision is the key to unlocking success for your business. It helps your people connect to and with your purpose – your why. The whole premise on which your business is built. The reason you exist. It puts heart into your organisation and it gives a face (when you have the customer in your vision) to who you're doing it for.

It unlocks discretionary effort within your team. Put it this way, how much more productive would your team be if they were connected to your purpose and believed in what you're doing and why you're doing it. Imagine, in turn, that they then put an extra 15 minutes in per day to contribute to that purpose? How much more effective would your business be? How much more could you achieve?

When you have a disillusioned or disconnected workforce, as so many organisations do, they're likely using your time to at best, scroll social media and search up their weekend plans, and at worst, search for jobs. Team members that are connected to your vision and purpose don't do these things, at least not to any detrimental impact on their role or the organisation. This is why we created our Customer-led Accelerator Program, to reorient your team to your vision and purpose, and get them all moving along the same path, in the same direction with a common shared purpose.

> **HAVING A CUSTOMER-LED VISION IS THE KEY TO UNLOCKING SUCCESS FOR YOUR BUSINESS.**

The other major pitfall we notice in organisations is incentivising the wrong behaviours. The best vision and values in the world mean nothing if you're rewarding your team for the wrong things.

This is where many businesses go wrong. They put their vision and values in a Kmart frame and stick them on the wall, then expect the world to change. Worse still, they pay consultants tens of thousands of dollars to come up with them, then do nothing with them.

Often it's because they don't know how to apply them. They don't know what good looks like. They think the words alone will save their business and their culture. But if the senior leaders don't know how to apply the vision and values, then how can they expect the team to? So the organisation gets a new vision and set of values, but the team's KPIs don't change. If you don't clarify what good looks like and then incentivise and reward staff around those things, you're doomed to fail. The team will continue doing what they've always done and you'll be tens of thousands of dollars lighter. Sad but true.

HOW DO YOU PULL IT ALL TOGETHER?

So how do you bring all of this together? How do you find your true north and bring your Customer-led Vision to reality? How do you get your staff and customers connected to your vision and your values and principles?

CUSTOMER-LED VISION: CREATING COMMON PURPOSE AND CONNECTION

Now we understand the importance of having a Customer-led Vision and how crucial it is if we want to deliver the best experience to our customers, let's take a deeper look at our Customer Strategy Framework™ discipline.

The core question

What are the goals and objectives for your organisation and where does the customer sit in your overall vision?

Why does it matter?

Putting the customer at the heart of your organisation requires a business-wide commitment from the top down. Your values, incentives, internal communications and measurements combine to position you as a truly customer-led entity.

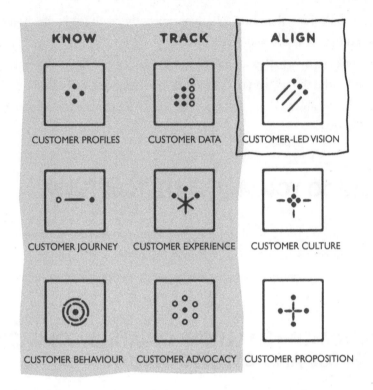

Figure 36: Customer-led Vision capability within the Framework

THE FIVE DRIVERS/INGREDIENTS FOR SUCCESS

There are five key drivers or ingredients you need in this discipline, for success. Let's take a look. As you read the statement, ponder your answer – what's your gut feel? Read over the best practice and explanation to see what good really looks like. Then, go back and consider again how strong you are in this area. What gaps and opportunities emerge?

#1 Your customer is clearly represented in your organisation's vision and purpose statements

Best practice: A simple, short and easily repeatable vision statement applies from boardroom to back office, transcending generations and motivating people to go above and beyond for the customer.

Do you believe your customer is important enough to have a place in your organisation's vision and purpose?

Do you consider your customer or do you only think about where you want to be in the marketplace in a certain amount of time, or how you want to be placed against competitors or what financial gains you want to be achieving?

In your organisation, you might feel as though integrating customer is too hard to do. Or that your team won't support it or believe in it or connect with it. You might think your industry is too cut-throat for it and that you'll be laughed out of town for putting anything wishy washy or heart-felt or customer-y in your vision. You might even think that the customer really doesn't matter that much, that it's way more about your technology and product, than any people-type metric.

But a little heart never hurt anyone.

If your organisation's vision is so compelling that even with a change in leadership, it lives on in the minds and hearts of the team rowing the boats – that's transcending generations.

#2 Your leadership team are aligned on the importance of customer in your organisation

Best practice: Unified under a common Customer-led Vision, the leadership team demonstrate the vision and values, driven by the same overall purpose and aligned strategy.

This is probably one of the most crucial elements to your customer-led journey success. It's imperative that the leadership team – every member – is connected to customer. This means having a deep understanding of where the customer sits in each division or function and what they can do to improve the customer's overall experience of the organisation.

Far from being a list of values in that Kmart frame on the wall, the leadership team must live and breathe the values, demonstrating to their people what it means to be a member of the team and what good, better and best looks like. The key is in the actions and behaviours demonstrated by these vanguards of your vision. Paying lip service is not enough.

Leaders must set aside individual agendas and personal interests and be whole-heartedly linked with the organisation's purpose and strategy, not their own. If you find something's not working in your organisation, take a close look at your senior leaders to check if they're playing on the team, or against it.

This element sets market-leading businesses apart from the rest.

#3 Your organisation's values drive a culture of being truly customer-led

Best practice: Unique behavioural traits are ingrained in the DNA of the organisation, directing strategic and day-to-day decisions and driving the organisation's reputation for being customer-led.

Once you have your senior leadership team on the same page, it's time to work on the people beneath them. We've found that people, for the most part, want to do a good job for their bosses and businesses. They're rowing their boats as hard as they can, they're just not clear on which island they're rowing to or what the best technique is to be most efficient and effective.

Setting the values (which should be done with your team heavily involved) is one thing, defining the behaviours that deliver those values is another level altogether. But the better you can define them, visualise and make them real, the better outcomes for you and your team.

Values must be in the DNA of the business. They must be lived and breathed by your team. The masters of being customer-led take it so far that they only hire people who match their values and behaviours. Recently we were listening to a podcast where the host and his guest were talking about how you can teach people skills but you can't teach them mindsets and that he would always employ someone with the mindset over someone who had even 5 or 10 years more experience in the skill-side of the role. Now that's going next level.

This must all come together to drive all decisions, be they strategic or tactical, big thinking or minute detail. The closer you can get to this, the more successful you will be. Even starting small with one department or one decision, will get you on your way.

The more unique the behaviours to your business, the more you'll stand out from the crowd and the stronger the customer connection you'll have.

#4 Your organisation's objectives are shared and reflect customer trends and needs

Best practice: Clear, achievable and measurable customer-led objectives cascade down through the organisation, focusing everyone's efforts around the customer.

We know we say this all the time but this one is an absolute no-brainer when it comes to becoming truly customer-led.

So often we see businesses where the leaders know what the strategic objectives are, but the staff are so disconnected from them, it's no wonder they're not achieving them.

To give you some hope that this isn't impossible – when you add customer into the equation, team members naturally connect. It's something about having a person at the heart of the objectives – a face, a name – that gives teams purpose and connection. Instead of doing it to drive x amount of revenue for the business, they're doing it to enhance the lives and experiences of their customers. It's what we call putting the heart back into business.

People love doing things for people, so it's not hard to focus your team's efforts around the customer once you get started. In fact, you'll find they'll be the ones coming up with the ideas and initiatives that will form the basis of your plans for world customer-led domination.

#5 You have a shared and consistent understanding of the core promises you make to customers

Best practice: A customer charter exists that directs business decisions and operations at all direct and indirect customer touch points, ensuring consistent delivery on your customer promises.

The customer charter is one of the most under-estimated and misused tools of the Customer-led Revolution. A customer charter is simply a set of promises you make to your customers. Intrinsically linked with your vision, purpose and values, it's how those things combine to create your customer experience.

The customer charter simply tells your customers what they can expect from you and guides your team to deliver those promises (supported by the other elements of this discipline as outlined above).

Making promises **can** mean they can get broken. And you know what? That's okay. Because if you don't make promises then people don't know what to expect from you. A promise is simply a commitment. We will do our very best to do this for you. Then you tell them, we won't always get it right because #human, but we're going to try our very best.

The power of this to a customer cannot be underestimated. Customers need to know what they can expect. They also love a business that has the balls to make promises, to stand in who they are and commit to trying. Everybody loves that.

SELF-ASSESSMENT: HOW DO YOU STACK UP?

Now that you're familiar with the five key ingredients for success and what best practice looks like, it's time to do a bit of self-assessment and ask yourself, how do we stack up?

To get an initial benchmark, check out the statements below and circle the one that best matches your current situation. Mark yourself on the harder side, there's no gold stars here, just learnings and opportunities.

We have customer thinking embedded in our vision + our strategy

CUSTOMER-LED VISION

| I don't think we even mention customers. They just haven't been that important to-date | We are generally committed to customers, but it is not overtly stated anywhere | We definitely mention customers in our strategy but not specifically as a priority | Customers are an important part of our strategy, definitely in the top five priorities | Customer, customer, customer + our vision + strategy is full of customer-centric objectives |

This quick assessment is a simplified version of our full-blown Customer-led Accelerator Program. But, straight away, this gives you an initial idea of how you stack up.

WHO SAYS CUSTOMERS CAN'T LOVE YOU?

We did some work for a major government client, helping them, among other things, to develop their customer charter. They had been struggling with a huge disconnect between their organisation and their customers for years. Being government, this wouldn't surprise you, but it bothered and frustrated the leaders of the organisation who wanted to do better.

Unsatisfied with being labelled 'government' and hiding behind the typical excuses of 'we're their council, our residents can't choose us' or 'they'll never be happy', they sought us out and embarked on a huge, brave journey to become one of the first customer-led councils in Australia.

And achieve it they did, with a significant reduction in customer complaints, fewer overall calls to the Customer Contact Centre, greater staff engagement and more letters of praise from their customers than ever before – and that's saying a lot for a government body!

Not only do they enjoy the efficiencies that these improvements give them, they're now sharing their success story with other like-minded organisations who want to be just like them. Brave. Incredible. Successful. And generous!

We believe customer charters must be built on heart. And being who we are, we pushed the limits of our client and delivered a charter that's core purpose was: For our customers to love us.

Love? Love? Said NO government organisation ever! You can imagine the furore that this statement caused. The brave leaders we worked with, after a few big deep breaths, embraced it with vigour. Middle management, stakeholders, not so much – they were skeptical, naturally. In the end, we got it through and the organisation is now exceptionally proud of the stance they took to be loved by their customers. And so are we.

Share it with colleagues and see what they think. It's a great way to open up the conversation on customer. What answers do you think you'd get if you asked your senior leadership team? Are you aligned or are you on completely different planets?

 Refer to the section 'How to use this book' for tips on who to ask in your organisation, how and why.

RED FLAGS AND ROADBLOCKS

Let's look at some of the red flags and potential roadblocks for Customer-led Vision.

Red flags	Potential roadblocks
■ Functional teams and individuals are pulling in different directions, seemingly working to their own agendas and not on a common path. ■ The values of the organisation appear counter to customer needs and/or people aren't behaving within the values, creating a disconnect. ■ Customer doesn't appear in your vision statement. It's all about your organisation using the customer to meet your needs, not the other way around.	■ Deep rooted cultural inertia that resists change and makes it difficult to get traction in a new direction. Doubters can appear anywhere in the organisation and most destructively, at the senior level. ■ The vision is created by a small number of people and doesn't reflect the inputs and views of the wider team and populous, limiting adoption and reducing impact. ■ Misunderstanding of what vision, purpose and principles actually mean to the organisation and getting caught up in the definition debate instead of getting on with the job.

WHEN YOUR ORGANISATION BUILDS THIS CAPABILITY

Imagine your organisation with a clear, compelling and fully embraced Customer-led Vision. Everyone in your organisation, from boardroom to back office, understands the part they play in helping the customer achieve success and that the organisation's success comes as a result. Teams are no longer competing against each other but working together to a common purpose. Politics are put aside for progress and self-interest is a thing of the past. Your people spring out of bed in the morning, understanding the crucial role they play, which enables them to go above and beyond just clocking in and clocking out to get their paycheck. Your customers know it too as your clear vision, purpose and principles magnetise the right customers to your organisation that value you for who you are and what you do. What a wonderful place this would be, don't you think?

With the capability of Customer-led Vision in place, let's now take this ALIGN discipline even further as we help you build out the DNA of your organisation to create an enviable customer culture that your competitors will find hard to replicate, and help your people thrive in the Customer-led Revolution.

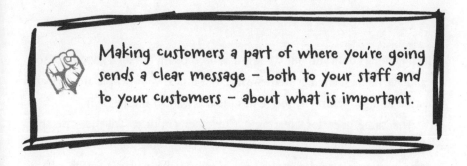

Making customers a part of where you're going sends a clear message – both to your staff and to your customers – about what is important.

Chapter 26

CUSTOMER CULTURE: CONNECTING YOUR TEAM TO THE ULTIMATE REASON YOU EXIST

The strategic question we're setting out to answer is:

How well is your organisation aligned with your customers, from boardroom to back office?

> Culture eats strategy for breakfast.
> *Peter Drucker*

It's a famous quote and one we know is used often, but it's a good one. You can have the best strategy in the world, but unless your people are onboard with it and get behind it, you're destined to wander off the path.

The same goes for creating a Customer Culture. That is, one that places the customer at the heart of everything you do. You can have a great customer strategy in place, unlocking the power of each of the elements within the Customer Strategy Framework™. But, without your people embracing it as their own, as part of how they think day-to-day, it becomes another one of those great pieces of work that sit on the shelf.

Culture is often overlooked or misunderstood. There is often a disconnect between what the organisation wants to achieve and the culture at play. Cultures that are stale, sluggish – even toxic, hold back progress. In many cases they've been left to grow organically, not intentionally.

The 'way we've always done it' is grounded in a deep cultural history, reinforced by incentives, behaviours, beliefs, values and systems. Often, these are deeply rooted in the organisation, under the surface and unspoken, but understood.

MONKEYS AND BANANAS

The best story of culture that we've encountered over the years is the one of monkeys and bananas. Imagine this. A laboratory setting with a large, luscious hand of bananas suspended from the ceiling of a barred cage, with observing scientists all around.

In the centre of this cavernous cage, under the yellowy goodness is a step ladder, leading up to them.

The scientists put five monkeys in the cage, lock the door and simply watch. They buzz around a bit for a while, working out the environment, but then suddenly one monkey spots the bananas. It sees the step ladder. The monkey thinks, 'Bananas, step ladder – let's go for it.' The other monkeys catch on and they are all going hell for leather towards the ladder and the bananas.

Just as the first monkey reaches the top and almost gets his hand on the bananas, all five monkeys get blasted with a cold-water cannon. They retreat back down and shake themselves off. WTF was that?

They dry off and go again. Monkeys love bananas after all. Maybe the water blast was just a once-off. So they set off and, you guessed it, just as they get within reach, they get blasted again. They retreat once more, cold and wet – confused.

This happens over and over again – until... all five monkeys are standing at the bottom of the ladder, looking at the bananas, looking at each other to see who will break rank. Then one inevitably thinks, 'I'm going to make it'. But before this monkey can even get near the first rung of the ladder, the other four monkeys start beating him up.

So, now we have five monkeys, standing at the bottom, knowing they want the bananas, but too scared to take action for fear of reaction. Does this story sound familiar yet? Well, it gets better!

The scientists take one monkey out and put a new staff member monkey in. She comes in, looks at the bananas, the step ladder and it's like, 'Guys – bananas, let's go!' What happens? The other four monkeys beat on her.

They take another staff member monkey out and replace it with a new one who looks at the bananas, the step ladder and is like, 'Guys – bananas, let's go!' Bash, bash, bash.

This happens until all of the original monkeys have been replaced. Now there's five monkeys standing around the bottom of the bananas, not reaching for them, who have NEVER seen a water cannon, yet still will not go for the bananas.

This is how culture develops. What silent assumptions are at play in your organisation today? How are customers perceived? What water cannons are you firing at your staff for behaviours they're not explicitly told to avoid, but inherently do?

#takesmorethanonemonkey... not sure if that hashtag will catch on.

EVERY ORGANISATION HAS A CULTURE – WHETHER YOU LIKE IT OR NOT

Culture is in the fabric of every organisation. You can choose to ignore it or embrace it. The high performers know this and use it as one of their truly sustainable competitive advantages.

It's the glue that binds everyone in the team together and establishes 'the way things are done'.

Sumantra Ghoshal, a leader in organisational culture, described it beautifully as 'the smell of the place'*. You know when you walk into a shop or an office, your 'spidey senses' pick up on the vibe of the place within moments. In your own business, you can get so used to it, you stop noticing altogether. Same with your team. It becomes so imperceptible that you forget about it entirely, only re-engaging with it when something goes wrong or your called to notice.

Strong cultures never lose sight of the smell of their place and continue to focus on it over time. It becomes a strong mesh that guides people on what they do, who they do it with and how they do it.

So then, what is a Customer Culture? It's when the customer is consciously embedded into the way things are done, at all levels. It showcases how important customers are and how they are perceived within the organisation. Customer Culture is the living outcome of how well your Customer-led Vision, values and behaviours are working for or against you. A robust culture will guide your team, even when you're not there. A weak culture accelerates inefficiency at all levels, with good people leaving – both staff and customers!

In working with experts in the areas of semiotics and linguistic discourse analysis, we've seen firsthand that the internal language used to refer to customers is a great indicator towards the orientation of that culture.

How do your people at all levels refer to customers? What labels do they use, officially through process and unofficially in the corridor? Chances are, the underlying beliefs

CUSTOMER CULTURE IS THE LIVING OUTCOME OF HOW WELL YOUR CUSTOMER-LED VISION, VALUES AND BEHAVIOURS ARE WORKING FOR OR AGAINST YOU.

---

* From his speech at the World Economic Forum, 1995.

at play are influencing the choices you make, the approaches you take – all seeping out and leaking back to your customers. We've run sessions with organisations where colourful words have been used to describe their customers – words like 'pain in the @ss, @ssholes and the like'.

Culture has traditionally been one of those unmeasurable things, relegated to the People and Culture realm. But what if you could benchmark it? Work out how aligned or misaligned your team is around the customer? (p278) There are ways and we'll touch on them soon.

CREATING A CULTURE OF CUSTOMER

We humans are rather simple beasts. At a high level, we avoid things we fear and move towards rewards and benefits. And this is where incentives are so important, yet we often see disconnects between what is measured and rewarded and the best win-win outcomes for customers.

Culture is an outcome of intentional choices. By looking at your incentives, you can shift behaviours. This can be either away from pain (stick), or towards benefit (carrot). We love working with call centre environments who are often rewarded for reducing call time or for the highest calls per hour. But, what if the customer's issue isn't resolved and they have to call back 5 to 10 times? Many call centre environments have cottoned on to this and have introduced a new measure – number of calls to resolution. Whether this helps or simply creates another problem is yet to be seen, but it's on the right track.

Incentives drive behaviour. And, while there can be all the best intentions behind the measure, there are often unintended consequences. It's worth reflecting on what your people are rewarded for today, and question – does it really help or hinder us in being customer-led?

Customer Culture is also driven by what gets attention. Creating cross-functional working groups to own and deliver improvement programs puts the customer top of mind. Not only does it engage wider than just traditional Customer Services functions, it creates shared ownership in the success of improving the outcomes for customers and the organisation.

CULTURE IS AN OUTCOME OF INTENTIONAL CHOICES.

DOES YOUR CUSTOMER FEATURE IN YOUR MEETINGS?

(p109)

In our second Customer-led Accelerator Program workshop with our Brisbane client, where we had been invited back to run the workshop with their middle management (after great success with the senior leaders), we uncovered something we believe is rife across many organisations and businesses.

At the start of these workshops, we do a round robin of the table for attendees to introduce themselves, tell us their department and why they're in the room. In this particular workshop, we had all of the Sales team in the room who are usually located across South East Queensland, from Brisbane and suburbs to Toowoomba, to north of the Sunshine Coast and beyond.

Part of this program is coming up with actions that the attendees can take in their roles, directly related to their KPIs and customers, to make a difference to the business.

We were conversing about their current practices and how much they worked together and shared their ideas, when we asked them how often they got together. Being spread across Queensland, some several hours away from the head office in Brisbane, we assumed once a month face-to-face (these were pre-Covid days). Since they didn't seem to know too much of what each other was doing in great detail, we thought this was a safe bet.

Do you know how often they got together? Want to hazard a guess? Would you say monthly? Bi-monthly perhaps?

Weekly. Yes, weekly. Every single Wednesday, every member of the Sales team would spend the entire day travelling to Brisbane to sit around a board table to meet. But that's not the most shocking thing.

What do you suppose they talked about? Our big thinking brains went to how they could work together more closely, perhaps some joint project catch-ups, referrals for business clients in neighbouring regions. Perhaps ideas around what was working and not working, potential partnership opportunities...

Nope.

Round robins. Yep. Your stock standard, go around the table and update each other on what they'd done in the past week. And what was planned for the coming week.

This is by no means uncommon. Many of the businesses and organisations we've worked for have done the same thing, but usually the team is at least based in the same building and the commute is no more than a couple of levels in the lift. So many businesses and teams get so caught up in telling their stories – look what I did, look what I achieved, look at me – that they spend little time looking forward or even backward.

But, it can play out differently when you shift the culture. Asking questions for one. Encouraging curiosity. What's worked, what hasn't? What went wrong? How could we do it differently? What's happening in the near future? What do we need to be aware of? What do we need to tackle now to safeguard ourselves later? Most of these questions are not asked in your typical weekly team huddle.

For our client's Sales team, our session shifted their perspectives in a big way. They now get together to look at customer improvements and leave the detail of the WIP update to a weekly consolidated summary report. As we often say, once you've seen the customer view, you can't unsee it. Winning!

Celebrating the wins and sharing them far and wide, even with customers, helps shift away from facelessness to greater connection. FOMO is a real thing and even the naysayers will eventually want to get on board.

A fundamental to creating a strong Customer Culture is to encourage exposure to customers. No, not the sort of exposure that gets you locked up. It's about having a program in place for your whole team, not just the customer-facing ones, to get out in the field and see what's happening. This can take various forms and when you start to think about the possibilities, the choices are endless.

For example, when working for a UK government department we created a Customer Knowledge Program, which gave each team member points for every time they chose a customer exposure activity. Depending on their level (Exec, Manager, Team member) they had different point targets, directly linked to their performance and bonus. The more exposure to customer, the better their bonus would be. Talk about walking the walk!

The menu of activities was varied to make it easy as possible to get involved. From attending focus group research, to going out and talking with customers (shock horror!), to listening in to live call centre enquiries, to reviewing customer comms – there were over 25 activities, each with points that reflected the intensity. Within 18 months, the whole team had met their targets and not only that, they also had a long list of improvement ideas, enabling the organisation to jump two levels on our Customer Strategy Maturity Scale. Impressive!

To truly have the customer at the heart of everything you do, the customer needs to be at the table. Not physically, but close to it. In our experience, we've seen customer reference panels created and used to great effect. This is where you gather a small group of target customers and use them to bounce off ideas and proposed changes, using their input to avoid costly mistakes or misguided investments. This is not a new concept, but it is one that seems to have been forgotten in recent years.

Finally, a Customer Culture is constantly defined and strengthened by sharing customer insights with the team. The good, the bad and the ugly. Celebrating success helps reinforce the desired outcomes and behaviours, while gathering around issues helps to rally the team to drive improvements. Linking wins back to activities done by the team, not an individual, brings a collective pride that removes internal barriers and fuels ongoing improvement.

 ## CUSTOMER CULTURE: THE KEY TO ENJOYING ALIGNMENT AND CONSISTENCY

Culture is king and by building it around your customer, it becomes an enduring source of advantage. As a leader, this is what will make your organisation the aspiration for your industry and create a legacy for the future.

The core question

How well is your organisation aligned with your customers, from board-room to back office?

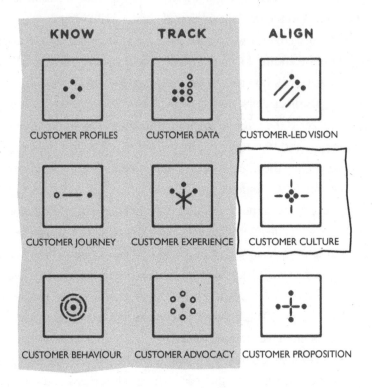

Figure 37: Customer Culture capability within the Framework

Why does it matter?

Being truly customer-led is an all of organisation effort. It requires an understanding of how well all functions stack together to create a unified and intentional customer experience through your structures, processes, people and incentives.

Let's break it down further into the drivers you can look at and what best practice looks like.

THE FIVE DRIVERS/INGREDIENTS FOR SUCCESS

There are five key drivers or ingredients you need in this capability for success. Let's take a look. As you read the statement, ponder your answer – what's your gut feel? Read over the best practice and explanation to see what good really looks like. Then, go back and consider again how strong you are in this area. What gaps and opportunities emerge?

#1 You have a structured approach to building customer empathy and focus across your organisation

Best practice: Staff are obsessively focused on customer at all levels of the organisation, with customer objectives being central to personal objectives.

Getting your people connected to your customer and their needs doesn't happen by itself or by accident. You need to formalise an approach that becomes an enabler for your team to come face to face with the reality your customers face. Much like the Customer Knowledge Program we referred to earlier in this chapter, it's about weaving these customer exposures into p277 the fabric of your everyday. Make it part of people's objectives. At all levels, across all functions.

#2 Your customer performance is regularly measured, shared and embraced by your entire team

Best practice: All levels of the organisation have a clear view of customer performance, from customer satisfaction per touch point, to gains made from customer experience improvements.

When speaking with internal comms people over the years, one of their biggest complaints is the infrequency of internal communications that link people to the outcomes. In our experience, think about how much you need to communicate, then multiply it by ten! There's a great quote painted under a bridge in Brisbane that says, 'The more I think about it, the bigger it gets.' In this context, the more you talk about customer, the more it becomes part of the agenda for everyone. They see how their role connects and the outcomes. Yes, we all like a paycheck, but, in general, most people also need to feel that they're making a difference.

Simple things like internal newsletter updates on customer feedback, interviews with customers, celebrating great customer outcomes or the latest research will all help to pique the interest of the team. Keep it real too – not just 'happy CEO shake hands with customer' photos. Highlight people on the ground and the great work they're doing, outside of the Customer Services function. If you don't have one yet, put up a customer billboard prominently in the office. Keep it simple, but visible with regular updates. Nothing worse than seeing the 'customer matters' board with data that is three years out of date!

#3 You have dedicated resources for improving your customer experience and internal capability

Best practice: A structured and planned customer improvements program drives enhancements to all aspects of operations, with dedicated resource(s) acting as customer champions.

One of our early mentors had a saying, 'The important things have the resources.' And this continues to be true. Your customer-led program needs to have resources formally allocated to it. Not just a tack on to someone's role but a formal recognition of the program and the need for it to have attention. Give the program a line in your budget – no matter how small the dollar amount. These seemingly small elements make a huge impact to demonstrate that this 'customer-thing' is real and valued.

Ideally, have a single person who is on point to own the program. However, in case you didn't get the memo, one person alone can't do it. Recruiting 'champions' from across the organisation helps to share the ownership, tapping into latent capacity and energy across the team. Formalise the group by putting terms of reference in place and, most importantly, give them some power to make change happen.

#4 Your non-customer-facing functions are invited to participate in customer-facing activities

Best practice: A structured approach exists to increase cross-functional customer awareness, including temporary job placements and information sharing to drive a customer-led culture.

If we had a dollar for the countless times we've heard from support function leaders (Finance, HR, IT) that they 'have nothing to do with the customer', we'd probably not buy bitcoin with it. The reality is that the customer is everyone's job. As the leader wanting to create the customer-led organisation, your job is to make sure they realise it. We've seen temporary job placements extremely effective here. Often, especially when there is low customer empathy or awareness, swapping a specific customer facing resource with non-customer facing helps bring a new level of awareness for both teams.

Another tool that is often under-utlised and somewhat forgotten is the 'brown bag' lunch sessions. Each week, teams share, over lunch, what they've been working on, wins they've had and how it all relates back to customer. These simple, yet effective sessions drive change in multiple ways, as presenting teams needs to think through their content (and realise what they've achieved), while the audience learns more and can then appreciate aspects outside their own domains.

#5 Your incentives, rewards and communications reflect the importance of customer

Best practice: Behaviours are reinforced by appropriate reward structures (eg. awards, incentives) that prioritise long-term customer relationships over short-term wins.

The ultimate carrot. Link your incentives and rewards to customer-led measures and activities. Traditionally, performance is linked to internally facing metrics – profit, sales, time to serve, some other objective-specific thing. And, don't get us wrong – these are important. But, we challenge you to think about the behaviours they create when they don't have links back to customer outcomes.

Short-term metrics often breed short-term customer relationships. We've seen the 'one and done' mentality across many organisations and it leads to very transactional views and operations – for staff and customers. Loyalty goes out the window as people focus on what they can get for themselves, regardless of the long-term cost.

Customer is the ultimate boss. The one with the wallet to choose you. The one you exist for. The patron. What matters to them should be the measures for your team. If they're not, it's time to dust off the HR hat and do a rethink!

SELF-ASSESSMENT: HOW DO YOU STACK UP?

Now that you're familiar with the five key ingredients for success and what best practice looks like, it's time to do a bit of self-assessment and ask yourself, how do we stack up?

To get an initial benchmark, check out the statements below and circle the one that best matches your current situation. Mark yourself on the harder side, there's no gold stars here, just learnings and opportunities.

Customers come up in conversation, but usually it's about how annoying they are!	Our main customer-facing functions know about the customer, but no one else does	We know customers are important + we try to remember them in our activities	We formally acknowledge our customers internally + keep them top of mind in all activities	We live + breathe our customers + have a defined customer charter that drives everything we do

This quick assessment is a simplified version of our full-blown Customer-led Accelerator Program. But, straight away, this gives you an initial idea of how you stack up.

Share it with colleagues and see what they think. It's a great way to open up the conversation on customer. What answers do you think you'd get if you asked your senior leadership team? Are you aligned or are you on completely different planets?

(pxviii) Refer to the section 'How to use this book' for tips on who to ask in your organisation, how and why.

RED FLAGS AND ROADBLOCKS

Let's look at some of the red flags and potential roadblocks for Customer Culture.

Red flags	Potential roadblocks
■ The majority of your people have limited exposure to customers, making decisions while sitting behind their desks without understanding the impacts it can have on the ground. ■ You see your people being incentivised for the wrong things which are often counter to customer needs, driving behaviours that are unhelpful to the organisation's ultimate purpose. ■ There's limited sharing of customer success stories across teams and throughout the organisation, instead with a focus on operational and tactical issues and fighting fires.	■ Inherent KPIs and legacy organisational measures inhibit the step change required to break the old paradigms to customer-driven outcomes. ■ Apathy at all levels of the organisation with low morale and a resistance to change and the 'we've heard it all before, here we go again' attitude held by disengaged and disillusioned team members (who may want the change but don't believe it's going to happen). ■ Your organisation doesn't prioritise becoming customer-led and give it the resources it needs for success.

WHEN YOUR ORGANISATION BUILDS THIS CAPABILITY

Picture a future where your organisation is thriving with a strong customer culture. Your people are working together, proactively innovating on improvements that create win-win situations for the organisation and for the customer. There's a strong connection to the human-side of what you do and deliver for customers that perpetually motivates your people to go above and beyond. Customer performance is celebrated by the organisation and customer issues are rallied around and dealt with swiftly and without blame. Your collegiate culture is the envy of others, helping you to attract and retain the best talent in your sector as you become an employer of choice. Is this the kind of organisation you'd be proud to lead?

With the capability of Customer Culture in place, let's now take this ALIGN discipline even further as we help you get clear on what you do, who you do it for, how you do it and where you sit in the wider competitive landscape. Let's move on to exploring your Customer Proposition.

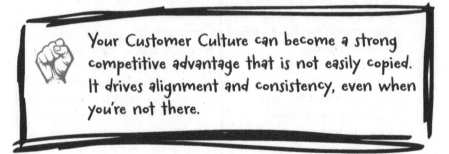

Your Customer Culture can become a strong competitive advantage that is not easily copied. It drives alignment and consistency, even when you're not there.

Chapter 27

CUSTOMER PROPOSITION: WHAT MAKES YOU UNIQUE AND DELIVERING ON THE PROMISE

The strategic question we're setting out to answer is:

What is your position in the marketplace and how do you present to the outside world?

Welcome to the final discipline in our Customer Strategy Framework™! You're almost there!

Customer Proposition is the closest thing to Marketing you'll get in our Framework, so this section is probably going to resonate the strongest for you.

If you're not clear on who you are, how can you expect your customer to be clear on who you are and what makes you different to everyone else in the marketplace?

In this chapter, we're going to challenge all you think you know about marketing and about 'selling' your offering to the world. In fact, we're going to redefine it for you so that your marketing will become a real asset to your business, not just a money-pit you pour your hard-earned cash into.

> Be yourself – everyone else is already taken.
>
> *Oscar Wilde*

SO, WHAT IS CUSTOMER PROPOSITION EXACTLY?

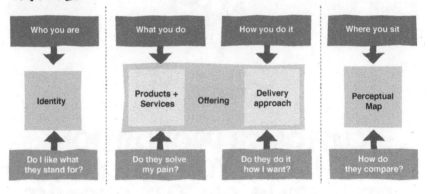

Figure 38: Customer Proposition – the three building blocks

Customer Proposition is way more than just marketing. In our experience, Customer Proposition is made up of three building blocks as seen in the diagram above:

1. a clear identity of who you are as an organisation
2. a clear understanding of your offering in the market, of what you do, who you do it for and how you do it
3. a clear view of your market position, where you sit perceptually among your competitors in the eyes of the customer.

In fact, element two – what you do and how you do it – is a direct reflection of who you are as a business. Which is why identity is not only one of the most important elements, but also the most commonly forgotten.

Identity is about who you are in the world. How you stand out. How you show up. It's about embracing what makes you different and special. Beyond your products and services, to who you really are. Your purpose. Your why. Your story.

Your identity directly reflects your values – they are like a mirror image of what is on the inside and how that shows up on the outside. So naturally, the clearer you are on your values and the more you and your team are living them, the stronger and more unique you will show up to the outside world.

Traditionally, Customer Proposition – in the marketing theory context – has been based on the elements of positioning – Product, Market, Service, Price (PMSP). Essentially – what you do, who you do it for, how you do it and the outcome or result.

But we believe it's so much more than that, though we do use the PMSP framework in our work with businesses to help whittle down the options and ideas.

IT'S NOT JUST ABOUT MARKETING OR SALES

In our view, traditional marketing is all about 'tell'. We 'tell' customers why they should buy us. Why we're better than the other options. Why they need us. We tell them. Tell, tell, tell.

While communicating what's special about us and why customers should choose us is not a bad thing, things have changed a lot in recent years, particularly with the emergence of the internet and user generated content.

We touched on customer trends earlier, and it's these trends that are (p11) changing the face of marketing and communications. And while some of us would rather things didn't change, there's really no choice but to get on board if you want your business to survive and thrive.

The fact is, customers don't want to be told anymore. They want a conversation.

It's not about telling, it's about connecting.

No longer is cut through gained by TELLING the loudest or spending the most money on marketing or having the biggest billboard in the biggest cities in the world (Times Square, anyone?).

We've been sold for years that billboards, television advertising, super-bowl exposure or bus advertising is the answer. These days it's search engine optimisation, pay-per-click, social media, influencer marketing and all that jazz.

The simple fact remains – if you don't define who you are and what makes you different to everyone else, the biggest bill-board in the world won't sell you to your ideal customers.

If you want to communicate on anything else but

IT'S NOT ABOUT TELLING, IT'S ABOUT CONNECTING.

price, then you simply have no choice but to define what makes you different. No one wins the price game. Competing on price is how many markets ended up in the commodotised mess they're in today.

If you find yourself in the price game, you'll want to step out of it as soon as you can (easier said than done but stick with us). If you're not playing in this space, keep right out of it if you want a sustainable, profitable business with longevity and market presence (not to mention your own sanity, mental and physical health).

So if it's not about price, then what's it all about?

1. First, it's about defining your customer promises and aligning them with your brand promises.
2. Then, it's about understanding where you sit against your competitors (more than just product and price), using a perceptual map.
3. And finally, it's about being clear on who you truly are as an organisation so customers are magnetised to you and can engage in a relationship with you.

It's these three building blocks that enable you to have a clear Customer Proposition to smash your goals and get ahead of your competition.

WHY IS A CLEAR CUSTOMER PROPOSITION SO CRUCIAL TO YOUR SUCCESS?

Having a clear Customer Proposition isn't just about your marketing messages. It helps your customers find and choose you over your competitors. Even more than that, it helps differentiate you from the competition and find the right customer that will value what you do and ultimately, pay more for it, buy more of it and refer more people just like them, who'll also buy it.

That's right – having a clear proposition doesn't just win you marketing awards or make your ads stand out more than the competitors, it helps you attract the right people – your tribe – meaning your customers (external) and your team members (internal).

It's more than just selling, it's 'being' – being who you are, truly and authentically. And more and more these days, customers want to connect with the businesses they transact with. They want to connect to your story and your purpose. They'll even pay more for it, over and above the basics of your product or service.

CUSTOMER PROPOSITION: FIND YOUR UNIQUE AND CUT THROUGH THE NOISE TO REACH YOUR IDEAL CUSTOMERS

Now we understand the importance of having a clear Customer Proposition and how crucial it is if we want to connect with the right customers and cut through the noise, let's take a deeper look at our Customer Strategy Framework™ discipline.

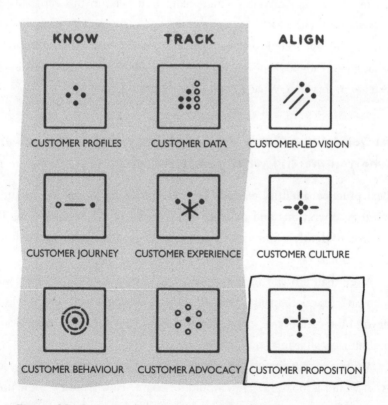

Figure 39: Customer Proposition capability within the Framework

The core question

What is your position in the marketplace and how do you present to the outside world?

Why does it matter?

Where you are positioned in the marketplace and how you differentiate from competitors is core to how well you connect with your customers. External communications drive how you show up and the promises you make to your customers.

THE FIVE DRIVERS FOR SUCCESS

There are five key drivers or ingredients you need in this capability for success. Let's take a look. As you read the statement, ponder your answer – what's your gut feel? Read over the best practice and explanation to see what good really looks like. Then, go back and consider again how strong you are in this area. What gaps and opportunities emerge?

#1 You have a clearly defined identity that communicates who you are and what you stand for

Best practice: Identity extends beyond marketing to connect business strategy, operations and delivery at all levels of the organisation. The team confidently embraces it to create deep and enduring customer connections.

More than a brand identity or a set of rules around how to use your logo and brand elements, your identity is all about you. Extending far beyond the confines of marketing, it encapsulates the entire organisation and impacts all teams and functions.

We like to talk about identity like this – if your business was a person, what would it look like? How would it behave? How would it show up in the world? How would others be able to find it in a sea of people and know that you are their kind of person? How would they know they'd want to be part of your tribe?

In your organisation, you might think you have a sense of this, perhaps even some ideas captured or written down. But to truly step into your identity, it must be codified and shared across the entire organisation. Only then can your customers truly have a consistent experience with you, where you and your team members – from frontline staff to the cleaner – show up as uniquely and genuinely 'you'.

This should extend all the way from your strategy to your operational delivery and everywhere in between.

#2 You communicate brand promises that you consistently deliver to customers

Best practice: All areas of the organisation understand what can and can't be done for customers, with external communications setting expectations that close the delivery-expectation gap and reduce negative feedback.

Once you have a clear identity that is understood and embraced by your team, it's time to refine and rework your brand promises. Why? So that your customers know what to expect from you and your team know what they need to deliver.

How many times have you been promised things by companies through their marketing and sales spiel, only to find there's a massive gap between the expectation they set for you, and their delivery? Think about times in your own buying experiences where this has happened – some might only be minor, others may have been chasmic but the reality is, they let you down.

The world becomes a better place – less stressful and more friction-less, when you deliver on the promises you make. Your team understands exactly what they can and can't deliver to your customer. Your customer, through your marketing and communications, understands your brand promises and what to expect. Supplemented by your identity, they also have a sense of how that interaction will go and how it will feel.

This helps you close the delivery-expectation gap and reduces negative feedback, poor reviews, customer complaints and team angst.

#3 You own a clear market position that differentiates you from competitors in the eyes of customers

Best practice: A visual map of where the organisation sits against competitors is used to drive a clear market strategy that is understood, shared and embraced by all levels of the organisation.

This one's a beauty. In a sea of sameness and in many cases, overwhelming choice, it's a challenge to stand out from the crowd these days. If you think it's hard for you, imagine being your customer in making sense of it all!

So many business leaders we've met have become so overwhelmed with the 'doing' within the business, they've forgotten (or not made time) to take a step back and look at the market and wider external environment. We can become very insular in our businesses.

Mapping out competitors in your marketplace and understanding where they stand against your own organisation, can help you identify opportunities and even threats, to your future. By identifying the gaps (against countless axis options beyond just price and quality), you can chart a clear market strategy and way forward that not only solves customer problems, but spells success for you.

A challenge, if you don't already have this existing in your organisation, is the pushback you might feel from different function leads within this process. But by looking at the world a different way, opportunities you never knew existed will arise.

So much of business, when we're busy and stressed and 'in the trenches' becomes accidental. Answering this question honestly might help you realise where some of your long-term issues stem from.

#4 You clearly articulate what you offer to customers in language they understand

Best practice: A clearly defined Customer Value Proposition (CVP) is aligned with marketing and development efforts that address customer pains, needs and priorities to create best fit solutions.

We love this one. So often we meet business leaders and function leads that love to talk about themselves (their organisations). So they should!

But they talk about who they are and what they do in their own language, not that of the customer. How often do you see businesses communicate the features and benefits of their offering, or their history or their story – but with no context to the customer? We've seen some of the biggest spends in marketing and advertising wasted, purely by the use of the wrong message.

Having a clearly defined Customer Value Proposition that addresses your customer pains, needs and priorities will help you drive more effective marketing communications and stronger connections with your customers. Use your Customer Profiles to apply this and you'll find the outcomes are even better!

But it's not just about marketing – use these same pain points, needs and priorities to inform your development priorities and you'll not only be communicating better, you'll be directly solving and addressing customer issues. And they'll love you for it.

#5 Your communications focus on solving customer problems, over selling features and benefits

Best practice: External communications focus on the who (the customer), not the what (the product) to engage the emotional aspects of the customer buying process and create a lasting connection.

By putting the customer at the heart of everything you do, including your communications and your own story, you'll find your efforts are far more effective and get you the results you want.

VACUUM CLEANERS THAT DON'T SUCK

Think of a product you use on a daily basis – let's take a vacuum cleaner. They essentially do the same thing – suck up dust and dirt. If you were simply looking at the features and benefits of the vacuum cleaner, you'd talk about how it sucks up dirt, how it has a handle that you can hold, a dust bag (or no dust bag), high-powered and the different attachments.

Now obviously there are a huge range of vacuum cleaners available on the market that have different levels and options that set the different price points. But who has an emotional connection to a vacuum cleaner?

Dyson customers do. Because Dyson essentially took your common vacuum cleaner and all the things people hate about them – having to empty the bags, difficulty in manouvering the ruddy things, cleaning the filters – and used technology to solve those customer pain points.

They transcended features and benefits to address the emotional aspects of the customer's needs and buying experience – and boy, has that worked for them!

The beauty of looking at your offering and how it solves customers' pain is that if you ask yourself honestly and take the time to find the answers, you may just find a whole tranche of opportunities you never knew existed.

SELF-ASSESSMENT: HOW DO YOU STACK UP?

Now that you're familiar with the five key ingredients for success and what best practice looks like, it's time to do a bit of self-assessment and ask yourself, how do we stack up?

To get an initial benchmark, check out the statements below and circle the one that best matches your current situation. Mark yourself on the harder side, there's no gold stars here, just learnings and opportunities.

This quick assessment is a simplified version of our full-blown Customer-led Accelerator Program. But, straight away, this gives you an initial idea of how you stack up.

Share it with colleagues and see what they think. It's a great way to open up the conversation on customer. What answers do you think you'd get if you asked your senior leadership team? Are you aligned or are you on completely different planets?

Refer to the section 'How to use this book' for tips on who to ask in your (pxviii) organisation, how and why.

RED FLAGS AND ROADBLOCKS

Let's look at some of the red flags and potential roadblocks for Customer Proposition.

Red flags	Potential roadblocks
■ You feel that your marketing isn't working and that customers don't have a longer term relationship with you – it's very much transactional, often relying on price to differentiate. ■ Your operations team finds it difficult to deliver on the promises your marketing team are making in your communications, leading to internal frustration, customer confusion and complaints. ■ Your customers (and even your staff) don't really understand what your organisation does and the value that it brings to the world, and how you're different from your competitors.	■ As a concept, identity is not understood or valued for the power it holds for your organisation, thrown in with marketing as a 'tell' concept rather than the heart of who you truly are, ignored by the wider team as just more marketing guff. ■ An apathy or resistance to change from the organisation's current state to where you want to be in the future, having mapped out your desired market position and the steps needed to get there. ■ A lack of understanding of your wider competitive landscape and not only your direct, but also indirect competitors, and differing views on where you sit based on opinion not fact.

WHEN YOUR ORGANISATION BUILDS THIS CAPABILITY

Imagine a future where your customers are seemingly magnetised to your organisation, already armed with a clear understanding and expectation of what you can do for them. Your marketing budgets are less about 'pushing your message' and are more about reinforcing who you are and the value of the relationship you have with your customers.

Your internal team can clearly articulate your market position and act like an extension of your sales force with everyone they meet. Your customer perceives you to own a clear space in the market and values your offering with price being one of the lowest determinants for them choosing you. Your profits are higher, your customer retention is off the chart and your staff retention is at an enviable level in your sector. You show up as the poster child of your industry. How powerful a force would your organisation be in the marketplace and how proud would you feel?

This rounds out the three capabilities that help you truly ALIGN your organisation around the ultimate reason you're in business – your customer. Charting your Customer-led Vision, creating a culture that truly has the customer at the heart of everything you do and fulfilling a clear Customer Proposition that's baked into your DNA will set you apart from the rest.

Making sure that everything stacks together in a meaningful and coherent way is a key component to becoming truly customer-led. Get one of the three strategic bricks out of place and it destabilises your organisation and ultimately your success.

*

Let's shift gears now and take all of this reflection across the three disciplines and talk about the journey ahead and how to make it happen. Strap yourself in as we share the benefits of our experience and direct you towards success and away from the battle scars we've encountered.

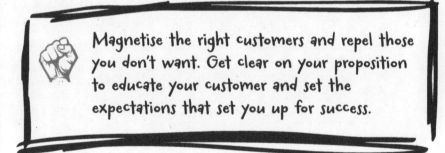

Magnetise the right customers and repel those you don't want. Get clear on your proposition to educate your customer and set the expectations that set you up for success.

Section 7

THE REALITY OF MAKING IT HAPPEN

So at this point, we've now covered all of the main concepts across all three disciplines and the nine capabilities that make high performing customer-led organisations succeed. By now, you should start to see ideas emerging, quick wins and some a-ha or (oh-sh!t) moments.

It's time to make this customer-led thing a reality. We're not going to lie to you, it won't be easy. But some of the smallest things can make the biggest difference and get you well and truly moving towards success.

Of course, you must know what success looks like before you start chasing it down. This is where so many business leaders and organisations go wrong – they want success, they just don't know what that success looks like.

We'd suggest you chart a course to success. That is, small points along the way that can help keep you on track and reorient you when needed. Small steps – way points – that you and your team can row towards (and recorrect if heading off track).

Chapter 28

THE SECRET TO GETTING TRACTION

How do you raise being customer-led on the strategic agenda? What if your leadership team don't think you have a problem to solve in the first place?

You will no doubt confront the challenge from those who don't believe they impact customers. The way forward is to engage them and raise awareness of the need. It's not that they don't care. From our experience, it's that they are not aware to care!

FIND, FOCUS AND FIX = A WAY FORWARD

From countless customer-led transformations, we've simplified the process into three main components. By breaking the complexity down into three main phases, as the customer-led leader, it helps you to frame up the journey ahead, without scaring the horses.

We call the process: FIND, FOCUS and FIX.

It starts with a benchmark of where you are today. How strong is your organisation across the nine customer competencies? Are you killing it? Would everyone in the leadership team agree?

This is where you **FIND** the customer capability gaps that are holding you back. In our experience with leadership teams of all shapes and sizes, across the nine areas of the Customer Strategy Framework™ there will be areas of agreement of your current level and areas of divergence. And this is the find – the gold.

Bringing together the team who is steering the organisation and discussing the gaps helps you to **FOCUS** your efforts on what will make the most impact. Going through this process objectively helps put individual agendas aside and enables a new level of strategic conversation – not trying to prioritise an uncontextualised laundry list of improvements.

Finally, with focus in place around the top customer competency gaps, you can then begin to create the actions to close the gaps and **FIX** the issues. The temptation here is to play 'give the other team the actions'. This doesn't turn out well. This is about each functional lead reflecting on how they can make improvements in their area to help close the capability gap. When combined, you have a shared action plan that will create long-lasting change.

Sounds easy right? And, to some degree it is. It just requires the team to step away from the day-to-day, see the organisation through a new lens and reorient the way forward to a shared direction. This direction is around the customer – the ultimate reason you exist. We like to call this direction 'true north'. Where your organisation is truly customer-led – with the customer out front and the business following.

> IT BREAKS DOWN THE POLITICS AND SILOS, RE-ENERGISES THE TEAM AND MORALE, RELEASING A NEW BREATH OF LIFE BACK INTO THE ORGANISATION.

For many organisations we've worked with, finding this shared destination is a liberating experience. It breaks down the politics and silos, re-energises the team and morale, releasing a new breath of life back into the organisation. For those doing well, it helps reaffirm the investment, helping them to refine even further to move up the customer strategy maturity scale.

BEING THE CUSTOMER CHANGE-MAKER

As a leader, you're possibly facing a level of resistance already in your organisation. You need to be the customer change-maker to get customer onto the agenda. It starts by opening the conversation around customer with your wider team. This is not about selling the concept, as in time, it will sell itself. This is starting with being curious and asking questions. For example, 'what's the one thing that peeves our customers off the most?' – and seeing what responses you get.

You will find that as you start to poke around you release the latent energy and desire for change that is in your people already. A Customer-led Revolution as it were!

Being the customer change-maker is about linking customer-led outcomes to your corporate objectives. If you have an objective to 'save money', find the link between being customer-led and efficiency. If the objective is around 'growth', what is the link between customer-led and the ability to extend your effective sales force through advocacy? It is these strategic hooks that validate the thinking and enable you to open the conversation.

Finally, it needs to be grounded in a robust, logical and defendable business case. Not some woolly, fluffy aspirational statements – this is solid numbers with real impact. It doesn't have to be too complex either, as you will lose the attention of your peers. It needs to speak right to the heart of the operation.

In our work with a UK government payments agency, our initial case (p49) was based on cost-saving. We did some simple modelling about the cost of reworking errors and how building customer capability would reduce the error rate. Errors meant money. Reducing them meant LOTS of money. That was the business case.

Gaining the support for doing the **FIND** phase is what the customer change-maker is there to do. With that engagement, you suddenly recruit a wider leadership on your journey for customer-led change. It is from here that you can start to secure the resources and begin to fix the issues. Before that, it is just a dream.

YOU CAN'T DO IT ON A SHOESTRING

If you think you can get your organisation to become more customer-led without a decent level of investment, you're setting out on a rough journey. This doesn't necessarily mean you need squillions of dollars. It's about giving permission to access the organisation's resources – be that people, time, expertise, cash – to further the cause.

What gets budget, gets attention. Many of the things you can do don't require tons of resources. They are shifts in mindsets. Changes in the way things are done. However, you won't get support unless you have robust customer foundations in place, that are made not from gut feel or opinion. This is where the Customer Strategy Framework™ helps you to prioritise where to focus your efforts over time.

We've talked about getting your leaders on the journey and your customer onto the strategic agenda. That is all good and agreeable – in principle. It is when your leadership peers have to support the investment of resources that true support is shown. We've seen lip-service agreements and 'yesses' countless times. But, as we said, what gets the budget, gets the attention.

QUICK WINS LEAD TO BIG GAINS

Now, we don't know about you, but we've never had a lot of success in getting mega dollars approved for customer-led transformation straight up (unless it is a crisis situation). As the leader, you need to chart out a journey of staged and planned 'wins', proving the way forward and the necessity of the investment.

In the early stages of establishing your customer-led program it is crucial that you get some runs on the board. Then, for each one, turn the amplifier up and shout about it to anyone that will listen. Depending on the complexity of your environment, this can be about extending beyond traditional comms lines and channels. Sharing wins back to customers, influential groups and key stakeholders can help to build the groundswell for your own revolution – and get more funding!

Much like a snowball creates size and mass as it rolls, you use these wins, intentionally engineered to create positive internal and external pressure, to keep it going. Nothing better than your CEO or senior responsible officers hearing great feedback from their historically painful customers or stakeholders.

In this way, you are creating a somewhat viral reaction. Much like a tree diagram, that multiplies at each layer, your program successes move from single events to eventually being 'the way we do things'.

To really accelerate your program, 'pin out' two or three key pain points from across your entire operation. Each of these 'pins' becomes an initiative of your customer-led program that will spark the internal revolution. As each pin releases energy, it emanates out. No longer is this a customer service bandaid, but a transformational approach that everybody owns.

It's like lighting fires. If you want to really get it going quickly, you light little fires in multiple spots. They quickly heat up and create the change and energy you so desperately desire.

LOW-HANGING FRUIT INTO SNOWBALLS

So here's our tips for making it happen – think of it as 'fruit snowballing'.

#1 Start with small wins in a defined area

Small wins are great, but they need to be delivered in a defined area. Otherwise, they can be lost in the sea of wider activity. Pick a specific function or a team. This will help you in two primary ways. Firstly, you get to work with a defined group and recruit another bunch of advocates for the Customer-led Movement. Secondly, their gains help you to prove the business case for ongoing and enhanced support and investment.

#2 Highlight existing good practice

We often see external consultants come in and poo-poo existing work in the hope of elevating themselves and their ideas. Effectively, they throw the baby out with the bath water. In most organisations we've worked with, there is some good work already happening. It might not 'fit' into any other program, but it can be integrated into the customer-led program. How? By celebrating the good things that are already happening. Communicate these and open up the conversation to unearth more existing good practice. Ask teams to share what they are doing. This helps to raise the profile of customer, but also bring it to consciousness across teams. It also reduces mindless waste.

#3 Pick off a customer pain point

This is usually obvious to everyone inside and outside the organisation. What is the one thing in your current offering (within your control) that if you addressed it, would make your organisation **an industry leader in the eyes of your customers and your competitors**? If you don't know or don't have consensus, open the conversation! Ask. Customers will tell you. If they don't, your staff will.

The quick wins will have given you the ammunition to prove the case, this is where you set out to nail one of the big ones. In our experience, there's MANY different things you can address, with different views on what matters the most. This is where we use the effort–impact matrix to help out.

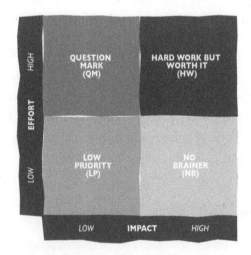

Figure 40: The effort–impact matrix

The one to choose should sit in the quadrant of low effort with high impact – the No Brainers. You can get to the others down the track. The reason we start here is that the timeframe for delivery is relatively short- to medium-term. Don't try to pick off the biggest and nastiest issues that are high effort and high impact. You might get started, but support will be tough. Nail the simpler one first to then accelerate the program and knock the big ones for six!

But – let's not get too far ahead of ourselves. The first step in the journey is still required. This is, to find your blindspots and get moving towards becoming the best customer-led organisation in your sector. Let's talk about getting started on your journey.

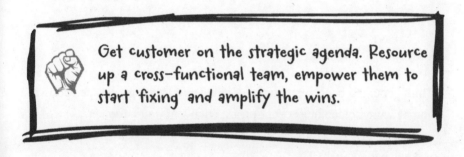

Get customer on the strategic agenda. Resource up a cross-functional team, empower them to start 'fixing' and amplify the wins.

Chapter 29

GETTING STARTED

Throughout this book, we trust you've found new learnings, new perspectives and new ways of looking at your organisation and your customer.

The beauty of a process like this is that you reveal your unknown unknowns.

It's the things you didn't realise were wrong or not working that are likely holding you back the most. The gaps in your efforts. The frictions in your team structure. The inequalities in your functions' voices and position within your organisation. The personalities. The practices and procedures that are working against, not for, you.

All the things. The gaps. The strengths. The good and the bad. It's powerful stuff.

WE DON'T KNOW WHAT WE DON'T KNOW

The fact is, we don't know what we don't know. It's as simple as that.

You know when things are working and when they're not. But when you're as busy as you are, it's often hard to see where the issues lie.

You know they're there, you just don't know where. You rely on your leaders and teams to inform you.

But the reality or truth is not always presented to you as individuals protect their jobs or avoid responsibility for poor decisions or practices. Or they simply don't know that there's anything wrong. There's a way around this by the way – we discussed earlier creating a culture where (p266) making mistakes and trying things is embraced and celebrated, rather than frowned upon or cast aside.

STEP BACK AND SEE YOUR ORGANISATION IN A DIFFERENT WAY

Stepping back and taking a look at your organisation or business in a different way can give you incredible insights that can save ailing performance figures or fractured internal cultures.

By looking at the world through the customer's eyes, you see things in their reality. And given they're the ones who ultimately make the decision about what to buy and who to choose, it's a useful perspective to have.

Once you see the world through the customer's eyes, you can't unsee it.

The fascinating thing is that so many business leaders are so busy looking from the inside-out perspective, they completely forget that there's an outside-in view too. And it's the one that truly matters.

> ONCE YOU SEE THE WORLD THROUGH THE CUSTOMER'S EYES, YOU CAN'T UNSEE IT.

YOU KNOW SOMETHING'S NOT RIGHT, BUT YOU DON'T KNOW WHAT IT IS

This process and framework helps you identify the things that have been keeping you up at night. The things that have been worrying you. The little comments or pieces of feedback or red flags you've seen but put to the back of your mind.

ASKING YOURSELF QUESTIONS YOU'VE NEVER ASKED BEFORE

It also requires you to ask questions of yourself and your team that potentially, you've never thought of before. Why wouldn't you have thought of them – you're a clever business leader, after all. Because you're not a customer-led transformation expert. You're an expert in what you do. That's why we're here.

We love this process because people are forever telling us – 'I'd never thought about it like that before'. And remember, once you see things from the customer's perspective, you can never unsee them. Once you ask yourself these questions, you'll never not ask them again.

GETTING OUT OF YOUR COMFORT ZONE

It's about getting out of your comfort zone. Admitting we need help as human beings, particularly as leaders, is also uncomfortable. To admit we don't have all the answers is not easy.

You'll feel uncomfortable about the things you find. There's no doubt about that. But once you push through the discomfort to find the key actions and outcomes that fit your organisation, there'll be no holding you back.

You're also likely to find out things about your procedures, your practices and even your team members that will be uncomfortable. Some will require immediate change, like getting rid of team members that are simply not on your side, or changing processes that will make things harder for the team in the short term.

It's about being uncomfortable, embracing that discomfort and pushing through to the other side.

THE MULTI-VIEW: YOUR VIEW OF YOUR ORGANISATION IS VALID, AS IS EVERYONE ELSE'S

This is an important one to remember. The more viewpoints you can have across your organisation, both from different functions and different levels, the better.

It's in the different viewpoints that often help you find the biggest issues or opportunities. For example, you identify that customer complaints are remaining unresolved for numerous weeks. Turns out that Frank from Operations thinks that customers are a pain in the @ss and doesn't want to deal with them, so he flicks them to Carol in Customer Services who tries to bat them back to him for his expert view and feedback. Or Simone in Sales has some great customer feedback that she's been wanting to share to improve the sales process, but her boss won't give her the time of day to allow her to share those ideas.

Your view of the organisation is from the high-line viewpoint, the bird's-eye view in many instances (depending on the size of your organisation). You simply can't see everything. And that's okay.

Your senior leaders and function heads see the organisation through their own expert lenses. The head of Operations sees the world differently to the head of Customer Services. Their views are equally as important and valid, but different.

Your team members see the organisation differently again. The customer-facing teams will see things differently (like customer service failures and opportunities, customer ideas and feedback) to the non-customer facing teams (like operational inefficiencies, team dead spots).

RICH INSIGHTS CAN BE GAINED FROM INVOLVING CROSS-FUNCTIONS AND LEVELS

All viewpoints are valid and useful and it's often why our clients get us to run our Customer-led Accelerator session with their senior leaders first, then have a follow-up session with their middle management level to unearth even more opportunities, challenges and roadblocks that would traditionally be lost in the management structure.

We'd encourage you to share your learnings from this book with your key team members, cross functions and levels, to gain the fullest perspective possible.

FIND YOUR BLINDSPOTS

One of the first steps in the process is identifying your blindspots. What are the things going on in the organisation today that are holding you back? What's missing? These responses will help you understand where you're starting from and what you should prioritise to get you started and on your way.

Step 1: Do the Blindspot roadtest

p337 Check out our mini Blindspot Roadtest tool that gives you a quick view of your organisation through the Customer Strategy Framework™. This exercise will give you an initial indication of the areas you're strong and weak and where you should focus your efforts for maximum impact. This is like our Initial Diagnostic Tool that we undertake for clients, but in a DIY format.

NEED TO GO DEEPER?

p334 If you would like to undertake a deeper view into your organisation, check out our industry-lauded Customer-led Accelerator Program, where we help you understand where you're strong and weak in each of the nine disciplines across your functions and senior leaders. You walk away with a prioritised list of actions you can take immediately to get you on your way to being truly customer-led. Even better, your function and senior leaders have their own list by function, aligned with each other – not fragmented and disparate as they likely have been in the past.

You'll walk away with a greater understanding of where you are today and what you need to do to get where you want to be. You'll accelerate your journey towards your true north, to being truly customer-led. With all your teams rowing at the right pace, in the right direction, with true heart, commitment and full belief in what they're doing.

Step 2: Grab two colleagues

Once you've done the Roadtest, pick two key people in your organisation to do the same. As we've done with you, encourage them to be open, honest and hard-marking. The gold comes from the honesty and deep reflection of what's working and what's not. Assure them no one is going to lose their jobs over this, in fact quite the opposite. Their role in helping you uncover your unknown unknowns is invaluable to the wider organisation and to their own functions. Encourage them to take notes about why they scored the way they did so you can discuss it.

Step 3: Catch up for coffee and ask the tough questions

Then set up a meeting over coffee (of course!) and talk through your findings.

Where are you aligned? Where are you different? What surprised each of you? What didn't?

What can you do next to take this process further and not lose the momentum you've already gained? Remember, you've now got these two peers on board too. Why not go the full hog and get all your senior leaders in the same room to do the full process? Or even the mini process to start? It's up to you.

PREPARE TO MOVE FORWARD

We never said this would be easy, but trust us, all the feelings you'll have after completing the Roadtest are completely normal (and let's be honest, as a senior leader, you're already feeling them all anyway as you continue to carry the success and health and wellbeing of your entire organisation on your shoulders).

Don't be afraid of the journey. Because those that push through the emotion into action, are the ones that fly. Trust us, we've seen it.

You've got this.

 Know where you're starting from and find the gaps to map out your path.

Chapter 30

IT'S A JOURNEY, NOT A DESTINATION

Take it from us, we've evidenced the false starts among the successes.

You can't just say you're going to be customer-led, do a few initiatives, then go back to the way you've always done things. It simply won't work. It's a journey of truly building your capability as an organisation. It is not a tick box exercise of either customer-led or not – it's not a binary zero or a one. It is an evolution of maturity as an organisation to meet the needs of the Customer-led Revolution.

Customer is not a one-hit wonder and certainly nothing like Milli Vanilli. (Does everyone remember them from the 80s – if you don't, then firstly you're making us feel really old and secondly, it's probably worth a Google!)

We've met countless business leaders (or function heads in charge of customer) who've told us, 'Yeah, we're all over this customer thing,' (thinking they've got the game all sewn up) or at the other end of the scale, 'We've tried it but it didn't really work,' (thinking one or two 'projects' would solve their problems).

Customers and their needs are always changing. You think you know them, then they change again. Same goes for the environment or ecosystem in which you're operating. Technology, the economy, society, trends, the environment – it's all changing at such a fast pace, it can make your head spin.

FINDING YOUR TRUE NORTH

To us, it's about finding your true north. The compass point that aligns and directs you to the place you want to be in the future. It's about removing the inconsistencies, friction and unhelpful cross-talk – getting the leaders and the whole organisation oriented towards a common goal. The true north. The true north around your customer.

It's about figuring out where you are today, unearthing the differing views of what that might be and bringing a new level of clarity and focus. It becomes a clear point of reference and guidance, away from internal politics and individual agendas.

True north is a set point. It's not impacted by gravitational force. It is what it is.

Your unapologetic destination. The place you are driven to be. The goals you are driven to achieve. Not some point that can change with the wind, or with one particular leader's self-interest or priority. An agreed point that is set by you and your senior leadership team. With your wider team involved to ensure engagement and drive a greater chance of success.

This is the key point of true north, of being customer-led. This is the difference.

We encourage you to be brave. Be unapologetic about where you want to be. Be driven in the way you get there. And with customer (and your people) at the heart, you'll be sure to succeed.

TRUE NORTH IS A SET POINT. IT'S NOT IMPACTED BY GRAVITATIONAL FORCE. IT IS WHAT IT IS.

Gearing up your organisation for the Customer-led Revolution is not only a journey, it's a journey you can't do on your own. It's an all of team effort, but you might not get everyone on board on day one. But keep the faith. Because we know you've got this.

BEWARE OF THE 'DO IT ONCE' VERSUS THE 'DO IT ALL AT ONCE' APPROACH

Some business leaders will look at this customer-led approach and do one of two things.

They'll get excited, map out a customer strategy or plan, then leave it to run alongside the other existing business strategies, like the HR, Sales, Marketing and IT strategies. They might even put a team on it, or they'll give it to the Customer Services Manager or the like to look after. In 12 to 18 months' time, they'll wonder why nothing has happened and why they didn't get the traction they expected.

Or there's the business leader who'll get excited, map out a customer strategy and/or plan, then expect everything to be done at once. They'll push their teams to adopt this new strategy and integrate the ideas and plans into their existing priorities and workload. They won't necessarily provide extra resources to achieve the objectives of said plan, but they'll expect everyone to adopt the changes and get moving.

Both will probably do a ra-ra presentation to staff to tell them of this new initiative and approach to their business. But over time, both will probably also lose focus – either due to the large lag time and lack of intentional accountability (as in the first instance) or in exhausting their team and burning them out (in the second instance). Either way, there's a danger – even with the best intentions.

THERE IS A BETTER WAY

Everything is changing at such a pace that neither of these options work. You can't set and forget with customer. Have a plan, yes but revisit that plan regularly, inputting new market trends, customer behaviours and feedback, internal changes, competitor actions and the like into your plan and don't be afraid to re-chart your course when needed. Static, passive plans simply won't work.

Nor does whipping your team so hard, going gung-ho and pushing hard with a concept that ideally needs to be integrated over time at a steady, intentional pace.

PREPARE FOR A MARATHON, NOT A SPRINT

Like any journey, it requires careful planning and preparation. An intentional strategy and approach. It's about identifying elements, like the right:

- **people to be involved**, from all levels of the organisation
- **pace of change** and implementation that suits your team dynamics, culture and environment
- **performance indicators** or KPIs to keep your team motivated and focused and practising the right behaviours to deliver your ideal customer experience
- **promises to make to your customer** that you know you can deliver, perhaps in stages to keep you motivated and to manage the customer experience over time.

Planning and preparation are key to success. Don't leave things to accident.

And, like any journey, you need the right tools in your kit bag to set you up for success and keep you on track. The right:

- **leadership representative** who believes in the case for customer and will continue to wave the flag when things get tough
- a roadmap to help chart the way forward
- **representatives across the organisation** that will help row the customer boat from the inside
- **plans** – both long-term and short-term that keep everyone focused and achieving
- **rewards** to help your team understand what good looks like and be rewarded for such behaviours and outcomes.

It's about building up your capabilities, almost like training for a big event. You can't expect to be great at this if you've never done it before. Nor can you expect your team to switch onto it overnight and just start kicking goals immediately. It's not going to happen. Training is the key. Keeping your eye on the prize and rowing towards those goals – perfecting your pace, your technique, your mindset. Invest in experts if required, even training for your team or your senior leaders, whatever it takes to get you and your team upskilled and journey-fit.

Chart way points along your journey to keep you and your team on track. Keeping them focused on the long-term goal or destination, while keeping them heading in the right direction, at the right pace. Way points guide them and help them reorient their efforts in small chunks, rather than finding themselves way off track and unable to get back. That's why checking in every 6 to 12 months simply doesn't work – if teams or team members are going off track, they'll be well and truly lost by the time these check-in points come around.

A critical, non-negotiable of this is to keep your customer strategy initiatives and plan on the senior leadership agenda. They need to be tracked and discussed just like any other part of the business, like Finance or Sales or Marketing – regularly and with conviction and commitment (not just lip service or box ticking). Giving it a firm and safe place on the agenda of the organisation will ensure you reach your way points, achieve your goals and continue your pathway to success.

BUT FIRST: YOU NEED TO KNOW WHERE YOU'RE STARTING FROM

Just like any journey you take, you need to know where you're starting from.

If we were to go on a holiday together to an agreed destination, but we hadn't agreed where we were starting from (the train station, the airport, what about which city?), then we'd be destined for trouble from the outset.

So many business leaders we know are great at setting the destination – the where to – but not all of them think about the start point.

Where you're starting from dictates the choices you need to make in the early stages of your journey – where are you leaving from, what mode of transport are you taking, who's coming along, who are your group leaders, when will the team follow, where are your rest points, where are your meet points – you get our drift.

Without this information – no matter how clear your actual destination is – you could find yourself in trouble before you've even started.

And if you know where you're starting from, then you can look back along your journey and see how far you've come. And that, friends, is magic.

DIAGNOSE WHERE YOU ARE TODAY, TO START YOUR JOURNEY

Because everyone plans differently – some of us will have a full spreadsheet, some will have mapped out a brief plan 'on the back of an envelope', others will have it all in their heads – it's important that you have a solid, robust process or diagnostic tool that helps you understand where you're starting from.

Not only do people plan differently, but we find in our process that different personalities and even department or function heads, have different views of where the organisation is starting. Some think they're well ahead of the other functions, others see issues and challenges that the majority don't.

By collectively mapping out where you are today, you can pack your kit bag with the right tools, and the right mindset and awareness of the roadblocks, to get you on your way in the right direction.

Using the Customer Strategy Framework™ as a diagnostic tool, it also helps you go beyond gut feel or personal opinion or even self-interest, to gain a holistic view of where you are today, taking all perspectives of the important people in your organisation, into account. Yes, that means not only Sales or Marketing or Tech, but Finance, HR, Operations and even Maintenance (depending on your industry). If you're a Tourism operation, your Food and Beverage, your Spa and Wellness, your Back Office and Front Office teams can all have incredible insights to share.

It's amazing just how many of these processes we've undertaken with organisations across the world that have uncovered deep-rooted and often cataclysmic unknown unknowns. Issues and blockages sitting right under the nose of senior management, yet undiscovered.

It uncovers deep-seated issues, roadblocks, communication failures and dead spots in your organisation, simply by bringing your leadership together to give their (unrestricted) views on where you are.

SKETCHING OUT AN INITIAL ROADMAP FOR THE JOURNEY

This is about getting the answers to the questions you've probably asked yourself over and over, for weeks, months or even years. For example:

- Why isn't our marketing working better?
- Why are we still getting bad reviews?
- Why won't our functions work better together?
- Why can't we seem to get ahead of our competitors?
- Why do our prices keep dropping?

All the questions you ask yourself regularly, be it in your leadership meetings or in the middle of the night. They're questions that plague business leaders the world-over.

You're not alone. But undertaking this process – you're more alone than you think. Why? Because only brave business leaders truly take the time to not only map where they're going, but find out where they're starting from. Asking the tough questions. Engaging their team, both senior leaders and middle management. Taking the time. Asking the customer.

Being intentional.

No more excuses. No more accidents. No more playing victim to markets or trends or competitors. Taking charge, charting your way to success, figuring out where you're starting from, then asking the questions – are we good at this or not today? What do we need to do to get better? This is where the magic lies.

> BECAUSE ONLY BRAVE BUSINESS LEADERS TRULY TAKE THE TIME TO NOT ONLY MAP WHERE THEY'RE GOING, BUT FIND OUT WHERE THEY'RE STARTING FROM.

Being customer-led is not simply a compliance piece or an off the shelf solution. Every organisation is unique, and sprinting to bandaid solutions won't get you there.

A CLOSING NOTE FROM THE DYNAMIC DUO

Firstly, a big warm thank-you to you. Picking up this book and working through it takes courage. Becoming customer-led is not for everyone, though most organisations could do with doing at least some or all of the actions covered in this book.

We've given you a crash course on why being a customer-led organisation is the key to your future success. What can be a seemingly daunting task, depending on where you're starting from, we've helped you break down into more manageable chunks.

The key is changing the mindset from customer improvements being a series of bandaids, to making customer-led a capability that can be built up and grown over time.

Throughout this book, we've introduced you to a range of core concepts and tools, with a view to giving you a clear roadmap for how to move forward.

As mentioned, this is the start of the journey – not the end. This goes for you <u>and</u> for us. Keep in touch with us as you step along and progress on your journey. We'd love to hear from you. If you get stuck, chances are we can share some wisdom – no doubt we've seen something similar before.

If you're having wins, we'd love to hear about them too, and shout about your success.

Yours in customer
Sueanne + Peter
The Dynamic Duo

ACKNOWLEDGMENTS

Writing a book is harder than we ever imagined and more rewarding than we can put into words. The long hours, the 'what's that word?', the wine, the coffee, the blood, the tears, the heart… For six months, this book went everywhere with us – literally. On business trips all over Australia to family camping trips on the Sunshine Coast. Early mornings watching the sun rise over Coolum Beach, or watching the world wake up creek-side in Moreton Bay; fireside sunsets over the rolling hills of Toowoomba and the golf courses of Mornington Peninsula; countless airport lounges, usually with a wine, and more cramped in-flight drop-down tables than we care to remember… you name it, we probably wrote it there.

What we didn't realise is that your book becomes an extension of yourself for a time. Never far from your mind, you find your thoughts, ideas and experiences are forever popping up their little heads – usually in the middle of the night or while you're driving! We could have written a book twice the length of this (in fact, we kinda did, until our Editor Karen got her hands on it!), we have so much to share. But alas, we hope we've got it just about right – not too overwhelming but enough to get you taking the actions you need to make your business better.

We dreamed about writing this book for years. And now it's here. There are so many people to thank, it's hard to know where to begin.

First up, we'd like to thank you, our reader. Our world is a better, more exciting, more challenging place because of brave leaders like you, who aren't afraid to take a chance, shake sh!t up and do things differently. You are our inspiration and our reason. It is for you, that this book is written.

To our families, friends and support crew, we thank you. In particular:

Greta and Trevor Turner, Pete's parents, without whom this book would not have happened. From taking the kids to swim classes and basketball games, to feeding us when we hadn't had time to eat, your unending support and help is the reason this book exists at all. Thank you.

From Sueanne – Pauline and Bernie Carr, my beloved parents. You may be gone from this earth, but you live in my heart, my mind and my soul. I am who I am today, because of you. Your limitless belief that I could do whatever I put my mind to, and your slightly embarrassing tendency to tell anyone who'd listen my life story, is where I get my strength on the darkest of days. Raising us in one of the poorest areas of Brisbane didn't stop you showing me the value of hard work, commitment and forging my own path to make my dreams happen. Mum, your incredible skills with a tile cutter and a chainsaw will forever inspire me to know – I can do anything I put my mind to. You are the woman I will forever aspire to be. Dad, your kind heart, your selflessness for those around you, your generous spirit and your determination to give the shirt off your back for those less fortunate than you, will forever inspire me to be the best human I can be. Let's not mention your regular purchases of treats for your grandsons – Poppy jelly and Freddo Frog birthday cakes will forever be a part of our lives. Thank you, my darling parents. You are the reason I am who I am. I wish you were here to see me now, and I hope I make you proud. I am yours, and you are mine. Forever. God bless, darlings. And thank you.

To George and Atticus, the lights of our lives. Everything we do is for you. You light up our days, you empty our bank accounts, you make us laugh and you make us cry. Your vivacious personalities, cheeky attitudes, and grit and determination are inspiring. We are so proud to be your parents and we hope that life gives you all that you ever dream of – be it a book deal or a quiet life in the country – your happiness is what matters most. Thank you for always checking in on us – 'How is the book coming along?' – the cups of tea, the warm hugs and most of all, the quiet under- standing when yet again we had to say no to a game on the Playstation or a swim in the pool. Our beautiful boys, this book is for you. Thank you.

From Sueanne – to my bliss, Leanne. Thank you for always being there. You have inspired me all my life, my stunning, strong, intelligent, ballsy sister who has always known her own mind and stood up for what she believes in. I always dreamed of being you one day and I hope I make you proud. I am a better person for knowing and loving you. Thank you for taking care of our beloved farver in his later years – he loved his dorters more than life itself, you know. Thank you, wee.

To Carmel, Jamie, Annette and Ryan – for always checking in, for bringing the wine and cheese (or coffee and cake), for listening to us complain, for helping us relax when we needed a break, for your unending belief in us and the countless 'you got this, guys!' Without your love, support, encouragement and ass-kicking, we're not sure we would have made it through. Thank you.

From Sueanne – to Mazza, Dan, Deb, Pete, Jen, Tuds, Marky, my SWB b!tches (Anna, Margie, Megan, Mel, Nerida, Tanya) – thank you for being there for me through all that life has thrown at me these past few years. It's in the quiet and the dark that I would reach for your hand, and know you were there to catch me. Thank you.

From Peter – a wise man (in fact, it was Sueanne's dad Bernie) once said to me, 'If you have just one great mate in your life, then you're the luckiest man alive.' Well then, the universe has looked after me well. Grateful for my brothers-from-other-mothers who keep me on the level – JB, Ryan, Gis, Trent, Wecks and the SS. From dark hours to happy hours. My liver still forgives you!

To all our friends, colleagues and bosses all over the world. Too many to mention here but you have been there throughout our professional and personal lives, cheering us on. Thank you.

From Sueanne – to my 'old' bosses who showed me what great leadership looks like and inspired much of the Align section of our book. In particular, Alistair Daly, Simon Thompson, John Bevan, Unni Menon, Debra Howe, David Morgans, Alex de Waal, Stephen Gregg and Alistair Cox. You encouraged me to step out of my comfort zone, to step into the light and to try. You were never threatened by me or my big ideas (or my big mouth), always open to my latest crazy plan. You are the leaders I aspire to be, you inspire me and you helped make me the person I am today. Thank you.

From Peter – for my mentors who played their vital part in shaping my journey, influencing and directing my (possibly intense!) energy over the years. Specifically, Prof Costas Markides, Prof Richard Jolly, and Dave Straker. You all provided the balance of big thinking, the need for authentic leadership and the need for making the theoretical real. And while we're here, a shout-out to some of my great bosses who saw my potential to soar and provided me with the perfect leadership and environments to shine. My heartfelt thanks to you, Greg Holder, Caroline Fawcett, Andrew Ryan, John Cowley and Ian Copeland. I carry pieces of you all with me, every day. Thank you.

To Jann, our marketing extraordinaire and very important person. Without your relentless commitment to CF, your determination to continue rowing the boat even when we weren't anywhere to be found, thank you. Our business would not be where it is today, without you. You kept everything going when all we could do was think about the book (and coffee). Thank you.

Thanks must go to Andrew Griffiths, our awesome business and book coach, who helped us make this book happen – finally. It was always in us, but without your butt-kicking, encouragement, guidance and support, we'd probably still be mind-mapping the contents page. Thanks, AG.

To Don Peppers, thank you for agreeing to have a coffee with two random Aussies back in 2018 in San Francisco. You gave so generously of your time and your wisdom, having never met or heard of us before. It was a great honour to spend time with 'the yoda of customer experience', as we love to call you. At the time, you told us, if we ever wrote a book and it was good, you'd do the foreword for us – and here we are! Thank you.

To our clients, of course – without you, we wouldn't have the stories to share, the experiences nor the incredible love and support of really clever people all over the world (that's you). From when we started out six years ago, you took a chance on us – a small business with big dreams and big ideas. You put your faith in us, and it is because of you that we are where we are today. It's your stories of struggle, of determination, of being brave, that we share within this book. It's your unending support, advocacy and repeat work that keeps us going, that inspires us and helps us pay the bills. It's you that drives us forward, it's your success and the impact we've made together that help us celebrate what we do, why we do it and who we do it for. Thank you, from the bottom of our hearts.

To the team at Publish Central, in particular Michael Hanrahan, for your extensive guidance (and unending patience) of these two crazy kids who wanted to write a book but had no idea how to. For the never-ending questions, the gentle explanations and the constant encouragement. Thank you.

To our wonderful editor, Karen, who guided us through the painful process of editing our book with such care, attention to detail and patience (lots of patience!). We wanted an editor that could tell us the truth, not just pat our egos and tell us our baby was beautiful (even when it wasn't). From the initial brief when we begged you to be as harsh as was needed (we wanted the best book, not just big egos!), you gave us the truth in a gentle, loving, but sometimes downright kick-@ss way, just the way we like it! Thank you.

Our book cover designer, Julia Kuris, who took our ideas for our cover and brought them to life right in front of our eyes. Your dedication to the project, your fantastic ideas (that we found hard to choose from) and your patience was appreciated, especially when it all happened before the book was even started. Thank you.

And finally – our book contributors who gave their time, knowledge, expertise and experiences, with honesty, warmth and generosity of spirit. From a random note from a random couple of strangers who fancied themselves as authors, you took time out of your day and your busy lives to help us. We cannot thank you enough. Your stories helped make this book better: Byron Thompson from Datagamz, Nic Emery from Crown Resorts, Craig Armstrong from Warwick Credit Union Ltd, Jackie Klus from Evolt, Yvette Mihelic from John Holland, James Harvey from Zepto, Alicia Avram from Bare, Neil Jorgensen from B&R Enclosures, Craig Errey from Solve Group Pty Ltd, Ben Alcock from Zepto, Nicole Imberger from Mirvac, Michael Dart from Energy Queensland, Sommer Moore from Boehringer Ingelheim, Peter Allaway from Transport for NSW, Stacey Burns from Hyne Timber, Kevin Arapa from Scentre Group, Graeme Baxter from Umbrella Solutions, Vivek Vasudevan from astify, Ron Ferdinands from ilume™, Jake Dutton from Telstra, Brett Power from Strata Choice, Richard Heinz from Scentre Group, Chris Kenny from Stockland, Andris Versteeg from Tic:Toc, Les Nelson from

The Travel Junction, Jessica Ramos from Hutchinson Builders, Ian Lyne from The Dinner Ladies, Travis Brown from Officeworks, Ross Thompson from Greenbox Group Pty Ltd, Johann Loibl from Carma, Craig Rochat from Land of Plenty Food Co., Bernice McLeod from Iron Mountain ANZ, Varghese Mathew from mx51, Cherylyn Russell from Russell Mineral Equipment, Lance Eerhard from BuyersCircle, Kate Shipton from RACQ, Gordon McAlister from ako Pty Ltd, Shelby Ueckermann from Wolters Kluwer Australia, Katrin Watson, M.A. from Indigenous Business Australia, Kym Vassiliou from Claro Aged Care and Disability Services, Rebel Bailey Senior from The Hollard Insurance Company Australia, Richard McInnes from Water Polo Australia, Greg Bowell from G8 Education Ltd, John Newton from Scotch College Adelaide, Neil Buzinkic from Reztor Restoration, Dawn McAleenan from Crosslinks, Chris Harnett from 1-Stop Connections, Stephen McGrath from Blueshift, Moana Rangi from icare NSW, Olga Duarte from SDN Children's Services, Geoff Wessling from TCCW Consulting Pty Ltd, Elizabeth Masen from Athlete Assessments.

PLEASE SHARE YOUR
STORIES AND EXPERIENCES

Now you know our approach and concepts for being a truly customer-led organisation. If you're energised and excited about embracing the Customer-led Revolution and you implement practices, ideas or actions in your organisation, we'd love you to share how this has worked for you. What changed in your business? What changed for your customers? For your staff? For you? Share your story with us and we'll share it with the world.

We're always looking for examples of best practice in this field of customer-led transformation. If you encounter any businesses, anywhere across the world, that you believe give an extraordinary customer experience, who truly embrace the Customer-led Revolution, we'd love to hear about them. We're building a database of these businesses to illustrate the ideas and concepts we've put forward in this book. Please email us at hello@customerframe.com

A LITTLE MORE ABOUT US

Hi, we're Sueanne and Peter – Co-Founders of Customer Frame – and we're here to do things *differently*...

Fueled by necessity, coffee and dogged determination, we started Customer Frame to combat an epidemic sweeping through the corporate and business world. The problem? The dehumanisation of *customers* and *staff*. We were tired of customers being seen as just-another-number (instead of a real person to be related to). And, we were tired of big corporations spending big bucks on big consultancies, but failing to empower their own people with the right skills to serve their customers well.

At Customer Frame, we're dedicated to helping organisations escape the trap of dehumanisation and put the customer at the heart of everything they do. We believe that a strong connection to your customers and your people gives you a truly sustainable competitive advantage.

With us, what you see is what you get. Authenticity is at our core and we wear *realness* to work every single day. We are unashamedly and unapologetically ourselves. So, why does that matter to *you?*

We don't believe in one-sided solutions, and we don't offer generic consulting based on little real-world experience! As our client, you'll benefit from the skills, hands-on industry experience and unique working styles of us *both*. You get the ying *and* the yang – the emotional and creative input of Sueanne, and the strategic, structured guidance of Peter.

Our clients call us the Customer Strategy superheroes, but we've found that wearing our undies on the outside doesn't go down so well in boardrooms... So if you're ready to take advantage of our superpowers in your own organisation, we'd love to hear from you.

WANT SOME MORE CUSTOMER FRAME IN YOUR LIFE?

If you feel like you've got great value and insights out of our book, there are a number of ways you can work with us. Check out the information on the following pages or visit our website www.customerframe.com. And of course, you can follow us on Facebook, LinkedIn and Instagram.

CUSTOMER-LED ACCELERATOR PROGRAM

After years of development, we are proud to present our signature program for CEOs, CCOs, business owners and senior business leaders who want to create a truly customer-led organisation.

Based on the Customer Strategy Framework™ outlined in this book, our Customer-led Accelerator Program fast-tracks your journey to get your leadership team on the same page and aligned around what matters most – your customer.

In an action-packed three hours, we'll bring your leadership team on a journey to:

- benchmark where you are today
- find the gaps that are holding you back
- focus your efforts on what will make the most impact
- fix the issues through a shared action plan that will create long-lasting change.

We will work through the nine customer competencies that separate high-performing organisations from the others and benchmark where you are today. Using our Customer Strategy Framework™, you'll get a gauge on where you are across the five stages of customer maturity and learn what you need to do to move up the scale.

We examine the gaps in perspectives across your leadership team – from Finance to IT, HR to Sales and everything in between. Even those who think they have nothing to do with customers will leave knowing, understanding and appreciating their role in the organisation's success.

Working collaboratively across functions, we will help you identify the competing priorities that are undermining your efficiency and effectiveness today. Through our structured process, we help you make sense of it all to focus in on the three strategic priorities that will make the greatest impact for your organisation.

With this shared focus, we then drive action at the individual function level, with your senior leaders leaving with a clear action plan for change that is aligned to and integrated with their peers.

It's an energising, entertaining and educating three-hour session that completely reframes the way you see your organisation and your customers, with everyone leaving aligned and clear on what needs to be done to smash your goals and accelerate your journey to enjoying all of the benefits of a customer-led organisation.

Get on the program that's helping courageous leaders to break down the barriers, align their teams and smash their goals.

TESTIMONIALS

What other brave leaders have said about the Customer-led Accelerator Program

An incredible three hours out of your week that will transform your business and get your whole team on the same page!
Jemma Elder, Board Director

I would say the best three hours out of your week, that you can really focus on what's important to your business from people who care and have got a significant amount of experience in this space.
Nerida Trappett, Director, Rivers Insurance

It was fantastic! It was interactive! I've never done that before. I've never been to a workshop that focused solely on the customer. Never. It's completely unique. I couldn't recommend it more.
Tyson Cobb, CEO, Practice + Pixels

CF is the best! I wasn't expecting such a detailed plan to go back to the office with, with a check point of nine items to start ticking off immediately. It was time well spent!
Suzie Majer, Talent Director, Majer Recruitment

If you want to break through all the fluff and truly understand your customers, you must speak to Peter and Sueanne – they are the gurus of customer experience. They have the ability to get into the nitty gritty with you while still keeping the big picture front of mind and the ultimate focus. I love the structure they have to understand your customers and then turbocharge their experience.
John Knight, MD and Co-Founder, businessDEPOT

BLINDSPOT ROADTEST: TAKE A QUIZ TO GET A SENSE OF WHERE YOU ARE TODAY

Throughout the book, you've undertaken some pieces of self-assessment to help you reflect on the various customer capabilities.

Here, we've brought it all together for you as a one-sheet tool – The Blindspot Roadtest – to help you see the complete picture and continue the conversation.

Using the Customer Strategy Framework™ as the core engine, The Blindspot Roadtest is a great way to engage your colleagues and begin to put customer on the strategic agenda.

Do it yourself, or do it with a group – one thing is for sure. You will begin to get a clear picture of what's working, what needs attention, where you're aligned and where you're not.

Head to customerframe.com/revolution to download this and other helpful tools to accelerate your journey.

HANDS-ON PROJECTS AND SERVICES TO BRING YOUR CUSTOMER-LED STRATEGY TO LIFE

Sometimes you just need help. We get it. Be it a kickstart for the whole journey or specific support in one of the nine customer capabilities that you want to build.

> The work is outstanding. You have been a pleasure to work with.
> You two riff off each other like Jagger and Richards.
> *Steve Wroe, CEO, Daylesford and Macedon Tourism*

We're *never* afraid to get our hands dirty in your organisation, and help you put this new, innovative approach into motion. Here are just some of the projects we're famous for…

We used to call ourselves an 'anti-consultancy', and our ethos is still the same. We use projects to help you propel forward to achieve your goals sooner. What sets us apart is that we pride ourselves on imparting the knowledge, skills and expertise to your team to help make your organisation stronger, resilient and sustainable.

If you're feeling blocked, confused or just need some help, book a discovery call and let's nut it out together. Email Sueanne and Peter at hello@customerframe.com to arrange it.

Customer Strategy	**Insight to Action**
■ Stuck at first base? We'll help you slingshot the process by creating a robust, clear and compelling customer-led transformation strategy that lays out the agenda and sets you up for success.	■ What do your customers really think of you at the 'moments of truth'? We'll help you put in an approach to activate your customer intelligence, so you're better informed and can engage your whole team to drive improvement.
Customer Profiling	**Journey Mapping**
■ Turn customers from a concept into a person. We'll help you understand who they are, how they think, and what they need so you can create tailored offerings that are truly irresistible.	■ Step into your customer's shoes to find hidden opportunities for improvement. We'll help you map out your customer's journey, compare it with your business processes, and find the gaps to fuel your growth.
Experience Development	**Experience Reviews**
■ Turn clients into raving fans with intentionally designed programs, products and experiences. We'll help you redefine your offerings to drive customer loyalty and engagement.	■ Take your customer experience to the next level with an expert 28-point review of your operation. We'll reveal the hidden issues and untapped opportunities that are holding back your success.

MASTERCLASSES AND TRAINING THAT PUT YOU IN THE DRIVER'S SEAT

Not only do we offer hands-on services to get the job done *for* you, but we also offer energising and engaging masterclasses and training to upskill and equip your team to do it yourself. Become a Customer Strategy Superhero in your organisation with immersive programs designed to help you master these skills and achieve your goals for the long-haul (even when we're not around).

Lauded by delegates across a range of industries, our Masterclasses and Training programs are designed using the same skills and techniques that we've honed and refined with our clients over decades of working on customer-led transformation projects.

Some of the specific topics we regularly deliver include:

CUSTOMER PROFILING AND PROFILE DEVELOPMENT

Turn customers from a concept into a *person*. We'll show you how to understand who they are, how they think, and what they need so you can create tailored offerings that are truly irresistible. We'll arm you with the tools to create your own profiles set to share across your organisation.

CUSTOMER JOURNEY MAPPING

Step into your customer's shoes to find hidden opportunities for improvement. We'll show you how to map out your customer's journey, compare it with your business processes, and find the gaps to fuel your growth.

These are intensive sessions, designed to give you the knowledge, tools and skills you need to do it yourself. This is not Lecture 101 stuff – you learn by doing, applying the concepts to your organisation. Our goal is always the same: to leave your organisation stronger, and more confident than ever to put customers at the heart of everything you do.

Want to find out how you can level-up to close the gaps and do it yourself? Email us at hello@customerframe.com

BUSINESS COACHING

There is no doubt that becoming a truly customer-led organisation takes guts, grit and determination. It also takes a lot of energy, mental, emotional and physical. It's not easy to achieve on your own, particularly when you're a senior leader with the weight of the world on your shoulders – a business to run, a team to support and a future to step into.

But you don't have to do it alone. We work with a limited number of business owners and senior leaders to help them build the customer-led business they aspire to and the one they deserve.

Through our unique styles and expertise – we call it the yin and yang – you'll enjoy the support of Australia's dynamic duo of customer experience to help you realise your business goals and market aspirations. The combination of Peter's strategic, data-loving brain, and Sueanne's creative, more emotional approach will bring a fresh perspective to your business.

If you'd like to find out more about working with us, please email hello@customerframe.com

NEED DYNAMIC, ENGAGING SPEAKERS FOR YOUR LIVE OR VIRTUAL EVENT?

Sueanne and Peter have delivered countless presentations, workshops, webinars and programmes across Australia and UK/Europe in the past 25 years. Entertaining and engaging offline or online, they're renowned for bringing something special to every event.

They are highly engaging in their styles, both on-stage and off, and have been revered for the energy, passion and learnings they bring to everything they do.

They leave audiences inspired, challenged and ready to take action. They draw on their combined 50 plus years of experience working with world-class organisations across the globe to small businesses and tourism regions, to bring real, actionable insights to every audience.

Last but not least, Sueanne and Peter have a down-to-earth style that portray their deep desire to help others create the best, most dynamic businesses possible. Clients tell them their presentations are second-to-none and are revered by all who attend their events.

From keynote presentations to workshops, Master of Ceremonies to facilitating panels, Sueanne and Peter will bring a special something to your event. Why not invite them to be the kick-off session for your next Senior Leadership Retreat or Strategy Session? It will be the perfect kickstart to your day and get your team on the same page.

Some of the topics Sueanne and Peter specialise in include:

- Are you ready for the Customer-led Revolution?
- The customer is yours to lose
- Advocacy – the crystal ball for your business
- Five customer trends to make (or break) your organisation
- The customer is not always right (and neither is your boss)
- The paradox of choice: how to stand out in the crowd
- From information to inspiration: visitor servicing principles to drive visitation

To find out more about getting Sueanne and/or Peter to speak at your next event, either face to face or virtually, email hello@customerframe.com or check out our speaker kit at www.customerframe.com/speaking

ARE YOU LOOKING FOR THE PERFECT GIFT FOR YOUR CUSTOMERS OR TEAM?

If you are looking for the ideal gift for your customers or team members, this book is one of the most valuable presents you could possibly purchase.

Bought in bulk, you can use them as relationship-building tools, simple thank-you gifts, as part of promotional campaigns and incentives or even gifts at your annual conference, senior leadership retreat or as a Christmas gift for the team. The power is in sharing the message and getting your team on board, to join you on the journey to becoming truly customer-led.

There are also ways to value add bulk book purchases, from special print runs with your company message printed in the book, through to having your own company message included as an introduction. Whatever your idea, we can make it happen.

If this sounds like the ideal opportunity to treat your customers or staff or the ideal promotional opportunity for your organisation, please email the Customer Frame team at hello@customerframe.com

WOULD YOU LIKE TO INTERVIEW SUEANNE AND PETER?

Sueanne and Peter love a chat and they love talking all things customer. They're comfortable being interviewed on a range of topics, including:

- the evolution of business
- the Customer-led Revolution
- the challenges facing business owners and senior leadership teams today
- moving from transaction to relationship
- moving from information to inspiration
- moving from selling to servicing
- putting the customer at the heart of your business.

If you would like to interview Sueanne and Peter about any of the above or their latest book, please email hello@customerframe.com